"I love it! I plan to order a copy for every teacher. Not just the memory techniques, but the best teaching practices are terrific."

Linda Kakes
Principal, Randol Elementary School

"*Memory Smarts* provides an opportunity for parents to improve their memory skills along with their children. The combination of visual, auditory, and kinesthetic activities addresses the memory needs of every child."

Dr. Robert Pruitt
Principal, Norwood Creek Elementary School

"The games are great. I found it exciting to do the exercises and have them work so well."

Diane Birkeness
Parent

"Jim Wiltens has let the genie out of the bottle. Now every kid can have their wish—the power to memorize facts easily …"

Diane Flynn Keith
Editor and Publisher, *Homefires, the Journal of Homeschooling*

Memory Smart

Nine Memory Skills
Every Grade Schooler
Needs

Text, illustrations, and photos by
Jim Wiltens

Deer Crossing Press
Redwood City, California

Library of Congress Control Number: 20022107635
$29.95 Pbk

ISBN 0-938525-08-5

First Printing 2003

Deer Crossing Press
690 Emerald Hill Rd.
Redwood City, CA 94061

Printed in the United States of America
10 9 8 7 6 5 4 3 2 1

Grateful acknowledgment is made for permission to reproduce the following previously published material:

The four vocabulary cartoon drawings in Chapter 6, from Sam Burchers, *Vocabulary Cartoons* (Punta Gorda, Florida: New Monic Books, 1998). Used with permission.

The illustrations of Clever Cat, Hairy Hat Man, and Annie Apple, as well as the Sammy Snake and Hairy Hat Man phonic fable in Chapter 4, from Lyn Wendon, *Letterland Programme One Teacher's Guide* (Cambridge, England: Letterland International, 1997). Used with permission.

Books by Jim Wiltens

Individual Tactics in Waterpolo

Edible and Poisonous Plants of Northern California

No More Nagging, Nit-picking, & Nudging: A Guide to Motivating, Inspiring, and Influencing Kids Aged 10–18

Goal Express! The Five Secrets of Goal-Setting Success

Memory Smart: Nine Memory Skills Every Grade Schooler Needs

Contents

History

Geography

Help Your Memory Be the Best It Can Be

Appendices

Acknowledgments

About the Author

What a Better Memory Will Mean for Your Child or Students

In school, children learn rules of grammar, multiplication tables, and the order of the planets in our solar system. They also learn that George Washington had wooden teeth, why water boils, where Brazil is located, how many legs a spider has, how to spell *kindergarten,* and even how the Internet works. These facts fall under the heading of content. Schools are heavy on content—what to remember. But the process of memory—how to remember—is rarely taught.

Did you take any memory classes in elementary school? When you consider that most academic tests measure memory, doesn't it make sense to include memory in the curriculum? Memory expert Harry Lorayne says there should be Four Rs in education: Readin', Ritin', 'Rithmatic, and Rememberin'. Rememberin' is incredibly important, because what you don't remember, you haven't learned.

Does Education Develop a Good Memory?

Both illiterate African children from Botswana and literate American school children were told a long involved story. They were then asked to repeat the story back immediately afterward, and then again one week later and one month later. The African children beat the American children hands down. The illiterate village children, who depended more on memory in their daily lives, had better memories.

You might be thinking, that's all very interesting, but my child is only 6—there's still plenty of time. In her book *Total Recall,* Joan Minninger writes, "The optimum time to learn to structure things and ideas is between the ages 6 and 12." Since mnemonic techniques are ways of structuring information, simplifying its retrieval, your 6-year-old is at an ideal age. The earlier children start developing these habits, the easier it is for them to learn.

A practical way to develop children's memory skills is to weave content and memory process together. When children are told that Christopher Columbus visited the Americas in 1492, only content is provided. When they are taught: *Christopher Columbus sailed the ocean blue in fourteen hundred and ninety-two,* they receive content in combination with a memory technique based on rhyming. Many American adults who have trouble remembering the dates of their own anniversaries or their children's birthdays still remember the date of Columbus's visit, not because it is a fascinating date, but because the fact was tied to a memory technique.

Much more can be done with memory. Teaching the content (subject) and process (memory technique) at the same time yields these kinds of results:

- Eight-year-old Stuart wasn't very good at the social skill of remembering names. After playing a memory game, Stuart could tell you the names of fifteen people he had just met.
- A group of fifth-graders memorized all forty-three presidents of the United States in order in twenty minutes.
- Heather, a fifth grader trained in memory skills, stood up in class and, without notes, explained the first ten amendments to the Constitution. She had studied the topic for less than an hour.
- Children in a memory-skills class learned all of the states and capitals of the United States—in several hours, something that usually takes weeks.
- Kindergarten and first-grade teachers use memory-based programs to accelerate learning to read by as much as 50%.
- Students studied 100 pages in a *National Geographic* magazine using a memory skill. Random numbers were then called out and the students could tell you which pictures went with the page number.

- Memory-trained students studied a textbook containing hundreds of pages and then recalled all the main points and examples in the text.

The memory skills presented in this book are patterned after people who developed exceptional memory strategies — people like Solomon-Veniaminovich Sherashevsky.

Sherashevsky's Story

It was the mid-1920s in Russia.

"Sherashevsky," said the red-faced editor. "How is it I give you all these assignments and you just sit there? Why do you not take notes like the other reporters?"

A surprised and somewhat embarrassed Sherashevsky sat up. "But I don't need notes," said Sherashevsky timidly.

"No notes," said the editor rolling his eyes. "You are a journalist. You are supposed to take notes. Today I have given addresses, names of people to interview, and much information about the assignments. All the others have taken notes but you."

"But I don't need notes," repeated Sherashevsky.

"No notes! Then tell me what I have read from my list," said the editor sternly.

"You said to visit 3821 Vladstock and talk to a Mr. Prosk. Ask him about the prices for potatoes for this coming winter. Next go to 58 Chinski Square and talk to two boys. Their names are ..."

The editor's face went from one of reproach to astonishment. Word for word, Sherashevsky repeated back the assignments given by the editor.

At the urging of his editor, Sherashevsky went to the local university. There he met psychologist A. R. Luria, Professor of Psychology at the University of Moscow. This meeting between psychologist and memory expert began a relationship that would last thirty years. During that time Sherashevsky participated in numerous experiments. In one, he listened to a list of seventy random words and repeated them back flawlessly — even sixteen years later!

In another test, he spent three minutes looking at a list of fifty-two numbers and then repeated the list several months later. That's equivalent to learning seven telephone numbers in a few minutes, then dialing them months later. When given the first four lines of *The Divine Comedy* in Italian, a language he was unfamiliar with, he committed the stanzas to memory in a few minutes. Even fifteen years later, with no warning, he was able to repeat the lines without error.

Strategies Can Be Learned by Anyone

People with exceptional memories, like Sherashevsky, use memory strategies. These strategies can be learned. For example, college students at Brigham Young University were taught several strategies used by Sherashevsky. The students then duplicated two of his memory feats, memorizing twenty digits in forty seconds and memorizing a fifty-digit matrix in three minutes.

Researchers studying an individual with an exceptional memory wrote in the *British Journal of Psychology,* "There has been no evidence to suggest that T. E.'s [subject's initials] memory performance requires an explanation in terms of unusual basic abilities … all of his feats could be explained by the mnemonic [memory system] 'tricks' that he employed. Furthermore, there is nothing to suggest that many people could not perform memory tasks as efficiently as T. E., if they had full knowledge of the … techniques used and were prepared to practice them … ." It turns out that T. E.'s interest in memory started when he was 15. He saw an advertisement in a newspaper for a book that would show the reader how to develop a "super power memory." T. E. bought the book.

Researchers referred to T. E.'s skills as *tricks*. Individuals skilled in these memory *tricks* have used them to remember the names of 400 people they have just met, to learn twenty-five foreign languages, and to memorize entire textbooks. If you don't know the secrets to these tricks, these feats are miracles performed by magicians. This book is about sharing memory secrets with children.

Beyond the Classroom

Memory shapes us. In addition to laying a foundation for academic success, it molds self-esteem. In his book *Self-Esteem Revolutions in Children*, Thomas

Phelan explains that at around third grade (or age 8), academic self-esteem, or how well children expect to do in school, becomes a durable belief. In turn, this belief in competency is a primary ingredient of self-esteem. And in school, for ten or more years, thirty hours a week, academic competency is measured. So anything that measurably improves academic competency, as memory skills do, also raises self-esteem for a lifetime.

Memory literacy is also important outside the classroom and down the road a few years. Memory skills improve your ability to process, organize, and retrieve information. These skills determine how well a person copes with the demands of life. Adults must be able to keep track of complex personal finances, children's activity schedules, and planning for retirement. On the job, whether waiting on tables and keeping orders straight during rush hour, engineering projects, writing assignments, organizing and directing the operations of a corporation, working in public relations in a social capacity, playing in a symphony, or teaching at any level of schooling, the person who knows how to organize and retrieve information will perform best. Make a commitment to help children become memory smart.

Mnemonics in Medical School

Many doctors survive the hellish memory requirements of medical school by using memory techniques. There are over eleven books for doctors, with names like *Medico Mnemonica,* loaded with techniques for remembering medical terminology and facts.

CDs on the Brain

The accumulated memories of an average lifetime would occupy 10^{17} bits of information or twenty million CD-ROM disks.

Chapter 2, "Nine Memory Techniques Every Child Needs," is the backbone of *Memory Smart*. It's a must-read chapter. It explains memory techniques and terminology used throughout the book. Go to Chapter 2 to find out what you need to know to be memory literate.

2 Nine Memory Techniques Every Child Needs

In Greek mythology, Mnemosyne is the goddess of memory. From her name comes the word *mnemonics* (pronounced knee-MON-iks—try saying it out loud). Mnemonics are techniques used to improve memory.

Memory Smart presents nine mnemonic techniques. Each technique improves memory by increasing retrieval cues.

Most people are familiar with *external* retrieval cues. Have you ever put a rubber band around your finger to make sure you don't forget about the water boiling on the stove? Have you set your child's lunch bag near the front door so it doesn't get left behind in the rush to get to school? Do you put a Post-It® note on the refrigerator to remind you of appointments like seeing a doctor or attending a parent-teacher conference? The rubber band, lunch bag location, and Post-It® note are examples of external retrieval cues that remind us of what needs to be done. *Internal* retrieval cues are the mental versions of rubber bands, lunch bag location, and Post-It® notes. *Memory Smart* explains how to work with *internal* retrieval cues. Here is an example of those cues in action:

Write down the names of the seven dwarfs in *Snow White and the Seven Dwarfs*.

1. _____   5. _____
2. _____   6. _____
3. _____   7. _____
4. _____

Was it hard to remember all the dwarfs' names? If it was a tough question for you, that's because fill-in-the-blank questions are low in retrieval cues. Beyond the request for information and the cue that there are seven dwarfs, the question doesn't do much to jog your memory. Those dwarf names may be tucked in the folds of your brain, but where?

Let's try the same question in a multiple-choice format. Look over the following list and circle the names of the dwarfs in *Snow White and the Seven Dwarfs*:

Sleepy

Floppy

Grumpy

Sloppy

Envious

Dopey

Hopeful

Sneezy

Happy

Jokey

Nasty

Bashful

Doc

Most people find the multiple-choice test easier than the filling in the blanks because multiple-choice tests are loaded with retrieval cues. You see the dwarf's name and recognize it. Recognition means it was in your memory all along.*

Teaching mnemonic techniques helps children set up *internal* retrieval cues, which make the process of retrieving information more like a multiple-choice test. Mnemonic techniques increase retrieval cues and improve concentration as well.

Memory and Concentration

Have you ever had the I-just-read-ten-pages-and-don't-remember-a-thing experience? Reading does not guarantee remembering. The typical advice you get for I-just-read-ten-pages-and-don't-remember-a-thing is to concentrate. But what does it mean to concentrate?

---

* The dwarfs in *Snow White and the Seven Dwarfs* are Sleepy, Grumpy, Dopey, Sneezy, Happy, Bashful, and Doc.

If you read at a superficial level, the content goes into your short-term memory. There, information is stored for thirty seconds or less, after which it disappears. For thirty precarious seconds, information sits in a basket on the front porch of your consciousness, but it needs a nudge to cross the threshold into long-term memory. Mnemonic techniques provide that nudge.

There are a number of theories for why mnemonic techniques work. One theory is that mnemonic techniques encourage active mental manipulation of information, which stimulates the brain into manufacturing special proteins. These proteins are related to long-term memory but their formation is not stimulated by casual reading. This exercise will illustrate the point. Look at the following list of nine words:

substitution
chaining
mapping
pegging
association
rhyming
initials
senses
chunking

Now turn away from the book and count to thirty. When you finish counting, write down the nine words. Did most of them vanish from memory? Soon after simply reading the words they are swept off the front porch of short-term memory.

Now put each of the words from the previous list into one of the four boxes below. You decide on the criteria for grouping words together:

After putting the words into categories, count to thirty, and then write down as many words as you can.

Did you do better the second time? That could be from actively manipulating the material, helping the brain move the words into long-term memory.

If you become even more involved with these nine words—say, you draw a picture for each word—then recall will be even higher.

By the way, these nine words are the labels for the nine mnemonic techniques presented in *Memory Smart*. Let's look at each technique in detail.

Infantile Amnesia

Infantile amnesia refers to the difficulty of recalling specific events before age 3. It doesn't mean that youngsters aren't learning but rather that they are assembling general patterns. Children exposed to a foreign language or violin lessons at an early age may forget the skill without practice, but if they return, even years later, they relearn the material more rapidly than their unexposed peers.

The Nine Mnemonic Techniques

SUBSTITUTION

The mnemonic technique of substitution is based on the observation that high-imagery words are easier to remember than low-imagery words. So what's a high-imagery word? It's one that instantly brings a picture to mind, like the nouns *pretzel, diamond,* and *waterfall.* Low-imagery words, on the other hand, like *sequence, loss,* and *certain,* take more effort to visualize.

Substitution replaces a low-imagery word with a high-imagery sound-alike word. For example, *substitution* is a low-imagery word—just try to draw it! *Submarine,* on the other hand, a high-imagery word, is much easier to draw. And it also sounds similar to *substitution.* Okay, it's not identical—but it doesn't have to be. Approximations create retrieval cues. Remember how much easier a multiple-choice test is than a fill-in-the-blank test? Using *submarine* in place of *substitution* provides a retrieval cue.

In the following exercise, circle the high-imagery words:

armpit	freedom
motif	prowess
Swiss cheese	fangs
cancel	skeleton*

Was it easy for you to determine which words were high imagery? You read *armpit* and bingo, there's an image. On the other hand, you read the word *motif* and you have to think for a moment—probably more than a moment. You might *still* be at a loss for an image. Face it, your memory is biased. It's partial to words that immediately spark an image. Give your memory a choice between *fangs* and *prowess,* and it will remember *fangs.* The mnemonic technique of substitution takes advantage of this imagery bias. Substitution converts abstract, hard-to-picture words and concepts into concrete, easy-to-visualize words.

---

* High-imagery words are: armpit, Swiss cheese, fangs, and skeleton. Low-imagery words are freedom, prowess, cancel, and motif.

Can You Visualize?

Answer the following question before reading any further:

How many windows are there in your house?

To answer this question, you probably imagined walking through the rooms of your house. In each room you stopped to count the virtual windows until you knew the total number. This shows you can visualize. If you still aren't convinced, ask yourself if you dream in words. Most people dream in pictures. Or, ask yourself how many capital letters in the alphabet have curves. Visualization may be a slippery skill, but you do have it.

An exercise at the end of this chapter requires memorizing a list that contains the nine mnemonic techniques used in *Memory Smart*: substitution, chaining, mapping, pegging, association, rhyming, initials, senses, and chunking. In the earlier exercise using those words, you probably found them hard to remember, even if you put them into categories. The problem with memorizing them is that words like *substitution* and *association* have low imagery value and are thus hard to remember. The solution is to use the mnemonic substitution technique.

Even Experts Do Better with High-Imagery Words

The memory expert known as T. E. was presented with thirty words and only three seconds to study each one. When tested, he recalled the high-imagery words perfectly, but only about 20% of the low-imagery words.

To help your memory, each of the mnemonic techniques covered in this book is represented by an easy-to-visualize symbol. As you noticed at the beginning of this section, substitution is represented by a sign with a submarine on it.

Here's another example of how substitution can be used. Let's say you're learning Spanish. In Spanish, the word for hair is *pelo* (pronounced PAY-low). Using substitution, you convert the sound of the Spanish word into a familiar sound-alike English word. *Pelo* sounds like *pillow*. Next, imagine a pillow in place of your hair. When asked for the word *hair* in Spanish, you visualize what replaces your hair, a pillow. This approximation is close enough to jog your memory. You respond "pelo."

Memory and language experts agree that using substitution is a great way to build a foreign vocabulary. In one study, by using substitution students increased their language retention for Spanish by 88%. Using a rote technique, they only improved by 28%. This means that your child, studying a list of 100 Spanish words, would be likely to remember 88 with the substitution technique but only 28 with rote repetition in the same amount of time.

But the uses of substitution aren't limited to learning a foreign language. Substitution can be used for any unfamiliar word. For instance, science classes are loaded with unfamiliar and often complex words: altocumulus, Paleozoic, metamorphic, stegosaurus, mitochondria, and femur, to name a few. Until children are fluent in a subject's jargon, they encounter many speed bumps to learning. The substitution technique smoothes linguistic speed bumps. It helps children at home and in school memorize new words in such areas as:

- Foreign languages
- Scientific terminology
- People's names
- English vocabulary words
- Geographical names

Using substitution is also a powerful way to memorize concepts. You've probably used it yourself without realizing it. If you've compared an atom to the solar system, the brain to a computer, or playing the stock market to gambling, you've used substitution. The substitute is a familiar image that makes the concept more memorable.

CHAINING

The symbol for the mnemonic technique of chaining is, logically, a chain.

Chaining is the mnemonic version of a memory charm bracelet. Like a charm bracelet, each link in a mnemonic chain has a piece of information attached to it. To retrieve that information, you work your way along the chain until you reach it. Chaining is used to:

- Deliver a speech without notes
- Remember sequential information like the names and order of the presidents of the United States
- Memorize an entire book's main points and examples

The beauty of chaining is that each piece of information acts as a retrieval cue for the next piece of information. When your youngster relates the story of *Goldilocks and the Three Bears,* you witness a simple example of chaining. The child begins with Goldilocks entering the house, then remembers the porridge, in the kitchen, followed by the chairs fiasco, in the living room, which leads, mentally, to the bedroom, the beds, and the denouement of the bears' discovery.

Two steps are required to create a mnemonic chain:

1. Create a mental picture for each piece of information.
2. Link the pictures together with action.

Let's say you want to remember nine items found in a survival kit: knife, fishing line, hooks, water bottle, hard candies, map, matches, space blanket, and compass. Here's how you commit this list to memory with chaining:

> A *knife* cuts *fishing line*. The fishing line is tied to a *hook*. The hook is dropped into a *water bottle* where it snags a piece of *hard candy* in a wrapper. The wrapper is peeled open to reveal a *map*. The map is ignited with a *match*. The burning map is covered by a *space blanket* to extinguish the flames. When the space blanket is lifted, there is a *compass* in place of the map.

Notice how actions connect items together, such as the *knife* cutting the *fishing line*. This action is the link. It's what makes chaining work. Like the trip action of dominoes falling over in order, each link (action) prompts your mind to go from one piece of information to the next. Often, the more outrageous the link, the more memorable it is.

Memorizing a Thousand Years of History

Maori Chief Kaumatara of New Zealand was able to recount the entire thousand-year history of his tribe—a feat that took three days. The mnemonic technique employed was probably chaining.

The next two mnemonic techniques, *mapping* and *pegging,* are versions of chaining.

MAPPING

Mapping is a special form of chaining. In classical literature on memory, mapping goes by the Latin name, *loci,* which means place.

The symbol for the mnemonic technique of mapping is a map with a dotted trail leading to an *X* (as in X marks the spot).

The invention of mapping mnemonics is attributed to the Greek poet Simonides. His discovery was prompted by a dramatic incident. Let's travel back in time to that occasion. It's 500 BC. Simonides is at the top of the poetry charts—a veritable rock star of rhyme. He has just finished a performance for a powerful—and vain—patron:

"Simonides, come," said Scopas, holding up an imperious hand to command silence in the banquet hall.

Simonides approached, his toga dusting the marble floor.

"Your poem is more than I could have wished for," said Scopas.

Simonides bowed politely.

"Yes, much more than I could have wished for," repeated Scopas more loudly for all his guests to hear. "I contract for a poem to entertain my guests with exploits of my career, which you do honestly." Scopas paused. "But then you praise the adventures of the gods Castor and Pollux for half the performance." Scopas smiled, a tight-lipped smile. "Yes it was much more than I could have wished for, considering it was I who paid for your muse and not the gods."

Scopas tossed a bag of coins at Simonides's feet.

"Since half the poem was mine," said Scopas, "I will pay my half." He paused. "Let the gods pay their half." Amused laughter erupted from the banquet audience.

Before Simonides could respond, a runner approached to whisper in his ear, "There are two young men with urgent business waiting outside. Make haste, as it pertains to life and death."

As Simonides crossed the threshold of the hall, a tremor shook the ground. Simonides stumbled forward. The columns leaned inward and the roof collapsed with a thunderous roar. Scopas and his guests were crushed. Only Simonides survived.

Later, when the grieving relatives arrived to claim the bodies, Simonides helped identify the unrecognizable corpses by using the mnemonic mapping technique.

"Scopas's sorrowful banquet was a lesson for me," said Simonides. "When asked to help identify the bodies, I reconstructed the banquet hall in my imagination. Then I walked the hall. As I gazed at each empty seat, the image of one of the doomed guests appeared: Epheus near the wine, Polonius reclining on a divan next to his beautiful wife, or Zeta in the alcove near the door." Simonides sighed.

"Later I realized this same principle could be employed by an orator such as myself to remember the order of ideas in a speech. First I needed a familiar locale, like the banquet hall. Since I am fond of walking, I chose a city street with distinctive landmarks: a well, the statue of Zeus, vendor stalls, and homes of friends. Then I dissected a speech into strong visual images. Prepared with these images I walked the street in my mind. At significant points, like the statue of Zeus, I deposited an image. One image per location, the images in the same order that they appeared in my speech. To retrieve the points of the speech in order, I simply walked the street in my mind and like a shopper collected each of the parts. I call this the 'method of loci'."

Simonides is considered the father of memory techniques. Orators of his time, lacking paper, committed hours of speech to memory. Simonides achieved patriarchal status by refining and teaching rhetorical memory skills in a memorable way. Think of the imagery he must have invoked by opening a lecture on memory with the drama of his shabby treatment by Scopas and ending with the gruesome scene of a building collapsing onto the audience. He must have made an impression, because later writers like Cicero wrote about it. His story may also have sent a message to future patrons. They would probably think twice about not paying for a performance.

Three steps are used in mapping mnemonics:

1. Choose a locale. Commit specific sites to memory—in the
    order in which you encounter those sites.

2. Create a mental picture for each piece of information you want to remember.
3. Link each picture to a site.

In mapping mnemonics you can use any of a variety of locales. You could use your own body, for example, designating the head, eyes, mouth, neck, and so on as the unique places to deposit your imagery. Here's a list of other places that could be used in mapping mnemonics:

- Interior of your house
- Playground and equipment
- Dollhouse
- Local park
- Baseball field or other sports arenas
- Pet's body (e.g., nose, ear, tail)

Mark Twain's Mental Parks

During Mark Twain's lecture tours across the United States, it was his habit to visit local parks before a performance. In the park he would choose specific objects like a bandstand, statue, and park bench. Then he would visualize images of the points he wanted to remember for his speech and associate them with the park objects, in order. To retrieve the information, he would stroll through the park in his mind and recall what he had associated with each landmark.

Camillo's Memory Theater

Camillo Delminio was famous in the sixteenth century. He was said to be able to talk with authority on any subject. As an aid to remembering, Camillo built what could be described as a memory theater or an elaborate dollhouse. It was large enough for two men to occupy. The interior of this structure had distinctive places, or loci. To use this theater to advantage, a trainee committed a series of locations to memory, then assigned an image to each one. These images were designed to jog the memory and were reputed to represent a substantial amount of the known information of the time. The theater, which had been partly financed by the king of France, disappeared mysteriously after Delminio's death.

PEGGING

The symbol for the mnemonic technique of *pegging* is, of course, a peg.

Pegging has two uses. It's used to memorize information that is best remembered in numeric order, and it's the technique of choice for memorizing numbers.

You can use pegging to teach a youngster something as simple as the months of the year, or help an older student memorize something as complex as the Periodic Table of Chemical Elements. Three steps are used in pegging:

1. First, convert numbers—1, 2, 3, 4, and so on—into memory-friendly images (referred to as pegs).
2. Next, translate blocks of information into images.
3. Finally, do a mental cut-and-paste collage. Imagine a peg superimposed on each image.

The various methods for assigning images to numbers are: rhyming patterns, formulas, shape similarity, and logical association. To illustrate the process, let's use logical association. Using this method, you assign an image to a number based on things often associated with that number. A unicorn has one horn. An airplane has two wings. A tricycle has three wheels. The following images could be applied to the numbers one through twelve:

One	Unicorn (one horn)
Two	Airplane (two wings)
Three	Tricycle (three wheels)
Four	Wagon (four wheels)
Five	Hand (five fingers)
Six	Ant (six legs)
Seven	Calendar (seven days in a week)
Eight	Ice skating (a figure eight)
Nine	Cat (nine lives)
Ten	Toes (ten toes)
Eleven	Football (eleven on a team)
Twelve	Carton of eggs (a dozen eggs)

Here's what a clock face would look like if you replaced the numbers with logical images:

A logical clock face

Close your eyes and try to see this clock face in your mind's eye. Check each number to make sure you have assigned the correct number to the right image.

When you have your pegs committed to memory, you're ready to hang information on them. But first your information must be turned into pictures. Let's say you want to teach a child the months of the year. Use substitution to turn the name for each month into a sound-alike word or phrase. This sound-alike must be something you can picture in your mind:

Month	Sounds Like	Picture
January	Jam berries	Jam jar filled with berries
February	Fern berries	Ferns covered with berries
March	March	Marching figures
April	Apes	Apes
May	May	Maypole
June	June	June bug
July	Jewel	A jewel
August	A gust	A gust of wind
September	Soap ten bears	Rubbing soap on ten bears
October	Octopus bear	Octopus wrapped around a bear
November	Nova bear	A nova exploding around a bear
December	Dice bears	Dice being rolled by bears

Now collage your pegs and images for the months of the year together:

Month	Images Collaged Together
January	A unicorn with a jam jar twirling on its horn throwing out berries
February	A plane covered with ferns and berries
March	Tricycles marching across a parade ground
April	Wagons filled with apes
May	Hands holding up a Maypole
June	A June bug
July	A calendar with jewels scattered across it
August	A figure-eight skater blown by a gust of wind
September	A cat soaping up ten bears
October	Toes on octopus-covered bears
November	A football team of exploding nova bears
December	A carton of eggs rolling dice with bears

When a child has attached the twelve monthly images to his pegs, he's ready. Ask him, "What is the third month?"

He says, "Three is a tricycle. Let's see, what is the tricycle doing? Oh yeah, it's *marching*. The third month is March."

Then ask, "What is the ninth month?"

He says, "Nine is a cat. The cat is *soaping* up *ten bears*. Soaping ten bears sounds like September."

A pegging system allows you to mentally scroll through your number-images, then retrieve the information-image attached to each number.

Mnemonic pegging can be used to memorize information that must be kept in numeric or linear order such as:

- Months of the year
- Amendments to the Constitution of the United States
- The Periodic Table of Chemical Elements
- A book's main points, in order
- Points you want to make in a speech

Pegs Training Dramatically Helps Recall

A group of children 10–12 years of age were shown twenty numbered pictures from a magazine. Ten minutes later they were asked to list in proper order the pictures they had seen. Two tests were conducted. The first test was before memory training. The second test was after thirty minutes of training in peg mnemonics. Different sets of pictures were used for each test. Here are representative results:

Student	Pictures recalled before memory training	Pictures recalled after memory training
Kim	4	14
Jeff	6	16
Cook	13	19

Pegging can also be used to remember strings of numbers, such as:

- Telephone numbers
- Addresses
- Dates

To remember strings of numbers, you need to learn a code. Chapters 11 and 12 and Appendix 3 present three different codes. These codes allow you to turn numbers into more easily remembered pictures or phrases.

How Many Numbers Can a Child Remember?

The typical memory span for digits is two items for a 2-year-old, five items for a 7-year-old, and seven items for a 12-year-old.

Peg Training

A 19-year-old man was trained in pegging mnemonics in seventy sessions over a period of five months. Given just five seconds per number, he could commit eighty numbers to memory. People without training are capable of remembering an average of seven digits.

ASSOCIATION

The symbol for the mnemonic technique of association is an ass—the donkey kind. Here again is an example of using substitution to get a visual image. Ass is the retrieval cue for *ass*ociation.

Does thunder make you think of lightning? If it does, then you have an association. One thing makes you think of another. This mnemonic technique relies on familiar pairs that are already bonded together in your memory: salt and pepper, windmills and Holland, and meat and potatoes.

The Russian scientist Pavlov did experiments using association. First he presented doggie treats to a pack of pooches. The prospect of food induced salivation. Then Pavlov rang a bell every time he produced the treats. In other words, he paired the ring of a bell with the presence of treats. Soon the dogs would salivate at the sound of the bell. They had formed an association between the bell and the treats.

Advertisers know the power of association. The most powerful advertising associates a product with something positive:

1. "How do you spell relief? R-O-L-A-I-D-S" (but you actually spell relief R-E-L-I-E-F)
2. It's the Pepsi _____ (fill in the blank)
3. Built Ford _____ (fill in the blank)

The substitution technique you read about earlier in this chapter is difficult to apply to some words. When that's the case, the mnemonic technique of association can save the day. For example, maybe you are trying to remember New Mexico and its capital. You have no trouble with the capital, Santa Fe. You use a substitution and think *Santa's sleigh*. But you also need an image for the state. New Mexico throws you. There doesn't seem to be a reasonable substitution. In this case you could make an association. An item commonly associated with Mexico is a sombrero, so a *new sombrero* could be the image you associate with New Mexico. You would finish up by chaining your association, a new sombrero, to Santa's sleigh. Imagine Santa in his sleigh wearing a new sombrero. When someone asks, "What's the capital of New Mexico?" You think, "New Mexico was a new sombrero that was worn by Santa in his sleigh. It's Santa Fe!"

RHYMING

The symbol for the mnemonic technique of rhyming is a musical note because musical notes are often associated with rhyme and rhythm.

Rhyming and rhythm are among the oldest mnemonic techniques. Songs and poems of ancient times were coded memory devices. Farmers learned rhymes to know when to plant. Histories were passed from generation to generation in rhythmic fashion. Shakespeare's "Double, double, toil and trouble, fire burn and cauldron bubble" has a cadence that marches into memory. Even Lewis Carroll's nonsensical *Jabberwocky*, "Twas brillig, and the slithy toves did gyre and gimble in the wabe: All mimsy were the borogoves, and the mome raths outgrabe," is easier to remember because of its rhyming quality.

What's Learned with Rhyme and Rhythm?

- ABCs are memorized by singing them to the tune of *Twinkle, Twinkle, Little Star*.
- *The Star Spangled Banner*. Try singing *The Star Spangled Banner* to a different tune like *Old Macdonald Had a Farm*. Without the original tune, the words are difficult to remember.
- Righty, tighty; lefty, loosey: The directions to screw the cap onto a jar—right to tighten and left to loosen.

Rhyme and rhythm can also be used to memorize:

- Multiplication tables
- Historical dates
- The number of days in the different months

> ### Memory and Rhythm
>
> It was said that a well-trained troubadour could memorize several hundred new lines of poetry after hearing them spoken only three times. Up until about the fourteenth century, except for legal documents, almost all material was written in rhyme. French merchants had a poem made up of 137 rhyming couplets, for example, that contained all the rules necessary to conduct commercial arithmetic.

INITIALS

The symbol for the mnemonic technique of initials is the single letter *I*, which happens to be the initial of the word *initial*.

The initials technique can be broken down into two categories: acronyms and acrostics. A classic acronym is HOMES, in which each letter represents one of the Great Lakes (Huron, Ontario, Michigan, Erie, and Superior).

Another initials technique, an acrostic, makes a word out of the first letter in each word. In the case of the Great Lakes, an acrostic is: Some Ears Hear Only Music (Superior, Erie, Huron, Ontario, and Michigan).

The initials technique can be used to memorize:

- Geographical facts
- Order of colors in a rainbow
- Classification system in life sciences

Your Order Please

J. C., a waiter, could remember up to twenty complete dinner orders. Researchers created a laboratory restaurant that offered as many as 600 different possible orders. J. C. made virtually no mistakes while others made many errors. J. C. used the initials system. To remember which salad dressings people ordered, for example, he used the first letter of each dressing to make up a word. He would remember an order for Bleu cheese, Oil and vinegar, Oil and vinegar, and Thousand island as BOOT. When J. C. was prevented from using this system, his ability to remember orders dropped closer to that of other waiters.

The Initials Technique
in the Cockpit and the Hospital

The initials technique of mnemonics is used in a variety of memory-intensive occupations. Airplane pilots, for example, are required to remember many facts. To help pilots remember the instruments and equipment required for Visual Flight Rules for day flight, they use initials to form the phrase GOOSE A CAT: Gas gauge, Oil pressure gauge, Oil temperature gauge, Seat belts and shoulder straps, Emergency locator transmitter, Altimeter, Compass, Airspeed indicator, and Tachometer.

A doctor or emergency medical technician might rely on I SHIP HAM to remember to take your complete medical history: Immunizations, Surgeries, Hospitalizations, Injuries, Past illnesses, Habits, Allergies, and Medications.

Senses

The symbols for the mnemonic technique of senses are an eye, ear, and hand, together. The eye (visual), ear (auditory), and hand (kinesthetic) are the delivery slots to our memories. Visual and auditory are self-explanatory. Kinesthetic includes hands-on experience as well as smell and taste.

Just as children have a preference for being left- or right-handed, they also have a preference for how they gather information. Visual processors take in information best by seeing diagrams, pictures, models, and the real thing. Auditory processors prefer listening to an explanation. They are strong on stories and benefit from discussing what they are learning. Kinesthetic processors need hands-on projects that involve manipulation and physical movement. How information is presented can help or hinder the memory process.

The Statistics of Processing

Approximately 65% of Americans favor visual processing, 20% favor auditory, and 15% are heavily kinesthetic.

If you provide information in the mode your children or students are most receptive to, they will feel more competent, learn faster, and have greater retention.

Visual, Auditory, and Kinesthetic Modes

For the following questions, put a *V* next to the question if it makes you think visually, an *A* if it requires auditory memory, and a *K* if it requires kinesthetic memory.

- When you type, where is the letter *w* located on a keyboard?
- What is the fourth word in "The Star Spangled Banner"?
- What color is your toothbrush?

The first question is most likely answered by relying on kinesthetic memory. Did you pretend to type, to see where your fingers would go? Identifying the fourth word in "The Star Spangled Banner" relies on auditory memory. Most people start the song inside their head until they come to the fourth word. Remembering the color of your toothbrush relies on visual memory. Did you close your eyes or defocus and see a picture of your bathroom and slowly pan in on the toothbrush?

Senses mnemonics takes a subject that is usually taught in one sensory mode and teaches it using the other senses. For example, the alphabet is traditionally taught as an auditory learning experience in which children practice the phonics of singing A, B, C, D, E, … . A new generation of learn-to-read programs, such as *Zoophonics,* assigns a physical motion to each letter of the alphabet. This alphabet sign language gives children a way to make learning the alphabet hands-on, or kinesthetic.

There's a big advantage to using senses mnemonics. The more senses you involve in learning, the more retrieval cues you put into place to recover a memory.

One theory says that memory resides on macrocolumns in your brain. These columns contain a few dozen to a few hundred neurons. When a memory is laid down, it might enter different macrocolumns as visual, auditory, or kinesthetic deposits. When you search for a memory, because there are different sites, the chances of finding it are greater. It's like having access to your local bank branch, an ATM machine, and online banking. By employing several senses you can make withdrawals from your memory bank at several sites.

When analyzing a lesson plan, teachers would do well to see how they're employing senses mnemonics. They can do this by simply jotting a V (visual), A (auditory), or K (kinesthetic) next to each presentation technique. A preponderance of one letter would show the need to come up with alternative methods for presenting to the other senses.

A Smelly Memory

Researchers had people look at photos while an aroma was spritzed into the room. Later, when asked to look at a selection of photos, people were more accurate in recognizing the pictures they had previously seen if the same odor was in the room. If another odor, different from the original, was in the room, people made more errors.

CHUNKING

The symbol for the mnemonic technique of chunking is a chunk taken out of an apple.

Chunking refers to the organization of information, making it easier to memorize. Consider the following diagram, labeled Pattern 1. Take ten seconds to memorize all the pieces. Then take another piece of paper and redraw them from memory.

Pattern 1

If you rearrange Pattern 1 into what you see in Pattern 2, you will find it much easier to remember the elements:

Pattern 2

Pattern 2 is easier to remember because it chunks, or connects, seemingly random elements into a familiar pattern.

If you were asked to remember a long string of numbers—1, 8, 4, 8, 1, 7, 4, 7, 1, 4, 9, 2—like most other people, you would have a tough time. This is because the average adult's short-term memory can handle only five to nine items. The twelve numbers listed above exceed your short-term limit, but you can increase it by chunking. Take those twelve numbers and group them as dates—1848, 1747, and 1492—and you'll have much better luck remembering.

Chunking, which can be used to memorize any subject, also makes it easier to transfer information to long-term memory.

Telephone Number Recall

In 1956, George Miller studied people's ability to recall various lists of digits, letters, and words. His findings showed that most adults could recall seven items or chunks, give or take an item or two. The telephone company was aware of this study when, in an effort to cut down on operator assistance, they reduced the standard telephone number to seven digits.

Symbols for the Nine Memory Techniques

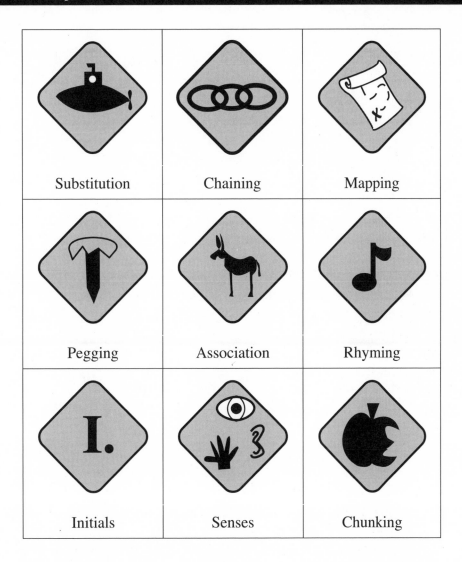

Substitution	Chaining	Mapping
Pegging	Association	Rhyming
Initials	Senses	Chunking

These symbols serve two purposes. First, they make it easier to remember the mnemonic techniques covered in this book. Second, these symbols appear throughout the book to indicate which mnemonic technique or combination is being used to memorize a specific subject.

Can you identify each symbol? Take a sheet of paper and cover the chart. Pull the sheet of paper down so you can see the first row of symbols but not the words. Identify the symbols, then do the same for the next two rows.

Two Ways to Read this Book

You can read this book for a general appreciation of memory techniques, or you can go for the long-term-memory benefits.

If you want this information in your long-term memory, do the exercises. The exercise below will enable you to remember the nine mnemonic techniques. Having this mental list will help you as you move to other chapters and read practical examples of how to use these techniques. Eventually you'll be able to sit down with a subject not found in this book and go through your mental outline and choose a mnemonic technique appropriate for the new material.

Memorizing the Nine Mnemonic Techniques

You have a choice. Do you want to use a chaining technique or a mapping technique to memorize the symbols? Use Exercise 1 for chaining. Use Exercise 2 for mapping.

EXERCISE 1

Let's chain the mnemonic symbols together. Imagine a hand with eyes and ears (senses). The hand is holding a wooden peg (pegging). Attached to the peg is a chain (chaining). Follow the chain to a submarine (substitution). The submarine's propeller is scattering musical notes (rhyming) in its wake. The musical notes enter an ass's (association) ear. The ass bites a chunk out of an apple (chunking). The apple is set down on a map (mapping). The map rests on a table shaped like the letter I (initials).

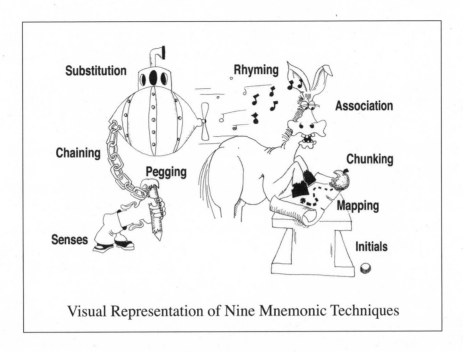

Visual Representation of Nine Mnemonic Techniques

Close your eyes and verbally go back through the chain. If you simply read, you will not push this fact across the threshold that separates your short- and long-term memory. Once you have the story committed to memory, explain which memory technique is represented by which symbol.

EXERCISE 2

Another way to remember the nine mnemonic techniques is to use mapping. For this we need some places. Let's use your body. Use nine distinctive places on your body:

1. The top of your head
2. Eyes
3. Mouth
4. Neck
5. Shoulders

6. Belly button
7. Fanny
8. Thighs
9. Knees

Without looking at the list, touch each body part in descending order. Do this touch test until you have the places committed to memory.

When you have all your body places memorized, you are ready to put an image at each place:

1. Imagine a submarine (substitution) on the top of your head.
2. Your eyes have pegs (pegging) in them.
3. An apple fills your mouth with a chunk (chunking) missing.
4. Your neck has a thick chain (chaining) wrapped around it.
5. Two folded maps (mapping) are on your shoulders like epaulets.
6. Musical notes (rhyming) are coming out of your belly button.
7. Your fanny is seated on an ass (association).
8. Your thighs have eyes, hands, and ears (senses).
9. The initial *I* (initials) is tattooed on your knee.

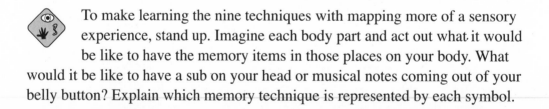 To make learning the nine techniques with mapping more of a sensory experience, stand up. Imagine each body part and act out what it would be like to have the memory items in those places on your body. What would it be like to have a sub on your head or musical notes coming out of your belly button? Explain which memory technique is represented by each symbol.

How Memory Smart Works

Equipped with a mental outline of the techniques taught in this book, you're ready for a specific topic—remembering names—which is in the next chapter. This is a must-read chapter because it involves a memory skill that is used in many of the other chapters.

Starting at Chapter 4, *Memory Smart* addresses subjects (content) that children learn in kindergarten and elementary school and embeds memory techniques (process) in those subjects. Each subject chapter stands alone. This means if you are teaching multiplication tables, go to that section. If you are helping a child memorize all fifty states and their capitals, go to that section. These stand-alone chapters contain all the information, illustrations, games, and memory techniques you need to teach that subject.

Before teaching a subject, read through the chapter. If you want to play the games or do some of the special projects, assemble the recommended supplies beforehand. Once you're familiar with a chapter, you can learn right along with your own children or your students.

If you are goal oriented, take a quick look at Chapter 28, *Become a Memory Black Belt*. This chapter contains a list of memory tasks that you can accomplish as you work your way through *Memory Smart*. If you completed Exercise 1 or 2 in this chapter, you have already earned a check mark in the extra credit section.

As a memory coach, you help children learn subjects faster and with better retention. But you do more than teach content. You teach process. As children use mnemonic techniques to learn additional school subjects, they build an example file of how their memory can be used. With sufficient examples, they will understand how to apply mnemonics to any subject. You're actually coaching children toward memory literacy.

Now, how do we remember names? Go to Chapter 3 to find out. The three S's technique presented in Chapter 3 is a vital memory skill used in many chapters in the book. It's a must-read chapter.

The Say, See, Stick Method for Remembering Names

Here's where we learn to remember people's names. You might ask, "How does remembering names fit into academics?"

A huge amount of school material is based on remembering names—names for scientific terms and names for parts of speech, names in geography and names in history. Vocabulary words are just names, and a foreign language is just new names for stuff you already know. Besides, one way for children to develop a better memory for names in school subjects is to start working on the social skill of remembering people's names. As children learn how to remember people's names, they also learn the techniques for memorizing terms used in all the school subjects they study.

Moreover, having the ability to remember people's names helps a child feel more comfortable in a group. This, in turn, helps a child enjoy school more, which ultimately contributes to better academic work.

Learn the Three S's for Memorizing Names

MEET SANDI

Ten-year-old Sandi was nervous. Her family had recently moved from Boston to California, and it was her first day at a new school. She didn't know anyone. But her mother had coached her on ways she could make friends, like remembering names. "The sweetest sound to anyone's ear is the sound of her own name," said her mom. "When you remember someone's name, especially if you have just met, it makes her feel good."

Sandi knew that her mother had a great memory for names. At the church they attended, she was a greeter, that is, she welcomed people as they came through the church doors. Her mother made it a point to learn the names of everyone in the congregation—more than 300 people. In the beginning, people were surprised at being greeted by name.

"Learning people's names makes you more comfortable being around those people," said her mom. "The faster you learn your classmate's names, the faster you'll feel comfortable."

SAY, SEE, AND STICK

Sandi's mom taught her three secrets for remembering names, and she called them the three **S's**—Say, See, and Stick.

SAY	Say a person's name five times out loud when you first meet them.
SEE	Turn the person's name into something you can see.
STICK	Stick the image you've created onto a unique feature of that person.

Sandi decided to make it a game and learn ten classmates' names on her first day at school. When she arrived at school, she was assigned a buddy, another student to show her around. Sandi started with the first S—Say the other person's name five times soon after meeting them.

"Hi. I'm Julie."

"Hi Julie [first chance to say the other student's name]. I'm Sandi."

Every time Sandi asked a question she used Julie's name. "Julie [second time], did Ms. Hemstead say the homework was due on Tuesday or Wednesday?" "Julie [third time], where are the bathrooms?" "I'm sorry, Julie [fourth time], I didn't hear you." "Julie [fifth time], do you buy lunch in the cafeteria or bring lunch?"

In saying the name five times Sandi made sure she heard the name correctly in the first place. While this dialogue may sound stilted in writing, in a real conversation with pauses, it sounds quite natural.

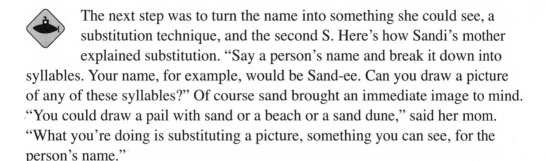 The next step was to turn the name into something she could see, a substitution technique, and the second S. Here's how Sandi's mother explained substitution. "Say a person's name and break it down into syllables. Your name, for example, would be Sand-ee. Can you draw a picture of any of these syllables?" Of course sand brought an immediate image to mind. "You could draw a pail with sand or a beach or a sand dune," said her mom. "What you're doing is substituting a picture, something you can see, for the person's name."

Sandi tried substitution on Julie's name. Jul-ie. The first part sounded like "jewel." The jewels that Sandi imagined were diamonds.

Now Sandi was ready for the last memory step, sticking the substitute image onto the person. Her mother explained by asking, "Remember the art project you did in fourth grade? You made a collage by sticking one picture on another? This is a similar idea. When you look at someone, find a distinctive feature. Maybe they have bushy eyebrows, or wide shoulders, or a prominent nose. Imagine the image you created, glued to that feature. Close your eyes and see that object on your new friend."

This is how Sandi attached the image of jewels to an outstanding feature on Julie.

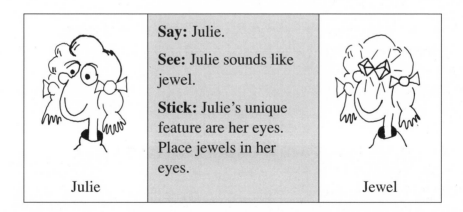

Say: Julie.

See: Julie sounds like jewel.

Stick: Julie's unique feature are her eyes. Place jewels in her eyes.

Julie

Jewel

Now when Sandi looked at Julie, she went to Julie's distinctive eyes and remembered the jewels. The jewels reminded her of the name Julie. In several days, Sandi knew the names of all the children in her class. Her mother was right.

When Sandi could ask, "Carolyn, may I play four square with you?" or "Tom, was I supposed to be in your study group?" it made her feel a lot more comfortable.

Using Substitution on Difficult Names—Schmurgling

Sandi didn't find all the names as easy as Julie's. Some names don't instantly produce an image. But substitution will work even for those names that don't. Some names require a close approximation. Whenever we need a close approximation, we *schmurgle* the name. To schmurgle, say a name in a sloppy way and listen for a word that can be turned into an image. Let's schmurgle a name that doesn't immediately bring an image to mind:

Say E-liz-a-beth. Notice how it is broken into syllables. Now schmurgle it. Say each syllable as if you were chewing a big wad of gum and a spoonful of peanut butter:

A-lizard-bath

Now that we have an image, *a lizard bath*, we stick this image onto an outstanding feature on Elizabeth. You notice that she has a long neck. Imagine her in a bath with a lizard. Elizabeth's long neck holds her head high above the bath water:

The Three S's—*saying* a person's name five times, turning their name into a picture you can *see,* and *sticking* that picture onto a prominent feature on that person—will make you a name whiz.

The Name Game

 When students in a memory class were asked if they would have trouble recalling the names of twenty people they had just met at a party, most raised their hands. Then everyone was asked to stand up and form a circle. The instructor introduced himself, saying, "My name is Jim." He then bent over and put his hands on the floor and asked, "What piece of playground equipment would I look like if I turned into steel? As a hint, part of that playground equipment has my name in it." The answer, a jungle *gym*. The image of this tall man bent over into a piece of playground equipment was memorable. Going around the circle, each person was given a substitute image for his name and a way to attach it to his features.

At that point, three bean bags were brought out. As each person was tossed a bag, they said three names in the following order:

1. The name of the person who tossed it
2. The receiver's own name
3. The name of the person to whom it would be tossed next

This got everyone saying names for several minutes. At the end of the game, people who would have had trouble remembering names at a party went around the circle and identified each person. Everyone was surprised at their ability to recall twenty or more names.

People who say they have a bad memory for names really mean that they have a bad strategy for remembering names. If they had a good strategy, they would be able to remember names.

The Most Common Memory Complaint

Few children are taught how to remember names. This may be why the most common memory complaint has to do with remembering names. In one study, 83% of people polled said that remembering names was a problem.

Year Book Memories

Within three months of graduating from high school, students were 90% correct in deciding that pictures of former classmates were familiar, but they could recall only 70% of their classmates' names that went with the pictures. Forty-eight years later, they were 70% correct in picking out photos of former classmates but they could only recall about 20% of the names.

Merely reading a book on exercise won't make you stronger. Similarly, reading a book on memory won't improve your memory. Improving physically or mentally requires practice.

Practice Turning Names into Images

Practice turning people's names into images. The following lists contain a number of common names. Starting with the beginner list, try coming up with an image for each name. You should be able to find a sound-alike substitution that is very close to the person's name for this list. Some names have already been substituted to get you started.

Beginning Level
Angela = Angel
Barry = Berry
Gail =
Rod =
Peggy = Peg
Daisy =
Mark =
Harry =
Doug =
Ray =
Jennie =
Jim =

If you found the beginner list easy, more challenging names follow in the intermediate and advanced lists.

As you start to work on the intermediate list, here's a tip. Say each name out loud. Saying the name out loud makes it easier to hear a possible substitution. When children say the word inside their head, they seem to have a harder time coming up with substitutions. In the case of a name made up of multiple syllables, saying the name out loud, syllable by syllable, may indicate multiple substitutions. In the case of Jackie, you should hear *Jack*, like the jacks you play with, and *key*. Both *Jack* and *key* then become your substitute image. You might imagine someone playing the game of jacks and using keys. As in the beginner list, some of the substitutions are already worked out for you.

Intermediate Level
Jackie = Jack key
Isabel = It's a bell
Kathy =
Ginger =
Manuel = Manual
Jose =
Dennis =
Max =
Don =
Sue =
Wendy =
Jennifer =

You are now ready for the advanced list. The advanced list requires that you listen for close approximations in the sound of the name in order to come up with a substitution. This is where schmurgling comes in handy. Tip: Try to get your approximation to start with the same sound as the target name. If the person's name is Fred, you are better off with *fried* than *red*. *Fried* starts with the same sound as the original name. This makes it easier to retrieve the correct name later.

Advanced Level
Kevin = Cave in
Fred = Fried
Chrissie =
Oliver =
Debbie = Dead bee
Silvia =
Frank =
Victoria =
Mitchell = Mitt shell
Tess =
Zoe = Zoo
Chris =

If you found some of the names on these substitution lists challenging, turn the page for solutions to the names that stumped you.

BEGINNER		INTERMEDIATE		ADVANCED	
Angela	angel	**Jackie**	jack key	**Kevin**	cave in
Barry	berry	**Isabel**	it's a bell	**Fred**	fried
Gail	gale (wind)	**Kathy**	cat	**Victoria**	victory sign
Rod	rod (fishing)	**Ginger**	ginger (bread)	**Oliver**	olive
Peggy	peg	**Manuel**	manual	**Debbie**	dead bee
Daisy	daisy (flower)	**Jennifer**	jeans fur	**Silvia**	silver
Mark	mark (ink)	**Dennis**	dentist	**Frank**	frank (hot dog)
Harry	hairy	**Max**	my ax	**Chrissie**	cross
Doug	dug	**Don**	dawn	**Mitchell**	mitt shell
Ray	ray (sun)	**Sue**	sew	**Tess**	test
Jennie	genie	**Wendy**	windy	**Zoe**	zoo
Jim	gym	**Jose**	hose	**Chris**	Christmas

PRACTICE SUBSTITUTING NAMES FOR A MONTH

Get a telephone book and put it under your bed. Every morning pull the book out, leaf through the pages, and randomly choose several names. Use substitution to convert these names into images. This is a simple way to become skilled at substitution.

Sticking Substitute Images

Now let's practice sticking substitute images. We'll start with cartoon characters and then advance to real people. In the beginning, a cartoon format makes it easier for children to focus on an outstanding feature. Here's how you play this game:

1. Cover up the two right-hand columns. All you should see are the cartoon characters and their names.
2. Use the cartoon character's name to create a substitute image.
3. Now choose an outstanding feature on the cartoon character and imagine attaching your image—as in Pin the Tail on the Donkey—to the cartoon character's face or body.
4. Uncover the right-hand columns to see some possibilities.

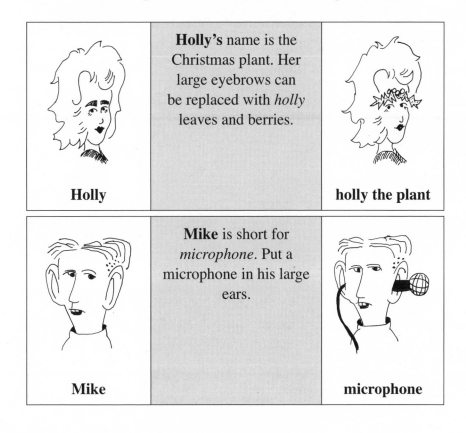

| **Holly** | **Holly's** name is the Christmas plant. Her large eyebrows can be replaced with *holly* leaves and berries. | **holly the plant** |
| **Mike** | **Mike** is short for *microphone*. Put a microphone in his large ears. | **microphone** |

Tom

Tom's name can be a drum, *tom-tom*. His flattop haircut is his tom-tom.

tom-tom

Sandi

Sandi sounds like *sand*. Her freckles stand out, so make her freckles beach sand or sandy.

sandy

Sue

Sue is close to *sew*. Take her expressive lips and see stitches or thread sewing them together.

sew

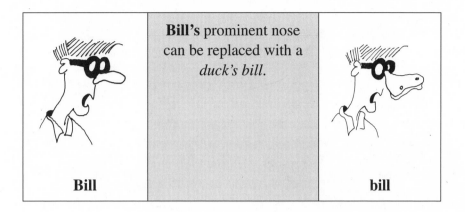

Bill's prominent nose can be replaced with a *duck's bill.*

Bill   bill

USE THE THREE S'S ON REAL PEOPLE

Now practice the Say, See, Stick memory technique on real people. In the photos you are about to see, use the following pattern to commit the names to memory.

SAY	Say the person's name five times. Do this in a make-believe conversation, as in "Glad to meet you, Amy." "How do you spell Amy?" "Amy, where do you go to school?" Remember that it is important to say the name out loud. Verbalizing helps place the name in long-term memory.
SEE	See the name. Turn it into a substitute image. The name Amy might be schmurgled to *aiming*.
STICK	Stick your image to an outstanding feature of the person in the picture. You might choose their forehead, eyebrows, nose, mouth, ears, or cheeks. The more unique the feature, the better. Amy has braces that will be there for awhile, so you might imagine Amy *aiming* through her braces.

Amy

Ben

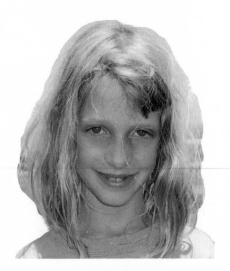

Delia

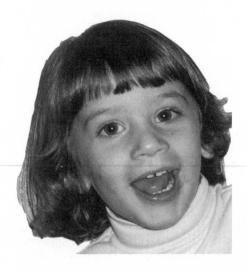

Nina

Bill

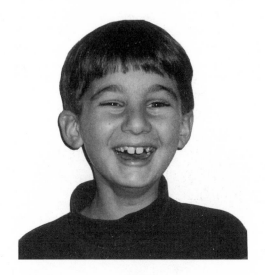

Nick

Renee

Susie

Some of the possible substitutions for the names of the people you looked at in the photos include:

Amy   *Aim*, like the sight on a rifle
Ben   *Bend*
Delia   *Dealing*, like a person dealing cards
Nina   *Knee*
Bill   *Dollar bill* or *duck's bill*
Nick   *Nick,* like a chip off a block
Renee   *Rainy*
Susie   *Sewing* or *sushi*

Hairy Identity

A group photo of soccer players was posted on the wall. Next to this photo was a picture of one player. People were asked to find this player in the group shot. After careful perusal, most people found the player in the second row. They were then asked if they noticed anything odd about the picture. "No," most replied. They were then told that all of the individuals on the soccer team were actually one person. The same person's face had been superimposed on each player, only his hair color or style had been changed. Of all the features on a person, the one that will change his appearance the most is his hair. Put Einstein's hair on Elvis Presley, and you will have a hard time recognizing Elvis.

Having a strategy for remembering names is a powerful social skill. Children who remember and use names come across as more confident and friendly than kids who call others "dude." Children with good name recall also are more poised in social situations. Have you ever met someone and then had to repeatedly ask his name because you forgot? If nothing else, it makes you feel awkward.

> ## Leaders Remember Names
>
> Having a good memory for names is often associated with leadership.
> * Napoleon could greet thousands of soldiers by name.
> * American politician James Farley claimed he was able to call 50,000 people by their first name.
> * Charles Schwab, manager of the Homestead Mill, knew all of his 8,000 employees by name.

DEVELOP SUBSTITUTIONS FOR SIXTY NAMES

The list following this paragraph contains sixty common names. These sixty names make up 50% of the names used in the United States. Become a name master. Devise substitutions for all sixty names. Then when you meet someone with one of these names you can quickly stick your substitute picture onto a prominent feature. (Several of the names are already worked out for you.)

Allen = alien	Andrew	Anthony
Bruce	Charles	Daniel
David	Donald	Douglas
Edward	Frank	Fred
George = gorge	Henry	Howard
Jack	Jim	John = long johns
Joe	Mark	Matt
Mike	Paul	Pete

Phil	Rick	Robert
Steve	Tom	Bill
Alice	Amy	Anne
Barbara	Carolyn = caroling	Catherine
Christine	Debbie	Diane
Donna	Elizabeth	Gail
Helen	Jane	Jean
Jennifer	Joan	Karen
Kate	Laura	Lisa
Marge	Marilyn	Mary
Nancy	Pat	Ruth
Sarah	Sue	Tina

4

Rapid ABCs: Learning to Read

In this chapter:

- Accelerate children's ability to read and write by making sure that the phonics programs they are using contain five mnemonic elements.

Most children in the United States learn to read and write by being taught phonics. Phonics means sounding out words by knowing the sounds that letters make. Learning to read, or more important, learning to *love* to read is influenced heavily by your choice of phonics programs. There are two types of phonics programs on the market, one relies on rote repetition for memorizing information. We'll call it mnemonic-poor. The second type of program makes extensive use of mnemonic techniques. We'll call it mnemonic-rich. Mnemonic-rich programs accelerate performance—often dramatically.

When a group of teachers in California were asked to compare mnemonic-poor and mnemonic-rich programs, they agreed that mnemonic-rich programs speed up acquisition of reading and writing skills by two to six months in a school year. What that means for an average first grader is that if your first grader was taught with a mnemonic-poor program, he would be able to read, "I like to swim," and maybe he could write it. But first graders taught with a mnemonic-rich program would be reading, "I like to swim in the swimming pool with my friends," and they would be able to write it.

Whether a program is mnemonic-rich or poor has nothing to do with when it came to market. Radio and television ads hype pricey new phonics programs that often incorporate little in the way of mnemonics.

As a parent or teacher, you need to be able to evaluate whether the phonics program you are using is mnemonic-rich or poor.

Mnemonic-Poor Phonics

If you walked in on a mnemonic-poor phonics class, you'd hear this:

"Look at this card," says the teacher as he holds up a card with the letter *A* printed on it. "My name is A and my sound is ahhh." This is the traditional way mnemonic-poor phonics is first introduced, followed by drills and repetition.

Mnemonic-Rich Phonics

Letterland, a program that originated in England, and *Zoophonics,* created in the U.S., are two mnemonic-rich programs. Both programs contain five characteristics that identify a mnemonic-rich program.

1. Pictures are superimposed over alphabet letters to make the letters memorable.
2. Children are taught the sound of a letter before they are taught the letter's name.
3. Each letter has a physical movement associated with it to make learning to read a whole-body experience.
4. Lowercase letters are learned before uppercase letters.
5. Stories replace rules to explain how combinations of letter sounds (e.g., ph, sh) result in unique sounds.

VISUAL PHONICS

To give you a gut feeling for understanding the importance of visual phonics, imagine you are being taught to read Chinese. In Chinese, each symbol represents a complete word. For example:

人	大	天
Man	**Big**	**Heaven**

Memorizing the symbol for each Chinese word is a daunting task until you realize that the words are pictograms, simple drawings of the object represented. Look at *man*—it's a stylistic drawing of a man walking. *Big* is *man* with an additional stroke that represents outstretched arms, suggesting the quality of bigness. *Heaven* is a *big man* whose head touches the sky, or heaven. Once you see the pictogram quality of a Chinese symbol, it's easier to remember.

English pictograms can also be used to make it easier for children to master their ABCs. In *Letterland* each letter of the alphabet has a recognizable shape woven into it. Letters are represented by animals, people, or objects that begin with the alphabet letter. Take *c, h,* and *a,* for example:

| **Clever Cat** | **Hairy Hat Man** | **Annie Apple** |

Using this approach, a mnemonic substitution technique, children quickly associate the characters of the alphabet with a letter shape. This reduces the abstract nature of the letter.

A two-and-a-half-year-old can memorize *Letterland* characters within weeks and point to the letters during bedtime stories, saying, "That's Clever Cat." "There's Hairy Hat Man." "Look at Annie Apple." So how do these pictograms translate into a child learning to read faster? This is where the visual and auditory aspect of modern phonics team up.

AUDIO PHONICS

In mnemonic-poor programs, children learn the alphabet name for each letter— *aee, bee, cee,* etc. In most cases, these sounds do not represent the sound of the spoken letter. If you tried to sound out the word *cat* using the alphabet names for the letters, it would sound like *cee … aee … tee*—not even close to cat.

Mnemonic-rich programs do not teach children *aee, bee, cee* until much later. Instead, these programs start by focusing children on the sound that a letter makes. When children see Hairy Hat Man, they also know the sound he makes. It's the beginning *hhh* in *hairy* and *hat*. In other words, the beginning of the character's name cues the child to the sound of that letter. This enables children to phonetically sound out simple words once they learn the names of the characters.

Music, tapes, and sing-along stories about the characters in programs like *Letterland* add further depth to the auditory component. But there's even more—kinesthetic enrichment.

HANDS-ON PHONICS

Involving children's bodies in learning also involves their minds. Many parts of the brain are used for even simple physical tasks, so appropriate movement helps children concentrate.

Here's one way new-generation phonics programs incorporate movement. In *Zoophonics,* each letter is represented by both a character and a unique physical movement. For example, the character for the letter *a* is Allie Alligator. To represent Allie, a child puts his hands together, then opens his arms wide, miming the opening of an alligator's mouth. Students' use of this sign language makes for a very active class.

Parent and teacher guides for mnemonic-rich phonics programs are packed with ideas for making learning a hands-on experience. Here are a few examples:

- Each child gets a necklace with a letter character—e.g., Dippy Duck for the letter *D*, Eddy Elephant for the letter *E,* and so on. When the teacher calls out a word, the whole class sounds out the word, then the children with appropriate letter necklaces stand in a line to spell the word.
- Each child wears a costume for the character letter represented, then lines up when needed to spell a word.
- Children may be introduced to the letters by cooking. For *Y* they make yogurt, *I* is ice cream day, and *A* day is apple crisp.

It Makes Sense

Another subtle characteristic of mnemonic-rich phonics programs has to do with lowercase and capital letters. Mnemonic-poor programs teach capital-letter recognition first. Mnemonic-rich systems start children with lowercase letters. The reasoning behind this change is that children see more lowercase letters in a book to start with, so it is better to start learning letters that will give the greatest early comprehension. In the first ten pages of the children's book *Curious George,* for example, there are only 22 capital letters but 427 lowercase letters.

Besides starting with lowercase letters, mnemonic-rich programs change the order in which letters are presented. *Letterland* doesn't introduce the alphabet in ABC order. *Letterland* starts with *c, a, d, h, m, t, s*. These seven letters enable children to build lots of words using the common vowel *a*. Similar letter shapes, such as *d/b, p/q, n/u, m/w,* and *s/z* are separated in the teaching sequence, so children are less easily confused. Anyone who has tried to teach a youngster the difference between *d* and *b,* or *p* and *q,* which are essentially flip-flop images of each other, will appreciate the significance of separating similar letters in the learning sequence.

Stories Replace Rules

Letter characters also simplify the process of learning complex spelling rules. Take a digraph, for example, which is what occurs when you put two letters together to create a single unique sound such as the *sh* in shout and *ph* in phone. These changes in letter sounds confuse children. Mnemonic-rich phonics programs use stories to explain these inconsistencies. To explain why *s* and *h* together make a *sh* sound, *Letterland* offers the following story:

> Sammy Snake [s] is a noisy letter, always hissing in words, but Hairy Hat Man [h] dislikes noise. He is a quiet letter. He even walks into words barefoot so that the sound of his footsteps won't stop us from hearing his quiet whispered 'hhh' sound. But when you see Sammy Snake [s] next to the Hairy Hat Man [h] in a word, that is different. Now he is busy hushing Sammy Snake up like this, 'sh', because Hairy Hat Man dislikes noise.

Why use stories rather than rules? Stories are more memorable than abstract rules. It's also easier to visualize a story with familiar characters.

WHY MNEMONIC-RICH PHONICS IS SUCCESSFUL

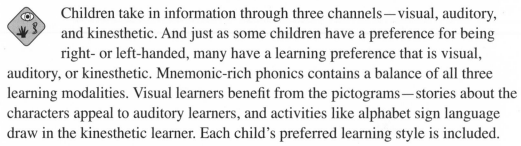

Children take in information through three channels—visual, auditory, and kinesthetic. And just as some children have a preference for being right- or left-handed, many have a learning preference that is visual, auditory, or kinesthetic. Mnemonic-rich phonics contains a balance of all three learning modalities. Visual learners benefit from the pictograms—stories about the characters appeal to auditory learners, and activities like alphabet sign language draw in the kinesthetic learner. Each child's preferred learning style is included.

Attention to all three learning styles also results in multiple encoding. In Chapter 2 you read that memories may be deposited on macrocolumns, groups of neurons in your brain. There may be different macrocolumns for visual, auditory, and kinesthetic deposits. When a memory is deposited in a variety of ways, multiple encoding occurs. A child who registers information visually, auditorily, and kinesthetically has more options for retrieval. So even a child who is a strong auditory learner still benefits from having the information presented in the other modes. Mnemonic-rich programs are balanced.

Mnemonic-Rich Phonics Programs

Letterland (603) 632-7377. www.letterland.com

Zoophonics (800) 622-8104. www.zoophonics.com

Addled Rats

Rats learned to run a maze with zero errors. Then discrete portions of their brains were scrambled. Scientists reasoned, "If we scramble the right spot, the rat will forget its maze knowledge." Scientists went through a lot of rats to try to locate the locus of maze-running memory in the brain. But when an addled rat ran the maze, while he made errors, he showed that he retained more maze knowledge than an untrained rat. Trying to pinpoint the maze-learning ability in a rat's brain failed, probably because rats learn mazes with more than visual cues. They also get kinesthetic cues ("I kind of leaned this way, then I took a couple of steps to the right … Yeah that feels right.") as well as olfactory cues ("The cheese smelled stronger when I went around this corner"). They might even register sound bouncing off the maze walls ("Sounds kind of hollow around the next corner"). The more senses a rat employs in learning something, the stronger the memory. This applies to humans as well.

Spell Like a National Spelling Bee Champion

In this chapter:

- Learn the spelling strategy of national spelling bee champions.
- Practice three techniques that improve concentration when learning to spell new words.

Are you a gifted speller? There's a quick way to check. Close your eyes and spell the word *dictionary*. Not hard? Close your eyes again. Now spell *dictionary* backwards.

It turns out that super spellers, the kids who win national spelling bees, can spell words backwards as well as forwards. This quirky ability is an indicator—it shows that super spellers have a different spelling strategy than the one used by most students.

Most students are phonetic spellers—they sound out words and then attach letters to the sounds. When asked to spell a word backwards, phonetic spellers find it awkward to impossible. Just try to sound out a word in the opposite direction!

Super spellers, on the other hand, create a picture in their mind of what the word looks like—sort of a mental flash card. This method allows spelling forwards and backwards with equal ease. They simply read the letters they see on their mental flash cards in either the forward or reverse direction. So what's the big deal? The big deal is that this visual strategy makes for a superior speller.

Wookie to the Rescue

Some children have trouble visualizing words. To make things easier, have them imagine a familiar background. Robert Dilts, a neurolinguistic programming trainer, relates an incident in which a youngster was having this very problem. The child was asked to name his favorite movie. It was Star Wars. Could he close his eyes and describe the Wookie? Yes. The child was instructed to see the word coming out of the Wookie's mouth. This movie-scene format opened up the child's visual spelling ability.

Super Spelling Strategy

 Here's how to help children become super spellers, using visual, auditory, and kinesthetic input—a sensory-based mnemonic technique:

1. Write the word on a blackboard or card, preferably in color. Letters that often cause spelling errors can be made to stand out by making them bigger or in a different color. Have your student look at the word and say each letter out loud. (Auditory)
2. Cover the word and ask the student to see the word in his mind and then spell it out loud. (Visual and auditory)
3. Ask the student to look at the word again and spell it backwards. (Visual)
4. Cover the word and have the student see the word in his mind and spell it backwards out loud. (Visual)
5. Have the student write the word. (Kinesthetic) To make a stronger kinesthetic experience, this writing might be done with shaving cream or with celery sticks that are subsequently eaten, or by tracing the letters in the air as the word is spelled.

You Don't Have to Be a National Spelling Bee Champ

Rita, a third grader, couldn't spell. Simple words like *was* and *there* came out "wz" and "thr". After a week of training in visualizing words, she put on a demonstration for a group of teachers. She began by spelling words like *phoenix*. This was an impressive improvement, but when she spelled the words both forwards and backwards, the teachers were left with their mouths hanging open.*

Mnemonic Techniques Help You Become a Better Speller by Making It Easier to Concentrate

Your conscious mind holds only one thought at a time. Think of your mind as a box. Each face of this box has an opening that is square, triangular, or circular. Swirling outside the box are thoughts. These thoughts are represented by pie-shaped figures, cubes, and balls. Only one shape will fit into this box at a time. Want a new figure in the box? Then you must first remove the one that is already there.

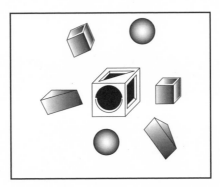

If you think you can hold more than one thought in your conscious mind at a time, try to find the eleventh letter in the alphabet, starting from A, while simultaneously counting backwards from Z to the eighth letter. To come up with

---

* Rita worked with a special resource teacher for three more years. Where previously she had done a half year of school progress in a year, she then was able to make a year's progress in a year. She didn't catch up with everyone else because she was already far behind, but she improved markedly. By sixth grade she could spell multisyllable words like dictionary and encyclopedia.

an answer, you either count from A and then move to Z, or you could jump back and forth doing some counting from A, some from Z and so on, but still, only one thought occupies your conscious mind at a time.

When children are asked to concentrate on a word, they're being told to hold one thought in their mind—to resist a barrage of outside thoughts that are bumping against their mind space, trying to dislodge the thought that's already inside. Mnemonic techniques make it easier to hold one thought in mind. They do this by encouraging students to manipulate a subject, making it hard for other thoughts to gain entrance. This manipulation can be visual, auditory, or kinesthetic.

Here are three ways to mentally manipulate a spelling word:

- Circle it.
- Play hide-and-seek with it.
- Write a helpful phrase.

Circle It

Focus students on the correct spelling of a word by having them circle problem letters. In each of these frequently misspelled words, circle the bold capitalized letters:

- Bel **I** eve instead of beleve
- Mis **S** pell instead of mispell
- Ar **C** tic instead of artic
- Liqu **E** fy instead of liquify
- Feb **R** uary instead of Febuary

Play Hide-and-Seek with It

Another way to get students to concentrate on spelling new words is to have them search for hidden words. Look at the word *believe*—*lie* is hiding inside it. The word within a word turns spelling into a game of hide-and-seek. Even dog and cat contain simple words.

Circle the hide-and-seek words inside these words:

Misspell   Parallel

Kindergarten   Environment

Through   Piece

Write a Helpful Phrase

Once children have learned about hide-and-seek words, they're ready to write helpful phrases or sentences that contain them along with the larger words. One hidden word in shelf is elf; a helping phrase might be an *ELF sitting on a shELF*. One hidden word in *believe* is *lie*; a helpful sentence might be *never beLIEve a LIE*. These helpful phrases and sentences can help children remember the correct spelling of a word. Here are frequently misspelled words used in helpful phrases and sentences:

- Don't MISS the second S in MISSpell.
- TEN kids in kindergarTEN.
- If he's ROUGH, he's ThROUGH.
- ALL the cars are parALLel parked.
- The envIRONment contains IRON.
- A PIEce of PIE.

Circle the hide-and-seek words in the following words, then construct a helpful phrase or sentence using the hidden word and the larger word:

Scowl	Courtesy	Freight
Determine	Minute	Capacity
Mischief	Laboratory	Organize
Nourish	Permanent	Absent

Explore   Impale   Computer

Meander   Stagnant   Bastion

Remembering the Spelling of Sound-alikes

Use hide-and-seek words and helpful phrases or sentences to determine which spelling to use for sound-alike words:

Principal vs. Principle

Inside every school princiPAL you will find a PAL. What do you think of that principle?

There vs. Their

tHERE is used to represent a place, as represented by the HERE. The other tHEIR has an HEIR, which is a word associated with people.

Vocabulary Cartoons

In this chapter:

- Use mnemonic techniques to memorize four vocabulary words.
- Learn about resources containing hundreds of vocabulary words with the mnemonics all worked out.
- Learn how to play vocabulary-building games.

Mnemonics provides a fast way to learn new vocabulary words and their definitions. In *Vocabutoons*, a mnemonic-based vocabulary study book, Sam Burchers describes tests that took place between 1995 and 1996 in Florida schools. Students who used mnemonic-based vocabulary study "scored an average 72% higher marks than did the control students that used rote memory study books." One teacher wrote that her students learned three times more words than in the traditional rote-memory class.

Say, Sentence, Stick

Remember the chapter on learning people's names? We used a mnemonic technique called Say, See, Stick. To remember vocabulary words, we will use a modified version of Say, See, Stick called Say, Sentence, Stick:

Illustrations in this chapter are reprinted with permission from the book *Vocabulary Cartoons*.

SAY	Say the vocabulary word, listening for familiar sound-alike words or rhyming words. To use this technique on the word *scrutinize* (which means to look very closely at something), we might say *scrutinize* sounds like *screw eyes*.
SENTENCE	Put the vocabulary word and its sound-alike or rhyming word into a sentence: U.S. customs officials have *screw eyes* when they *scrutinize* baggage.
STICK	Create an image, or a memorable or outrageous scene, that applies to your sentence: "U.S. Customs officials have **SCREW EYES** when they **SCRUTINIZE** baggage."

Here are three more vocabulary words:

Minuscule = Very small or tiny	**Horizontal =** Parallel to level ground	**Goad =** Anything that pricks, prods, or urges
SAY *minuscule,* which sounds like *mini school.*	SAY *horizontal,* which sounds like *horizon.*	SAY *goad,* which rhymes with *toad.*
SENTENCE: A *minuscule mini school.*	SENTENCE: A *horizontal* position is parallel to the *horizon.*	SENTENCE: Never *goad* a big *toad.*
STICK:	STICK:	STICK:

"Roger's **MINUSCULE MINI SCHOOL**."

"Something in a **HORIZONTAL** position is parallel to the **HORIZON**."

"Never **GOAD** a big **TOAD**."

REMEMBERING THE DEFINITION FOR A VOCABULARY WORD

To remember the meaning of a vocabulary word:

1. Say the word. Listen for its sound-alike substitution: *"Scrutinize.* Hmmm, sounds like *screw eyes."*
2. Bring up the image represented by the sound-alike word: "Let's see, the screw eyes were on a customs official. He was looking at luggage with a magnifying glass."

3.　The image will remind you of the caption for the picture: "Customs officials have *screw eyes* when they *scrutinize* baggage." The picture and the sentence remind you of the definition for the vocabulary word. For *scrutinize,* a customs agent looking very closely at something is a clue to the word's definition, to look very closely at something.

SOURCES FOR MNEMONIC VOCABULARY WORDS

Two books that use mnemonics to teach vocabulary words are *Vocabulary Cartoons* for elementary school students (grades 3–6) and *Vocabutoons* for learning SAT words. These books contain hundreds of vocabulary words for which the mnemonics have already been worked out for you.

Why Teach Vocabulary Words

The refrigerator had four words prominently taped to the door: clandestine, mattock, singe, and exempt. Strange words for a fridge? Turns out that the owners of this refrigerator are pro-vocabulary—mom and dad proactively teach new words to their children. Clandestine, mattock, singe, and exempt were the vocabulary words for the week. In a year, their children learn over 200 advanced vocabulary words. When pressed for a why, Herb, the father, explained it this way: "Did you know that Maidu, an American Indian language, has only three words to describe the color spectrum—lak = red, tit = green-blue, and tulak = yellow-orange-brown? Children with a limited vocabulary are like Maidu speakers using a limited color language to describe a rainbow. A limited vocabulary limits expressiveness and precision."

Vocabulary Bingo

 Make learning vocabulary a game. All you need to play vocabulary bingo are:

1. Three or more players
2. A bingo card for each player
3. Definition cards
4. Numbered markers

BINGO CARDS

Bingo cards can be made on a computer or hand drawn. One card, like the sample shown below, is needed for each player.

Minuscule	Scrutinize	Goad	Horizontal
Badger	Queue	Erode	Solitude
Veer	Gossamer	Procrastinate	Mettle
Mode	Endure	Belittle	Vocation

Each square contains a vocabulary word. Players must have previously learned the meaning for the vocabulary words, using the mnemonic technique described earlier. If desired, add additional columns and rows to include more words.

Definition Cards

To make definition cards for the bingo game, take one of your bingo cards and, as shown below in the example, write definitions under each vocabulary word.

Minuscule	Scrutinize	Goad	Horizontal
Very small	To look very closely at something	To prick, prod, or urge	Parallel to level ground
Badger	**Queue**	**Erode**	**Solitude**
To tease, annoy, and harass persistently	To form or wait in line; a line	To wear away	Alone or isolated from others
Veer	**Gossamer**	**Procrastinate**	**Mettle**
To change direction	Delicate, light, or flimsy	To put off until a later time	Courage
Mode	**Endure**	**Belittle**	**Vocation**
A way of doing something	To carry on despite difficulties	To put down; minimize	Job

Cut along the lines. After cutting you should have sixteen cards, each with a single vocabulary word and its definition.

NUMBERED MARKERS

Here's how you make numbered markers. If you have sixteen spaces on a bingo card, you need sixteen consecutively numbered markers. For example:

1	2	3	4
5	6	7	8
9	10	11	12
13	14	15	16

Cut the cards out along the lines. You will need a set for each player and the referee.

TO PLAY VOCABULARY BINGO

1. Each player, including the referee, receives a bingo card.
2. Each player, including the referee, gets a complete set of numbered markers. If there are sixteen squares on a bingo card, then each player receives sixteen markers numbered from one to sixteen.
3. Shuffle the definition cards. Place them face down on the table.
4. The referee picks a definition card and reads the definition. Maybe the definition is "to look very closely at something."
5. Players look for the word on their bingo card that fits the definition: *scrutinize*. Then they place marker number one on their choice. The referee reads another definition. Players put marker number two on their choice, and so on.
6. A continuous column, row, or diagonal of markers is a *Bingo!*
7. The referee keeps track of which vocabulary definitions have been read by placing her numbered markers on the correct word on the bingo card for each definition. When a player calls *Bingo!* she can make sure that the player chose the

correct definitions by asking the player which column, row, or diagonal he got the bingo in. The referee asks for the sequence of numbers starting at the top of the card for columns and diagonals or the left side of the card for rows. The sequence of numbers should be identical on the referee card. If it isn't, the player made an error. In this case, play continues for the other players. The person who made the mistake sits out the rest of the game.

OTHER WAYS TO PLAY VOCABULARY BINGO

- Switch around. Put the vocabulary definitions on the bingo cards. The referee calls out the vocabulary words.
- When it is confirmed that a player has a *Bingo!* she has to describe the mnemonic image for each word in her winning row to win that game.
- Don't even use bingo cards. Have two players face each other, with the deck of definition cards between them. Player #1 picks a card off the shuffled definition stack and reads the definition to her partner. Player #2 calls out a vocabulary word. If Player #2 is correct, he gets the card. If he's wrong, the card goes into a discard pile. Now player #2 pulls a card from the definition deck and reads it to player #1, and so on. The player with the most cards at the end wins.

7

The Building Blocks of Grammar

In this chapter:

- Learn nine terms used in English class: noun, pronoun, adjective, verb, adverb, conjunction, preposition, article, and exclamation.

Children learn the eight parts of grammar in English: nouns, pronouns, verbs, adverbs, adjectives, conjunctions, prepositions, and exclamations —as well as articles. When explaining English grammar, teachers often use these terms, so students who remember these terms have an easier time understanding the subject. To help students in this memory task, the mnemonic technique of substitution is used to convert each grammar term into an image. This image is then put into a scene. These scenes make it easier for students to remember grammar terms and their definitions.

Nouns

Nouns are words that represent people, places, and things.

Noun sounds a little like *hound*, so use the image of a *hound* to represent a noun.

Since nouns represent people, places, and things, imagine your noun hound retrieving a:

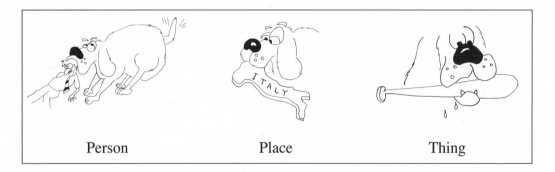

| Person | Place | Thing |

Now clump all the images together to remember what a noun is:

Noun hound with his collection of
people, places, and things

Pronouns

Pronouns are a kind of shorthand for nouns. If you had to write a person's name each time you referred to that person, it would become tiring, and it could take up a lot of paper. For example:

> Arnold Zimplezowski is a weird guy. When Arnold Zimplezowski goes into an elevator, Arnold Zimplezowski faces the back wall instead of the door.

Since we said Arnold Zimplezowski's name at the beginning of the sentence, we know who we're talking about. So we could exchange his full name for the pronoun *he*. The he is shorthand for his full name:

> Arnold Zimplezowski is a weird guy. When he goes into an elevator, he faces the back wall instead of the door.

There are also pronouns for places and things. If you are writing about a place like Texas, you don't write Texas each time, you simply write *there*. If you are writing about a baseball bat, you don't have to write *baseball bat* each time, you write *it*.

Pronoun sounds like *pro hound*. Imagine a hound dressed up in a suit and tie—as a professional, or a pro. To remember what pronouns do, imagine your pro-hound taking shorthand dictation. Remember pronouns are like shorthand for the nouns they represent. Visualize three words on the pro-hound's steno pad, the pronouns *he, there,* and *it*. Of course he could also write other pronouns like *she, our, they,* and *that*.

Adjectives

Adjectives give additional information about a noun. If you are told to go into the backyard with my dog, you might appreciate specific information about the dog, such as that he is a big, sweet, gentle dog. The adjectives *big, sweet,* and *gentle* add information to the noun.

Adjective sounds like *add* and *injection*. Imagine a vet adding something by injecting into a hound (noun). *Ad*-jectives *add* or *inject* something into the description of a noun.

Verbs

Verbs are action words. Verbs run, pinch, bite, bounce, undulate, and explode. Verb sounds like *vibe*.

Verbs sounds like *vibes*. Imagine vibes coming out of a boom box. The boom box is surrounded by action words that get excited by the vibes. The first action word, *dance,* starts dancing to the beat. Then all the other action words start doing their thing. *Bounce* starts bouncing. *Fall* falls over. *Explode* explodes. *Pinch* pinches. *Undulate* undulates.

Adverbs

Adverbs add additional information to verbs, adjectives, and other adverbs. In general, adverbs answer one of four questions: how, when, where, and to what extent. Examples of adverb usage include:

The elephant walked slowly (the adverb *slowly* adds "how" information to the verb *walked)*—lots of adverbs end in *ly.*

I'm always happy (the adverb *always* adds "when" information to the adjective *happy).*

She tilted the telescope skyward (the adverb *skyward* adds "where" information to the verb *tilted).*

He rowed too slowly (the adverb *too* adds "to what extent" information to the adverb *slowly).*

Adverb sounds a little like *Admiral Verb.* Imagine Admiral Verb at the back of his ship. He's towing three rowboats. Each one represents what adverbs modify—verbs, adjectives, and other adverbs. In one boat is our image for verbs—vibes coming from a boom box. Another boat contains the image for adverbs—another Admiral Verb. The last boat holds the image for adjectives—an injection needle.

Prepositions

Prepositions tell how things relate to each other. Prepositions include *under, in, on, over, to, about, by, with, of, before, after, through,* and *between*. To tell if a word is a preposition, place a word before the phrase "the mountain." If the word you're testing is a preposition, the phrase should make sense. Try this test on the words *under, on, over, purple,* and *high*. Under the mountain, on the mountain, and over the mountain all make sense. They pass the preposition test. But the phrases "purple the mountain" and "high the mountain" do not, so they don't pass the test.

Prepositions sounds like *prayer positions*. Imagine a Buddha in the traditional cross-legged prayer position. See him in three positions: *under* the mountain, *on* the mountain, and *over* the mountain—these three positions represent the basic test described above.

Articles

Whenever you see an article, you can be sure that a noun will follow, although sometimes an adjective is in the way. In English, the three articles are: *a, an,* and *the*. An article tells whether you're writing about a specific noun or a noun group. If you say "the dog," then you know it's a specific dog. If you say "a dog or an ape," then you know it's any dog or ape.

Articles sounds like *art tickles*. Imagine an artist tickling the noun hound with his paintbrush. In this case, the article indicates a specific dog.

The artist also could be tickling a group of hounds with his paintbrush, as illustrated to the right. In this case the hound could be any hound.

Conjunctions

Conjunctions connect other words, clauses, phrases, or even complete sentences. Commonly used conjunctions include *and, or, but,* and *because.*

The word conjunction sounds like *cons* (convicts) and *junction.* Imagine two cons on separate railway cars. Each con is holding on to one end of the word *and.* The word *and* is the junction between the cons that keeps the cars joined together.

Exclamations

Exclamations are single words or short phrases that usually express some emotion. Simple exclamations include *Oh! Super! Wow!*

A sound-alike image for exclamations is *clam nation.* Imagine a nation of clams all saying: Oh! Super! Wow! Radical! Ahhh!

Remembering the Grammar Terms

If you would like to be able to rattle off all the parts of speech, use the mapping memory technique.

 Start by visualizing nine distinct locations—in your house, a park, or parts of your community. Let's say you choose your house.

1. You go into the front yard, where you find the *noun hound.* Since he represents people, places, and things, these items are piled in the yard with the noun hound.

2. The entrance hallway is blocked by the *pronoun pro-hound* in his suit and tie looking very professional. He's taking shorthand dictation, writing the words *he, there,* and *it—* shorthand for people, places, and things.

3. In the living room, verbs are *vibes* coming from a boom box. Action words like *bounce, undulate,* and *pinch* are dancing to the vibes.

4. The kitchen is reserved for adjectives. Adjectives are represented by a big *injection* needle. Adjectives add to nouns, so a noun hound is getting an injection in the kitchen.

5. In the bathroom, you find *Admiral Adverb* in the bathtub. Adverbs modify adjectives, verbs, and other adverbs. To represent this, Admiral Adverb's ship is pulling three rowboats. One rowboat has the vibing boom box (verbs). The second rowboat has an injection needle (adjectives). The third rowboat has another Admiral Adverb (adverbs).

6. In the bedroom are prepositions, represented by the *prayer positions* of a Buddha figure. He is sitting *under* a mountain, *on* the mountain, and *over* the mountain.

7. Opening the hall closet, you discover millions of clams, a virtual *clam nation* (exclamation), and they open up and shout, "Hey!" "Gee!" and "Wow!"

8. In the garage you find an *artist tickling* (article) first one noun hound and then several noun hounds.

9. The backyard has railroad tracks running through it with two train cars held together by *cons* making a *junction* (conjunction) with the word *and*.

Now imagine walking through your house. What image do you have at each location in the house and what does it stand for?

Getting Physical with Punctuation

In this chapter:

- Learn a sensory method for teaching five punctuation marks.

Punctuation marks are abstract squiggles. They're usually taught using an auditory technique. But some children are slow auditory processors (that is, they learn more slowly when they only hear words). If a child doesn't have a strong auditory preference, he will find it easier to remember information if it's presented in another sensory mode. "Moving punctuation" gives students a hands-on experience for what punctuation marks do.

Punctuation As a Moving Experience

Have students choose a book that has lots of punctuation marks in the sentences, then start reading it out loud while walking. Ask them, when they come to a punctuation mark, to act as if they have come to a street sign. These street signs tell them to perform various physical actions, as described in the following pages.

PERIOD

A period indicates the end of a sentence. It's like a miniature stopping point. The walking reader comes to a complete *stop*—of both walking and reading—then he continues walking and reading until he again comes to another period.

COMMA

A comma indicates the briefest of interruptions in a sentence. The physical action for this interruption is a slight *skip,* with a corresponding hesitation in reading.

QUOTATION MARKS

Quotation marks tell the reader that some character, real or imaginary, is about to speak. The end quotation mark tells us that the dialogue has ended. The sign for quotation marks is to *open* your *mouth* wide, as if you were going to speak.

QUESTION MARK

A question mark at the end of a sentence leaves the reader in no doubt that a question is being asked. When students reach a question mark, they *shrug* their shoulders, a common physical response to a hard question.

EXCLAMATION POINT

Exclamation points are used to mark an outcry or an emphatic comment, like "Look out!" If someone yelled that with all the energy that deserves an exclamation point, you would probably *jump*. Exclamation points are represented by the physical act of jumping high in the air with both feet off the ground.

Add Emotion to Lessons to Make Them Memorable

In memory theory, the more senses you involve, the more memorable the experience. Lessons on punctuation are usually sedentary activities. Sensory input is minimal. By physically involving students in the lesson, you help them activate more memory sites for recording information. This memory-enhancing effect is caused by more than movement. As the students move, they also smile or laugh outright at their antics. This experiencing of emotions has a fixative effect on a student's memory. When you can incorporate emotion into a lesson you add glue to a memory thread, and it's more likely to stick. Emotions are one form of sensory mnemonic techniques.

9

The Ultimate in Reading Comprehension: How to Memorize a Book

In this chapter:

- Learn how to remember the main points and examples in any book.
- Practice by memorizing a booklet on African animals.

How often have you read a *Wow!* book, yet a month later you remember less than 1% of the material? How would you like to read a text and be able to recall the major points and examples? As memory expert Harry Lorayne says, "There is no learning without memory." Here's how you can experience the ultimate in reading comprehension.

Steps for Committing a Book to Memory

1. Highlight main points
2. Create images
3. Chain images together
4. Practice

HIGHLIGHT MAIN POINTS

When choosing the first book to memorize, make it an easy one—one in which the author uses stories, pictures, graphics, and metaphors to make important points. This type is easier to visualize than a book with abstract material. As you read the book, highlight significant points with a marker. Be conservative in using the highlighter. Choose to highlight material that is essential to understanding the main points of the book. Our goal is not to memorize the book verbatim but to be able to refer to all the major points and supportive examples. In other words, to retain all the useful information.

Worried about Overload?

The average person will store in her memory 500 times as much information as is found in the *Encyclopedia Britannica* by the time of her death. That sounds pretty impressive until you find out that the average brain capacity can store approximately 2.8×10^{20} bits of information, which works out to ten million books of a thousand pages each. Most people store roughly 10^9 bits of information. Lots of room left.

CREATE IMAGES

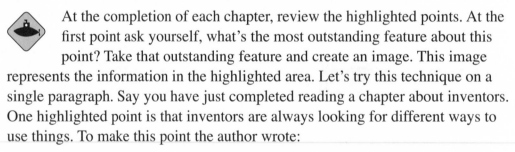

At the completion of each chapter, review the highlighted points. At the first point ask yourself, what's the most outstanding feature about this point? Take that outstanding feature and create an image. This image represents the information in the highlighted area. Let's try this technique on a single paragraph. Say you have just completed reading a chapter about inventors. One highlighted point is that inventors are always looking for different ways to use things. To make this point the author wrote:

> The Frisbie pie company sold pies to Yale University. Someone discovered that with a flick of the wrist, the empty pie tins could be made to glide through the air. Pie-tin-catch became a campus fad. An entrepreneur, Fred Morrison, developed a plastic version of the flying pie tins. Capitalizing on the current interest in UFOs and flying saucers, he marketed his flying saucer toy as the Pluto

Platter. Later it was renamed for the company that had sparked the fad, but instead of Frisbie, the name of the pie company, the spelling was changed to Frisbee®.

Create an image for the preceding paragraph. One possible image is to visualize a college kid wearing a Yale sweater throwing a pie to an alien sitting atop a flying saucer-like Frisbee®:

The Pluto Platter, better known as the Frisbee®

To create memorable images, make them outrageous and filled with *action!* See your pie-throwing Yale student slinging a pie that splats cherry-red against a four-eyed polka-dotted alien.

Your next highlighted paragraph in this chapter on creativity reads:

Creative people keep track of their ideas. Leonardo da Vinci was a creative genius in painting, sculpture, mechanics, science, and architecture. He carried a notebook everywhere he went to record his ideas. His surviving notebooks cover 7,000 pages.

The main information here is the importance of keeping a notebook with your creative ideas. Leonardo da Vinci is given as an example. So how about an image of Leonardo writing in a notebook that is balanced on a stack of notebooks to represent the large number he filled up? To remember that this is Leonardo da Vinci, a lion stands behind Leonardo (Leo = lion):

Leo and Leonardo

Here's a tip. In the margin of the book you are memorizing, opposite each highlighted section, make a simple sketch of your visual image. When you check back later, especially if the book has a lot of chapters, these sketches will refresh your memory.

CHAIN IMAGES TOGETHER

After creating an image for each important point in a chapter, you're ready for the next step. Starting at the beginning, link the images together. Remember the frisbee-seated-four-eyed-alien in a previous example? To create a transition or link to your next image, you might imagine the pie thrown by the college student hitting your alien and bowling him head-over-flippers into your next scene. This linkage acts as a transition between images. Like boxcars in a train, each image is coupled to the next. To be effective, this linkage needs to be an action, preferably a flamboyant or outrageous action. As in life, actions that are flamboyant or outrageous are more memorable.

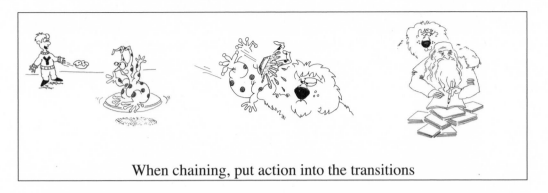

When chaining, put action into the transitions

When using the mnemonic technique of chaining, it's important that students visualize the images they create. Sometimes kids think they are visualizing when in reality they are saying the words in their mind, a form of self-talk. Memory experts agree that a mental image is a must. An example of creating a mental image would be the process you go through when asked how many capital letters in the alphabet have curves. In response, you may start by mentally singing the alphabet song, but at each letter you'll stop and visualize it to see if it has curves.

PRACTICE

As you add images, periodically run through the chain. Be sure you remember what each image represents. Chains can be practiced anytime and anywhere:

- Commuting to school
- Walking around the block
- Laying in bed
- Exercising (swimming, jogging, biking)

If your chain is long or complex, the links may fade with time. If this happens, simply review the margins of the book you memorized. Sketches next to the highlighted paragraphs will quickly refresh your memory. Better still, make a master sheet that shows all your sketches in the proper sequence. Tape this sheet to the inside cover of the book. If you really want to remember a book, practice at periodic intervals. Check your memory after a week, a month, and a year.

> ### Relearning Takes Much Less Time
>
> A psychologist read passages of ancient Greek to his toddler every day. This education began when the boy was fifteen months old and continued until he was 3. Then they took a break. When the child was 8, he memorized the previously heard selections along with new ones. It took him 27% less time to master the previously heard passages compared with the new ones. At 14, the boy was 92% faster in memorizing the old passages, and at 18, he was 99% faster. It is easier to relearn material you already know.

Memorizing a book isn't easy. It takes discipline. Combining the mnemonic techniques of substitution and chaining make this genius skill possible.

Research shows that most young children have trouble remembering material because they lack effective memory strategies. Children taught to memorize a significant book learn not only the content of the book but a process they can use for a lifetime of learning.

Memorizing a Book with Help

What you are about to read is a short story divided into seven mini-chapters. After each mini-chapter you will find an illustration. This illustration is a substitute image, a condensation of all the information in the mini-chapter into a visual format. Commit that image to memory. Then continue reading till you come to the next image. At this point, link the previous image to the new one. Use action to make the link. It's important that you close your eyes and see one scene move to the next with your action link. Repeat this process to the end of the story.

If you are working with children, explain that the world-traveling adventurer who wrote the story they are about to read finds it important to learn everything he can about places he visits. If you want to be Indiana Jones, this knowledge protects you and makes your adventure more enjoyable. In Africa this means learning about the animals.

Impala on the run

Running Hamburgers

Impala are the hamburgers of the African plains. Lions, leopards, hyenas, and wild dogs put impalas at the top of their fast-food menu. But this is one fast food that's really fast. Impala cover 30 feet in a single bound. When chased, glands on impalas' rear hooves leave a scent trail. This scent, left on grass or brush, helps impalas locate the herd, should they become separated. Staying with the group is important for survival. The herd has lots of eyes, ears, and noses to detect predators. It's a case of safety in numbers.

If you're on the ground with big game animals, it's wise to pay attention to the impalas. Skittish behavior may indicate that you are sharing the area with a predator. That predator may decide that you are easier to catch than an impala.

An amazing feature of impala mothers is that they can delay giving birth until all the females in the herd are ready to give birth. This delay is a species survival feature. Impala parents can do little to protect their newborns from predators. But if all babies are born simultaneously, predators eat their fill and the surviving babies get a 24-hour reprieve, enough time to turn wobbly legs into running legs.

Substitution Imagery for Impala Paragraphs

A lion chases an impala—this represents the impala's food status to predators. The impala leaps over a high jump bar—indicates the ability to cover distance. A spray can of perfume is held by the impala—signifies the scent trail they leave so they can find each other. Pregnant impalas watch the chase—represents simultaneous birth ability of the herd.

Cape buffalo checking things out

BUFFALO AT THE WATER COOLER

Locating cape buffalo means looking for water holes. Buffalo love water. To stay healthy, they drink 10 gallons a day. During droughts, herds of cape buffalo can suck a pond dry. This is why they may stampede to reach water. First one there gets his fill.

They also like mud, often rolling in it. Then as the mud dries and flakes off, it traps pesky bugs. While searching for a herd of cape buffalo, we came across a mud hole they had wallowed in. Our tracker pointed out nearby trees that buffalo had brushed up against. Drying mud held a number of ticks. We determined how long ago the buffalo had been at a spot by how dry the mud was on the surrounding trees.

Our tracker also told us that cape buffalo are schizophrenic—you never know what one is going to do. If you meet one, he may give you a cud-chewing stare and saunter back into the bush, or he may drop his head and charge. You'd think it isn't likely that you'd accidentally run into this creature. After all they are big—over 1,600 pounds. But buffalo are good at hide-and-seek. While stalking one herd, we didn't notice a lone individual until he came out of the grass 20 feet in front of us—dangerously close. Fortunately, he was in a cud-chewing mood.

Substitution Imagery for Cape Buffalo Paragraphs

Imagine a cape buffalo sipping from a glass—this indicates the cape buffalo's need for water. He's sitting in a bathtub filled with mud—his way of cleaning ticks off. His face is hidden behind a mask—indicating his uncertain nature and his ability to hide.

Hippo yawning

TENDER-SKINNED HIPPOS

Hippos look like they were designed by a cartoonist—tiny eyes, huge mouth, and blubber body. Don't laugh. Any animal that weighs over two-and-a-half tons is not to be messed with. Hippos can be seriously dangerous on land or in the water. If you encounter a hippo on land, avoid getting between her and the water. If the hippo charges, try to leap over something, as they won't step over a raised object. Of course the hippo might smash through it, but she won't step over it. She also might not appreciate your canoeing on her section of river. Hippos are known to come up under boats and flip them over.

Next time you see a hippo, pay particular attention to the skin. It has a pinkish color. Natives used to think that hippos leaked blood out of their skin, which gave them the color. Actually, it's a pink oil secreted by the hippo to protect it from sunburn. It would be interesting to know what the SPF factor is!

Substitution Imagery for Hippo Paragraphs

Imagine a hippo approaching some steps but not going up them—represents unwillingness of hippos to step over objects. The hippo is holding a canoe overhead—showing that they can flip boats over. The hippo is carrying a pink parasol—showing that they have personal sun protection in the oil covering their bodies.

Warts on a warthog

WARTS ON A WARTHOG

Even funnier looking than a hippo is a warthog. They're called warthogs because they look like pigs with big warts on their faces. The warts are fleshy knobs sticking out from the face. Look at the photo of a warthog and notice the big warts just below the eyes. These warts serve a purpose. When warthogs fight among themselves, the warts help protect their eyes against another warthog's tusks.

Another strange warthogian feature is its proportions. With a big head and a tiny rear end, it looks like someone made a design error. But there's a reason for this too. Warthogs dig holes in their territory. These holes are just the right size for a warthog rump. When chased, a warthog runs to a hole and backs in, like a cork in a wine bottle. Their big heads, and more important, their sharp tusks, plug the hole from the front. This makes it hard for enemies to dislodge them without risking a slash from the tusks.

Substitution Imagery for Warthog Paragraphs

Imagine a warthog admiring its warts in a mirror. These warts serve a purpose that goes beyond good looks—protection of the eyes. The warthog is digging a hole—which represents its way to escape predators by backing in and facing an enemy with its nasty tusks.

Zebra camouflage

ZEBRAS IN BLACK AND WHITE

In the wet season, African grass turns a brilliant green. Zebra grazing against this green backdrop are eye-catching. Considering that zebras are a favorite food of lions, the high contrast of their black and white coats against a green background would seem to be a disadvantage. Actually, zebras are hard to see—if you are a lion. This is because lions are color blind. They see in shades of black and white. To a lion, the grass is dark gray, and the pattern of the zebra blends into this background.

Zebra stripes serve several functions. When running from predators, zebras stay in a herd, much like impala. The kaleidoscopic pattern of a moving herd makes it difficult for chasing predators to focus on a single animal. Baby zebras also recognize their mom's stripe pattern. Each pattern is as unique as a human fingerprint. This is why mother zebras give birth away from the herd and wait half an hour before returning. In thirty minutes, a baby zebra learns to recognize its mother's stripe pattern.

Substitution Imagery for Zebra Paragraphs

Imagine a zebra standing in tall grass, its body partially obscured—representing the camouflage striped pattern that color-blind predators see. The zebra holds a kaleidoscope—signifying the confusing pattern that chasing predators see when looking at a fleeing zebra herd. The zebra holds a baby zebra—indicating the imprinting of a mother's unique stripe pattern on her youngster.

An old bull elephant

ELEPHANT VS. CAR

Approaching a wild elephant is not smart. In an area I visited, two tourists tried to sneak up on a slumbering elephant. One tourist approached the front of the elephant. The other stood nearby filming. Suddenly the elephant woke up. Oh-oh.

When an elephant prepares to charge, he does a couple of things. First he fans his ears out on either side of his head, making him look bigger. You wouldn't think an animal that weighs six tons would need to look bigger. Your next clue that you are in trouble is when the elephant lowers its tusks low to the ground. In elephant body language this means, *Lo-o-ok ou-u-u-t!* The tourists experienced all these warnings in the blink of an elephant eye. The elephant charged. One tourist dove underneath his car. It's good he went under the car. The elephant hit the car with his tusks, piercing the door like tissue paper. Then the elephant flattened the roof of the car with one blow of his trunk. If the tourist had made it into the car he would have been both shish-kabobed and squashed. Many tourists think they're safe inside a car, but several big African animals can destroy an automobile.

Substitution Imagery for Elephant Paragraphs

Imagine an elephant with its ears fanned wide, tusks lowered—this represents an elephant's display response prior to charging. The elephant is bouncing on a squashed car—indicating the story of the tourists' car that was flattened by the angry elephant.

Lion with a taste for tires

LIONS AND TIRES, OH, MY!

It is not only elephants who mess with cars. Driving through Africa, we came across a car stranded in the middle of the road. Lions sauntered around the car. The people inside were scared. When the lions left, they motioned to us. They explained that they had stopped to help someone repair a flat. The person with the flat told them that a lioness had done the damage. The good Samaritans helped repair the tire. When they got back into their car the lions returned. That's when a lion chomped their tire. We went to get help.

What makes you safe in a car is not steel and glass. A lion could bat out your windshield with one swipe. But lions don't see cars as food, so they leave the occupants alone. This is obvious when you are in an open vehicle. One night, while sitting in the back of a truck bed, we were surrounded by a pride of lions. They looked but showed little interest, even though they could have easily leaped into the truck bed where we were sitting. If you do something to attract the lions' attention like stand up, make a lot of noise, or get out of the truck, then you could be a lion's blue-plate special.

Create a Substitute Image for the Lion Paragraph
What are the key points?

What's your image?

Using the Africa Story to Teach Chaining

1.   When teaching children how to chain a story, read the Africa story to the students. This keeps them from jumping to the next paragraphs before fixing the substitution image in their mind.

2.   Show each substitute image at the end of a section. Explain how the illustration contains the information in the preceding paragraphs you read.

3.   Have students close their eyes and imagine the picture. Give them at least ten seconds. If you think students are having trouble visualizing, have them draw a picture of what they imagine.

4.   As you come to the next substitute illustration, have students imagine some action from the previous illustration that draws them into the next image.

5.   At the end of the story, have students go back to the first image. Ask them to repeat the series to you or to a partner.

6.   When students have the chain memorized, have them go back and explain what the images stand for.

If your students completed the last exercise, congratulations are in order. They memorized a section in a book. Now have them try the technique on a book of their choosing. If they are using a book that they are not allowed to write in, have students list the page numbers with the important information. Next to the page number they draw the image they come up with.

Memorize Life-Changing Books

The best teachers lead by example. To teach children how to memorize books, memorize a few yourself. Choose a book the way you would choose a friend—pick a good one. These three questions will help you decide which books to memorize:

1. Ask people you admire, "What are the three best life-changing books you've ever read?" Maybe they'll mention the book *Learned Optimism,* by Martin Seligman. If the book sounds interesting, leaf through it. If it contains valuable information, memorize it.

2. Ask yourself, "Will the ideas in this book help me become the person I want to be?" Memorizing a creativity book like *Cracking Creativity: The Secrets of Creative Genius,* by Michael Michalko, installs a workshop of creativity tools in your mind. Just as a craftsperson has hand tools readily available, so a creative person has unique thinking tools.

3. Ask yourself, "Will having ready access to the ideas in this book help me?" If you choose a book like *Drawing on the Right Side of the Brain,* by Betty Edwards, you have an outline of how to teach yourself and others to draw. As an art instructor, you could pull it up at any time. If you are a biologist, a geologist, an electrician, a beautician, a salesperson, a tree surgeon, or a dragon trainer—what book contains information that would help you if it was in your mind all the time?

10 The Fastest Way to Learn a Foreign Language

In this chapter:

- Memorize twelve Spanish or French words.
- Use two memory techniques to quickly learn any foreign word.
- Find out which 100 key nouns are the first you should learn in a foreign language.

Barry Faber speaks twenty-five foreign languages, including French, Spanish, Italian, Norwegian, Mandarin Chinese, Hungarian, and Indonesian. One of the secrets behind Faber's amazing multilingual ability is revealed in his book, *How to Learn Any Language*. He uses substitution mnemonics.

You're already familiar with substitution mnemonics. You used it in Chapter 3 to memorize people's names. Remember the Say, See, Stick technique? This same technique is used to learn foreign vocabulary words. Here's how you would use that method to learn the Spanish word for hands, *manos* (pronounced MAN-ohs.)

SAY	Say the word out loud several times. Say it slowly and break it down into syllables—*MAN-ohs*. As you say *MAN-ohs*, listen for syllables that sound like English words.

SEE	The first syllable of *MAN-ohs* is the English word *man*. Visualize a man. For the second syllable *-ohs*, imagine two *O*s. The *man* and the two *O*s are your substitute images, the things you can see.
STICK	Now stick the substitute image to the meaning of the foreign word. The substitute image for manos is a *man* and two *O*s. The meaning of manos is hands. Imagine a *man* with *O*s in place of his *hands*.

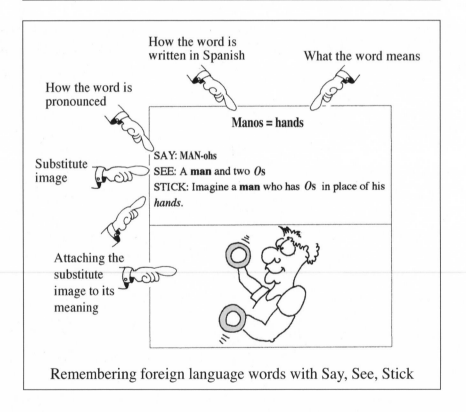

Remembering foreign language words with Say, See, Stick

The Ten-Second Rule

In the Say, See, Stick memory system, sticking is a process similar to creating special effects for movies. In movies, a film editor superimposes one frame of film over another to create a special effect. Memory experts superimpose one image over another in their mind, then view the combined image on a mental screen. Memory experts recommend that this inside-your-head-viewing should take a minimum of ten seconds. Images have a better chance of making it into long-term memory if you concentrate on them for that long.

Research findings suggest that protein synthesis takes place inside the brain when a long-term memory is being formed, but only when a threshold amount of stimulus occurs. Too quick a scanning of information may not provide a sufficient stimulus.

Remembering a Foreign Word

To retrieve a foreign vocabulary word from your memory, first go to the image that the word represents. If you are looking for the Spanish word for hands:

1. Visualize a pair of hands.
2. Then ask yourself what image is associated with the hands. In this case, the image is of a *man* clapping two *O*s together.
3. The image of the *man* and two *O*s prompts you to say, *MAN-ohs,* the correct pronunciation for hands in Spanish.

USING SAY, SEE, STICK ON HARDER WORDS

Manos was an easy word to use substitution on because the first syllable easily suggested an English sound-alike word. But some words are not so easy. For difficult words, use the schmurgle technique.

Schmurgling means to say a word out loud in a sloppy manner. For example, the Spanish word for knee, *rodilla,* is pronounced ro-DEE-ya. If schmurgled, *rodilla* sounds a little like *rodeo,* so *rodeo* becomes the English sound-alike approximation to help us remember ro-DEE-ya. In classes, students often ask,

"But it's not the exact pronunciation. When you try to say knee in Spanish, aren't you going to say rodeo instead of ro-DEE-ya?" The answer was given in Chapter 2. A schmurgled word gives you a place to start, just as a multiple-choice test jogs your memory for the correct answer. Schmurgled substitutes also jog your memory. You'll learn to make the adjustments necessary for proper pronunciation.

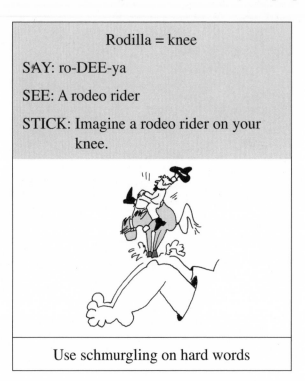

Rodilla = knee

SAY: ro-DEE-ya

SEE: A rodeo rider

STICK: Imagine a rodeo rider on your knee.

Use schmurgling on hard words

USING SUBSTITUTION TECHNIQUES TO LEARN SPANISH WORDS FOR PARTS OF THE BODY

Memorize the following list of Spanish words for parts of the body. Each card follows the format of Say, See, Stick. (If you'd rather learn another language, look in Appendix A, where there is a list of French words for parts of the body.)

Ojo = eye

SAY: **O-hoe**

SEE: A **hoe** and someone going **Oh!**

STICK: Imagine someone sticking a hoe in your *eye* and you going **Oh! Hoe.**

Nariz = nose

SAY: **na-REES**

SEE: The universal symbol for **no** and a bowl of **rice**

STICK: Imagine the **no** symbol on a *nose* and **rice** in front of the nose.

Boca = mouth

SAY: **BO-ka**

SEE: A **bow** and a **caw**ing bird

STICK: Imagine a **bow** in your *mouth* held by a bird going "**caw**."

Cabeza = head

SAY: **ca-BAY-sa**

SEE: A taxi cab saying something

STICK: Imagine a **cab** in place of your *head* trying to **say** something.

Manos = hands

SAY: **MAN-ohs**

SEE: A **man** and two *O*s

STICK: Imagine a **man** who has *O*s in place of his *hands*.

Brazo = arm

SAY: **BRAS-oh**

SEE: A **brass O**

STICK: Imagine a **brass O** around your *arm* like a bracelet.

Estómago = stomach

SAY: **es-TO-ma-go**

SEE: An **S**-shaped **stomach**

STICK: Imagine an **S**-shaped **stomach.**

Rodilla = knee

SAY: **ro-DEE-ya**

SEE: A **rodeo** rider

STICK: Imagine a **rodeo** rider on your *knee*.

Oreja = ear SAY: **o-RAY-ha** SEE: A **ray** gun saying **"Ha"** STICK: Imagine a **ray** gun in your *ear* saying, "**Ha.**"	Pelo = hair SAY: **PAY-low** SEE: A **pillow** STICK: Imagine a **pillow** in place of your *hair*.
Pecho = chest SAY: **PAY-cho** SEE: A **peach** STICK: Imagine a **peach** on your *chest*.	Pierna = leg SAY: **pee-AIR-na** SEE: A **pear** and the symbol for **no** STICK: Imagine the symbol for **no** on **pears** on your *leg*.

TEST YOURSELF: SPANISH WORD TEST

On the next page you will find a Spanish word test. It consists of two columns. The left column contains images we've made for remembering Spanish words for parts of the body. The right column contains simple cartoons for what that Spanish word represents. Start by covering the left column. The first picture in the right column is of cartoon eyes. What is the Spanish word for eye? The retrieval process for this information is as follows:

1. Ask, "What image did I stick onto the eyes?" This jogs the image of you saying "Oh!" because you had a hoe in your eye.
2. You realize the answer is pronounced *O-hoe*.

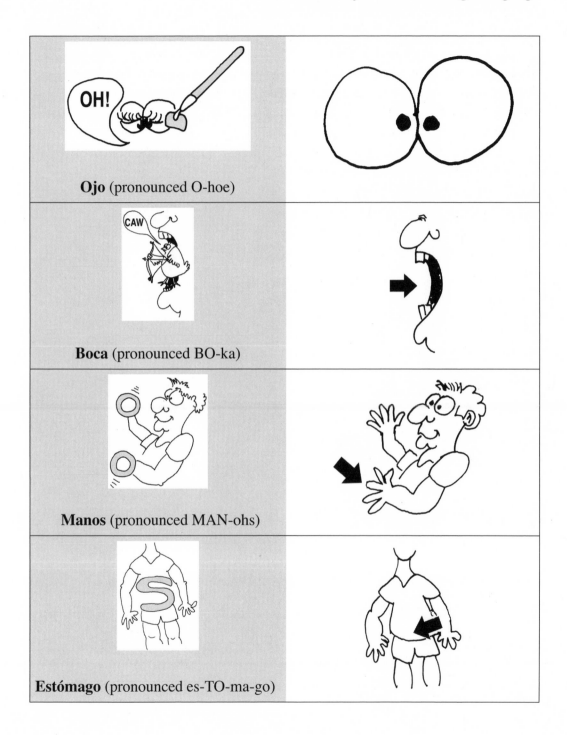

Ojo (pronounced O-hoe)

Boca (pronounced BO-ka)

Manos (pronounced MAN-ohs)

Estómago (pronounced es-TO-ma-go)

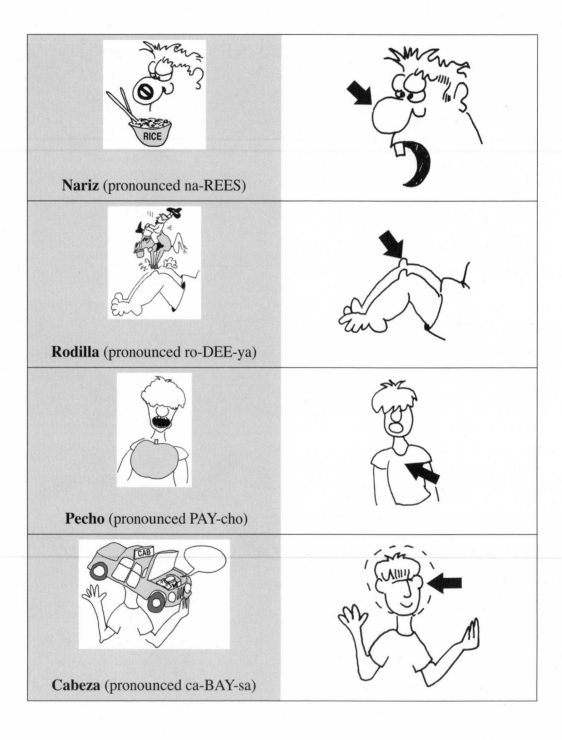

Nariz (pronounced na-REES)

Rodilla (pronounced ro-DEE-ya)

Pecho (pronounced PAY-cho)

Cabeza (pronounced ca-BAY-sa)

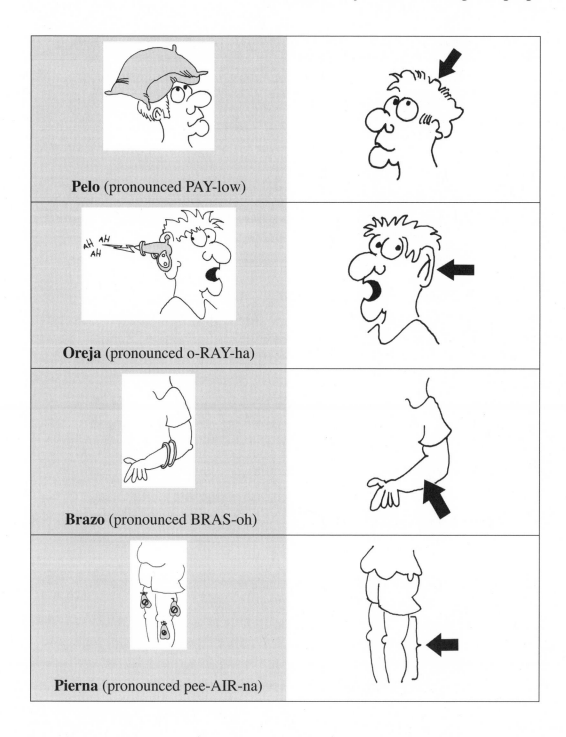

Pelo (pronounced PAY-low)

Oreja (pronounced o-RAY-ha)

Brazo (pronounced BRAS-oh)

Pierna (pronounced pee-AIR-na)

The Foreign Language Card Game

To play the foreign language card game you need:

1. Twenty-four foreign language cards
2. A referee sheet

To make your foreign language card game, choose either the Spanish (pages 119-121) or French word test illustrations (the French word illustrations are found in Appendix A), and then:

1. Use a copy machine and heavy stock paper to duplicate the illustrations. Make two copies of each illustration.
2. Cut out each card. A card will have the mnemonic substitution picture on the left and an illustration of which body part is indicated on the right, as shown below.

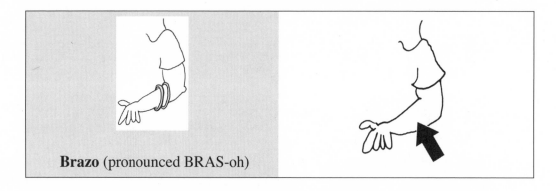

Brazo (pronounced BRAS-oh)

3. Fold each card along the center line. One side of the card shows the body part. The other side of the card has the foreign word and the mnemonic substitution picture.
4. Glue the folded pieces together. Do this to all the cards. You now have twenty-four cards—two each of the twelve cards.
5. Now, duplicate the referee sheet. The Spanish one is on the next page (the French referee sheet is in Appendix A).

Ojo O-hoe (eye)	**Nariz** na-REES (nose)	**Pelo** PAY-low (hair)
Boca BO-ka (mouth)	**Cabeza** ca-BAY-sa (head)	**Oreja** o-RAY-ha (ear)
Manos MAN-ohs (hands)	**Brazo** BRAS-oh (arm)	**Pecho** PAY-cho (chest)
Estómago es-TO-ma-go (stomach)	**Rodilla** ro-DEE-ya (knee)	**Pierna** pee-AIR-na (leg)

Rules for the Foreign Language Game

(Beginner Level): Two Players

1. Deal out all the cards onto a table. You should be able to see all twenty-four cards. The sides with the Spanish words are face down.
2. One player is the referee. The referee uses the referee sheet and calls out the name of a card in Spanish.
3. The second player looks for the card called out by the referee and puts her finger on the image that represents the Spanish word. If she is right, she takes that card. If she is wrong, the referee takes the correct card.
4. When all the cards have been removed from the table, the player counts the number of cards she got right. Then referee and player switch roles. In each game, the players try to get more cards than in the previous one.

(Intermediate Level): Three Players

1. Deal out all the cards onto a table. The sides with the Spanish words are face down.
2. One player is the referee. The referee uses the referee sheet and calls out the name of a card in Spanish. The other two players try to be first to place their finger on the correct card.
3. The first player to put his finger on the correct card takes that card. Players may put their finger on only one card when the referee calls a name. If a player makes a mistake, he is not allowed to switch his finger to another card. If both players make a mistake, the card remains on the table.
4. When there is a tie, the referee determines whose finger was on the card first. The winner becomes the new referee.

(ADVANCED LEVEL): THREE PLAYERS

1. Spread the cards out on a table. The sides with the Spanish words are face down.
2. One player is the referee. The referee calls out the name of a card in English. Each of the other two players tries to be first to put a finger on the correct card.
3. The first player to put a finger on the correct card must say the name in Spanish. Turn the card over to determine if the player is correct, or have the referee use the referee sheet to see if the word was said correctly. If so, the player takes the card. The winner becomes the new referee.

Make Your Own Foreign Language Substitutions

Once children understand the technique of using mnemonic substitution on a foreign language, you want them to make their own substitutions. Try drawing a substitute picture for the following four Spanish words.

Perro Pronounced: PEAR-roh (dog)	**Gato** Pronounced: GA-toe (cat)
Mañana Pronounced: man-YAN-a (morning)	**Pan** Pronounced: PAN (bread)

Some children enthusiastically adopt the substitute technique. Others need practice with the creativity and visualization that is required to master this skill. Compare your ideas for the Spanish words in the above boxes with those that children came up with. For perro: a *dog* eating a **pear;** gato, a *cat* sitting on a **gate;** mañana: a **man yawning** in the *morning;* pan: a loaf of *bread* in a **pan.**

Conventional vs. Mnemonic Language Techniques

Michael Gruneberg, a memory expert, has written a number of foreign language books. He has taken hundreds of words and phrases and applied the substitution system to them. In one study, for one term, 13-year-old students who had been identified as low-ability language students were given one session a week using his Spanish mnemonic system and another session using conventional teaching methods. When students were tested, conventional techniques improved students' ability by about 24% compared with 69% improvement using the mnemonic techniques. Gruneberg's highly recommended books include *Spanish by Association, French by Association, German by Association,* and *Italian by Association.*

Using Substitution on Very Difficult Words

It is difficult to use the Say, See, Stick technique on some foreign words. Some foreign words simply do not lend themselves to a visual image. Either the sound-alike English substitution or the meaning of the foreign word fails to provide an image. In these cases, use a modified substitution technique: Say, Sentence, Stick.

SAY	Say the foreign word, listening for a sound-alike English word.

SENTENCE	Use the sound-alike English word in a sentence that includes a reference to the meaning of the foreign word.
STICK	Create an image, a memorable or outrageous scene in which your sentence is being said.

Here are two examples of Say, Sentence, Stick:

Gafas = sunglasses	**Ayuda** = help
SAY: **GA-fas,** which sounds like **give us.**	SAY: **eye-U-da,** which sounds like **hey you there.**
SENTENCE: **Give us** those *sunglasses*.	SENTENCE: **Hey you there,** *Help!*
STICK: Imagine a two-headed cyclops in an optician's shop saying, "**Give us** those *sunglasses*."	STICK: Imagine a man floundering in the water and yelling to someone on shore, "**Hey you there,** *Help!*"

Expanding a Child's Foreign Language Vocabulary

Encourage children to create their own sets of substitute foreign language cards. On the next page you will find a list of the first 100 words to teach a child in a foreign language. Translate this list into the foreign language being taught. This list focuses on frequently used nouns. Nouns are picked because they usually have a counterpart in a foreign language and because beginners find it easier to use the substitution mnemonic system on nouns. Nouns like *cow* and *boat* are easy to visualize. Trying to visualize words like *the, in,* and *of* is more challenging.

When teaching a foreign language, it makes sense to start teaching the words most commonly used.

The Most Commonly Used Words

"The most commonly used words in the English language are based on a computer study," explained Edward Fry, Ph.D., author of *1000 Instant Words*. "The study was done by *American Heritage Dictionary*. They looked at five million words from books used in grades three through eight, plus popular magazines, literature, and some adult material. These words were then ranked by frequency. The first 100 words on the list make up 50% of words used in written literature. The first ten words on the list are so important that you would find it difficult, if not impossible, to write a paragraph without using these words. The most frequently used words are called structure or glue words [like *the, of, and, a, to*]. Glue words may not translate directly into a foreign language, but nouns work well." The title of Dr. Fry's book, *1000 Instant Words*, refers to the importance of a reader being able to instantly recognize these words because they come up over and over again. The most commonly used word in the English language is the glue word *the*. The most common noun is *word*.

THE FIRST 100 NOUNS TO LEARN IN A FOREIGN LANGUAGE

The following list contains nouns ranked in order of how frequently they are used in writing. There may not be a counterpart word in some foreign languages.

1. Word	26. Father	51. Fish	76. King
2. Number	27. Tree	52. Mark	77. Town
3. People	28. City	53. Dog	78. Box
4. Time	29. Earth	54. Friends	79. Field
5. Water	30. Eye	55. Horse	80. Wood
6. Day	31. Light	56. Birds	81. Fire
7. Year	32. Head	57. Room	82. Person
8. Sound	33. Story	58. Door	83. Road
9. Name	34. Life	59. Ship	84. Stars
10. Sentence	35. Paper	60. Waves	85. Street
11. Man	36. Sea	61. Wind	86. Scientists
12. Boy	37. River	62. Rock	87. Wheels
13. Home	38. Children	63. Space	88. Island
14. Hand	39. Feet	64. Morning	89. Week
15. Picture	40. Car	65. Farm	90. Building
16. Air	41. Book	66. Voice	91. Ocean
17. Animal	42. Girl	67. Pattern	92. Class
18. House	43. Mountain	68. Numeral	93. Note
19. Page	44. Idea	69. South	94. Machine
20. Letter	45. Face	70. Table	95. Base
21. Food	46. Song	71. North	96. Plane
22. Mother	47. Family	72. Money	97. Boat
23. Country	48. Body	73. Map	98. Game
24. Plant	49. Music	74. War	99. Circle
25. School	50. Color	75. Ground	100. Moon

The Tower of Babel

There are 122 different languages in use around the globe today—if you count only the languages spoken by one million or more people.

Teaching Youngsters How to Remember Telephone Numbers and Addresses

This chapter explains how to teach two important pieces of information to 4- to 6-year olds:

- Telephone numbers
- Addresses

Why are telephone numbers and addresses hard for youngsters to remember? For two reasons. First, numbers are abstract, which makes them inherently difficult to remember. Second, youngsters don't have a strategy for storing numbers in a sequence. In one study 2-year-olds remembered two numbers, 7-year-olds remembered five numbers, and 12-year-olds retained up to seven numbers.

Picture Numbers

 When teaching very young children how to remember their telephone number and street address, you want to get rid of abstractions. Convert the numbers zero to nine into concrete images. What does a zero look like? How about a tire? Number one has the shape of a candle. A two has the silhouette of a swan. A three has the outline of a heart with the tip missing. Four looks like a sail on a sailboat. Five is a hook. Six represents a coiled snake. Seven looks like a boomerang. Eight is a snowman. Nine is a lop-sided balloon. The following chart shows the shape of each number transformed into a picture, or pictogram:

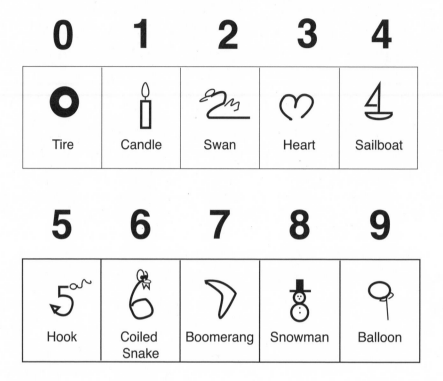

It's possible for a 3½-year-old to learn all ten pictograms in fifteen minutes. Simply go over each number and point out how the shape looks like the intended picture. Then test your child by doing one or more of the following.

PRACTICING WITH PICTOGRAMS

- Use a copy machine to enlarge and duplicate the pictograms. Then cut out each one. Make a set of cards from zero to nine. Write the appropriate number on the back of each pictogram card. Lay the cards number side up. Now randomly call out a number and see if your child can tell you what picture is on the other side. See how many cards he can collect by being correct.

• Have the child draw the picture that goes with each number.
• Get small toys for each of the represented numbers and ask your child to pick up a four, an eight, and so on.

ADDING BODY LANGUAGE TO PICTURE NUMBERS

Many youngsters are highly kinesthetic. They like to use their bodies in learning. You can take advantage of this inclination by adding a physical action to your pictured numbers. For example, the number 1 is represented by a candle, so the action for that number is to pretend to light a candle. A 2 looks like the silhouette of a swan, so imagine petting a swan. Three is a heart, put your hand over your heart. Having an action for each number allows youngsters to act out their numbers. Take a look at the chart for the numbers 0–9 to see what action you can use with each of your number images:

Tire	Candle	Swan	Heart	Sailboat
Hold a tire around your waist like an inner tube.	Light a candle.	Pet a swan.	Put your hand over your heart.	Steer a sailboat with the tiller.
0	**1**	**2**	**3**	**4**

Hook	Coiled Snake	Boomerang	Snowman	Balloon
Shape one finger into a hook.	Weave your arm like a snake.	Throw a boomerang.	Roll a snowball.	Hold a balloon.
5	**6**	**7**	**8**	**9**

To get youngsters physically involved with the numbers:

- Have them act out the numbers by using the physical movements.
- Make up four-digit numbers. Have the child act them out, charades fashion. If the number is 6281, she might move her arm like a snake for 6, pretend to pet a swan for 2, mimic making a snowball for 8, and for 1, mimic lighting a candle.

Using Picture Numbers to Learn a Telephone Number

The next step is to take your child's telephone number and convert it into a picture sequence. Here's the number 996-9448 represented by pictograms:

9 9 6 - 9 4 4 8

Turn your telephone number into pictograms:

My Phone Number in Pictograms

Telephone number: ___ ___ ___ ___ ___ ___ ___

Pictogram phone number: ___ ___ ___ ___ ___ ___ ___

PUTTING YOUR TELEPHONE NUMBER ON YOUR BODY

Now that we have turned your telephone number into a pictogram, we need to memorize the sequence. For this we'll use a mapping technique, because it prompts both number recall and the proper sequence. To create an easily remembered map, specify ten places on the body. The following body locations will give you room for an area code and phone number: top of the head, eyes, mouth, neck, shoulders, tummy, fanny, thighs, knees, and feet.

A youngster can learn the sequence by playing a game. Have her pat each body part two times, starting at the head and descending. Demonstrate this sequence and have her copy you, in Simon-Says fashion. Go slow for the first run through. Go faster on each successive pass. You'll get a lot of giggles by speeding up the pace.

Now that you have ten body locations, put each image of the telephone number on a specific body part, beginning at the top and working down in order. For the 996-9448 number, your child imagines a balloon on her head, and another in her eye. Her mouth holds a snake. A balloon is tied to her neck. There's a sailboat on her shoulder and her tummy. She sits on a snowman. If you want your child to know her area code, begin with the area code at the top of the head followed by the phone number.

To increase motivation, have her practice decoding her phone number by starting at the head and dialing the number on a play phone. Graduation occurs after she calls home on a real phone.

TEACHING YOUNGSTERS THEIR TELEPHONE NUMBER: SUMMARY

1. Teach the pictograms for each number.
2. Convert a telephone number into a picture sequence.
3. Teach children ten places on their body.
4. Have them imagine each number image on a part of their body.

Some young children may have trouble learning the visual picture substitutions; they may be auditory learners. In this case, see Appendix B for a chart similar to the visual chart, but with substitutions that use a rhyming technique more appropriate for auditory learners.

Using Picture Numbers to Learn a Street Address

To learn an address, start with the picture number system explained at the beginning of the chapter. Now take each of the digits in a house address and convert it into a picture. Let's say you live at 2310 Farm Street. The numbers translate into swan, heart, candle, and tire:

Next, use a mapping method. Choose four distinctive locations that logically lead up to your house. These locations might be the street, followed by the sidewalk, your driveway, and finally your front door. At each location, starting with the street, attach the visual image for a number. The street has a swan swimming down it. The sidewalk is the site for a giant beating heart. Your driveway is covered by wax from a burning candle. The front door is blocked by a massive tire.

To recall the street number, the child imagines walking up to his house. As each obstacle is passed, the child translates that image into a number.

Now draw out your street number in pictures:

My Street Number in Pictograms

Street number: ___ ___ ___ ___ ___

Pictogram street number: ___ ___ ___ ___ ___

REMEMBERING A STREET NAME

Now that the child has the street number memorized, he needs to remember the street name. If the name of a street is hard to remember, use a substitution technique. Farm Street is easy. Imagine a farm complete with cows, pigs, and sheep. Put this image on the roof of your house. More abstract names, like Lafayette Street, will require a more creative concrete substitute. Here's where *schmurgling*, explained in Chapter 3, comes in handy. Something that sounds like Lafayette Street but provides an image for the child might be *laughing feet*. Put these laughing feet on the roof of the house. Now the child imagines looking on the roof for the street name.

Does your street name make a ready picture? Or will you have to use substitution to make a meaningful image? Draw a sketch of your street name.

My Street Name as a Picture

Studies show that youngsters have good recognition memories. If you show a child a bunch of pictures and then mix these pictures with other pictures she hasn't seen, she can tell you which items she saw and which are new. On the other hand, if you ask children to recall what they saw without prompts, they perform horribly. "What pictures did you just see?" "I don't remember." What's happening here is that information is going into their brain, but they don't have a way to find that information. It's like a library that adds books but doesn't enter them into a filing system. The books are there, but they're hard to find.

The methods you've learned for teaching youngsters how to remember a telephone number and an address provide filing systems. For the telephone number, a child uses his body as a filing system, "What image is on my head?" "On my eye?" and so on. For the address, we use the street, sidewalk, driveway, and door as a filing system. He imagines what is in the street, on the sidewalk, in the driveway, and at the door to retrieve his street number.

How to Remember Any Number

In this chapter you will learn how to remember:

- Anything with numbers

Imagine that you are offered $1,000. All you have to do is memorize a list in ten seconds. You have a choice of lists. You can choose one with numbers or one with words. Which of the following lists would you find the easiest to memorize in ten seconds?

Number List	Word List
186,282	To Fiji on a fan
685	Joyful
2150	Initials
740	Kris
4145	Retrial

Most people choose the word list because of a simple memory principle:

Words are easier to remember than numbers.

 An appreciation of this principle inspired an early memory scholar to ask, "If words are easier to remember than numbers, how can I convert numbers into words?" The earliest answer to this question can be traced back to a system developed in Hindu culture when the Sanskrit alphabet was popular. Whether inspired by the Hindu system or an original invention, an analogous system appeared in Europe in the seventeenth century. Over time, this system evolved. The most recent version was devised in the 1840s by an Englishman, Dr. Richard Grey, called the consonant code.

In this system, the numbers zero through nine are assigned letters. These letters can be formed into words. Once you know the secret code, you can translate numbers into words and words into numbers. Knowledge of the code allows you to translate a number like 2150 into the word *initials*.

When children master the consonant code, they can use it to remember:

- Telephone numbers
- Locker combinations
- School ID numbers
- Dates
- Addresses
- Mathematical constants
- Numbers associated with distances, speed, quantity, etc.

Popcorn

Business people are well aware of the fact that you can convert hard-to-remember telephone numbers into memorable words. This conversion is possible because of the grouping of letters under numbers on a telephone keypad. If you are asked to dial POPCORN, you tap the letters P-O-P-C-O-R-N. On a telephone keypad, these letters correspond to the numbers 767-2676. Unfortunately, this technique only works with a limited combination of numbers.

The original consonant code is a sophisticated mnemonic technique. It requires some effort to learn initially. To make it easier for children to understand this technique, a simplified consonant code is presented here. If you want the full version, with all the mnemonic bells and whistles, go to Appendix C.

Breaking the Consonant Code (Simple Version)

Think of the consonant code as a secret decoder ring that you got in a box of Cracker Jacks®. There are ten digits (1, 2, 3, 4, 5, 6, 7, 8, 9, and 0) on the ring. Opposite each digit is a letter.

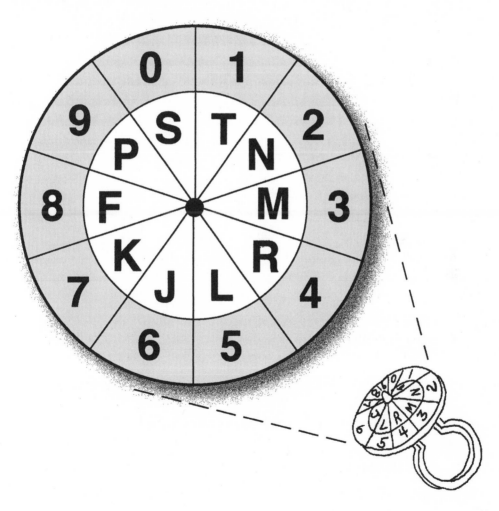

Once you know the code, you can change a number like 2150 into the letters NTLS:

$$2 = N, 1 = T, 5 = L, \text{ and } 0 = S$$

You might say, "Well, NTLS isn't very memorable." That's because there is one more step. Vowels (a, e, i, o, u, w, and y) are inserted into the letter group to create a word. Vowels have no number value. So they can be used freely to build words. Adding vowels, the letters NTLS are transformed into the word iNiTiaLS.

To translate the word *initials* back into numbers, you reverse the process:

$$i = \text{no digit}, N = 2, i = \text{no digit}, T = 1, i = \text{no digit},$$
$$a = \text{no digit}, L = 5, S = 0$$

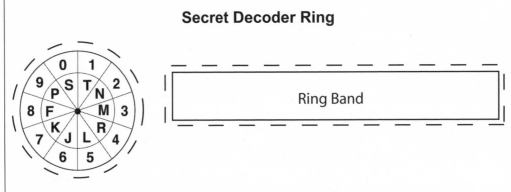

Secret Decoder Ring

Ring Band

Decoder

1. Cut out the decoder and the ring band along the dashed lines.
2. Wrap the ring band around your finger and tape it together. This is your ring.
3. Put a dab of glue on the ring and glue down the decoder.

Now use your decoder to translate numbers into words.

MEMORIZE THE CODE

Here is a way to commit the consonant code to memory using mnemonics:

Digit	Consonant Sound	Mnemonic Aid
1	T	T has *one* down stroke.
2	N	N has *two* down strokes or it looks like a 2 turned on its side.
3	M	M has *three* down strokes or it looks like a 3 turned on its side.
4	R	R looks like a backwards 4 or a golfer saying Fore! Look at the R at the end of the word four.
5	L	Roman numeral for 50 is L, or hold up your left hand and stick out your thumb so that your index finger and thumb make the outline of an L (five fingers on a hand).
6	J	A cursive *j* is a mirror image of 6.
7	K	Look closely at a capital *K* and notice that it's made up of two 7s.
8	F	A cursive *f* has two loops like an 8.
9	P	P is a mirror image of 9.
0	S	S makes a sound like the Z used in zero.

Put the Code to Work

Try using the code on the number 206, the number of bones in the human body. Stop reading now and see what words you come up with:

206 =

One possibility for the number 206: The code translates the number 206 into the letters NSJ; add a few vowels, and you have the words *NoiSy Jaw*. Now stick this image to the subject it applies to. Imagine a skeleton. His *noisy jaw* is creaking up and down. The next time you need the number of bones in a human body, imagine your skeleton. Imagine him moving his *noisy jaw*. Once you have the words, use your decoder ring to translate the letters back into numbers.

As illustrated in the previous paragraph, when you translate a number into a word, stick that word to what it represents. Create a memorable image. If the street number you are looking for is 690, imagine JeePS parked in front of your destination. If your locker combination is 12-35-20, imagine a TiN-MaLe-Nose from *The Wizard of Oz* sticking out of your locker. These images make later retrieval easier. Try coding the following numbers. Then stick the code words to what they represent before looking at the possible solutions:

Length of the longest river, the Nile at 4,145 miles

Length of the Great Wall of China, 2,150 miles

Height of the tallest mountain, Everest, 29,035 feet

Deepest depth in the ocean, Marianas Trench, 6.85 miles

Speed of sound, 740 miles per hour

Speed of light, 186,282 miles per second

Start of World War Two, 1939

POSSIBLE SOLUTIONS TO THE NUMBER FACTS

Fact	Numbers turned into words	Stick
Nile River: 4,145 miles	ReTRiaL	Imagine the Nile River filled with lawyers demanding a *retrial*.
Great Wall of China: 2,150 miles	iNiTiaLS	Imagine carving your *initials* into the Great Wall of China.
Mt. Everest: 29,035 feet	NaP SMiLe	Imagine a climber reaching the top of Mt. Everest and taking a *nap* with a *smile* on his face.
Deepest ocean depth: 6.85 miles, Marianas Trench	JoyFuL	Imagine a *joyful* whale diving to the bottom of the ocean.
Speed of sound: 740 mph	KRiS	Imagine a *kris*, a long wavy knife, breaking the sound barrier.
Speed of light: 186,282 miles per second	To FiJi oN a FaN	Imagine racing at the speed of light *to Fiji on a fan*.
Start of WWII: 1939	ToPo MaP	Imagine a topo map with Hitler plotting WWII.

This chapter contains a simplified version of the consonant code. The original code, while more difficult to learn, is an even more powerful number memory system. Go to Appendix C to learn the original code.

You Don't Have to Be Born with an Exceptional Memory to Get Exceptional Results

As an adult, Rajan Srinivasan Mahadevan recited the first 31,811 digits of pi from memory in under four hours. Rajan's father said that his son showed a precocious memory at an early age. During a birthday party for his sister, Rajan recited the license numbers for about twenty cars at the party and their corresponding owners. He was not yet 6 years old. As an adult, he can remember around forty-three digits when they are presented to him auditorily as compared to sixty digits that he sees in print. This is impressive considering that the average person can remember between five and nine digits. But an impressive memory for numbers can be learned. In one scientific experiment, a man was trained in a technique for remembering numbers. After 230 hours of practice over six months, he increased his recall ability from seven to seventy-nine digits. His ability was as good as that of lifelong memory experts.

Learn the Multiplication Tables in a Week

In this chapter:

- Learn how to teach times tables for 2s, 3s, 4s, 5s, 6s, 7s, 8s, and 9s the mnemonic way.

Learning the multiplication or times tables—2s through 9s—is a major memory task. Most students take weeks, months, or years to learn them. Using a mnemonic system, students can memorize them in a week!

It's important to understand that children learn more than the multiplication tables in this section. They also learn how to use a variety of mnemonic techniques that can be applied to a variety of other subjects.

Multiplying by 2

To learn the times tables for the 2s, the products of 2 x 1, 2 x 2, 2 x 3—all the way up to 2 x 9—have been put into a rhyme:

2, 4, 6, 8,
Who do we appreciate?
10 plus 2, 4, 6, or 8,
Flying pigs are really great.

The first line—2, 4, 6, 8—represents the products of 2 x 1, 2 x 2, 2 x 3, and 2 x 4. This is followed by the rhyming line *who do we appreciate?*

Who do we appreciate?

The next line—10 plus 2, 4, 6, or 8—represents the products of 2 x 5, 2 x 6, 2 x 7, 2 x 8, and 2 x 9. The products are 10, 10 plus 2 (12), 10 plus 4 (14), 10 plus 6 (16), and 10 plus 8 (18).

The final line is again a rhyming line, *flying pigs are really great*.

Flying pigs are really great

Once children have memorized the rhyme, they simply count their way through the rhyme to find a product. If they need 2 x 5, they count through the first five numbers that appear in the rhyme: *2, 4, 6, 8, Who do we appreciate? 10* … here they stop, because 10 is the fifth number in the rhyme. The product of 2 x 5 is 10.

The rhyme is silly. This silliness makes it more memorable than simply learning to count by 2s. Children like silly, and it makes math more fun.

Multiplying by 3

The final products of 3 x 1, 3 x 2, 3 x 3, all the way up to 3 x 9, can be learned with a chunking technique. The chunk to remember is the numbers:

3, 6, 9

 These numbers—3, 6, 9—are the products of 3 x 1, 3 x 2, and 3 x 3. This 3, 6, 9 pattern appears as you continue to multiply by three. Here's how it works. The next three multiplications in the sequence—3 x 4, 3 x 5, and 3 x 6—give the products 12, 15, and 18. Notice that the 1 and 2 in the number 12 add up to 3. The 1 and 5 in the number 15 add up to 6. The 1 and 8 in the number 18 add up to 9. It is a repetition of the 3, 6, 9 pattern. A similar coincidence appears with the products of 3 x 7, 3 x 8, and 3 x 9: 21, 24, and 27. Notice that the 2 and 1 in the number 21 add up to 3. The 2 and 4 in the number 24 add up to 6. The 2 and 7 in the number 27 add up to 9—again a repetition of the 3, 6, 9 chunk. An understanding of this progression makes it easier for students to check themselves and memorize the pattern.

Here's a memorable way of presenting this multiplication mnemonic to students. Tell the following story:

Pharaoh 369

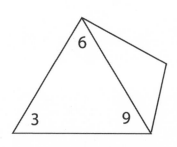 Archaeologists have discovered a pyramid. It's the tomb of a Pharaoh known as 369. An ancient scroll explains that the Pharaoh was obsessed by the numbers 3, 6, and 9—in that order. He believed they were magical numbers. When archaeologists measured his pyramid they found that each edge was 369 feet long. Next they discovered that the pyramid was made up of 369 massive sandstone blocks. The numbers 3, 6, and 9 appeared everywhere on his pyramid, even on the face. Inscribed on the east face of the pyramid were the mystical numbers 3, 6, and 9. One number in each corner.

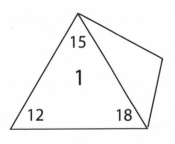

But the archaeologists are confronted with a riddle. The other two faces of the pyramid have numbers that don't seem to fit the 3, 6, 9 pattern. On the northwest face, there is a large 1 in the center of the face. Chiseled into each corner, they find the numbers 12, 15, and 18. This puzzles the archaeologists. Why the numbers 12, 15, and 18 if the Pharaoh believed that 3, 6, and 9 were the magical numbers? Then one archaeologist excitedly says, "Look, it is still the 3, 6, 9 pattern. Take the 12 and imagine the 1 and 2 are separate numbers. Now add the 1 and 2 to get 3. Do the same for 15: 1 + 5 = 6. And then for 18: 1 + 8 = 9. It's 3, 6, and 9 again! The 1 in the center reminds you to start each corner number with a one and then add a number to get the sums of 3, 6, and 9."

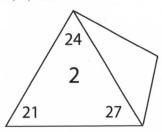

Now look at the final face of the pyramid. There's a 2 in the center of this face. Each corner also has a number: 21, 24, and 27. Having solved the riddle on the previous face, do you have a clue to how this final face also fits into the 3, 6, 9 pattern? Can you help the archaeologists figure out the riddle for this face?

If you haven't figured out the answer for the third face of the pyramid riddle, here goes. In the first corner they find the number 21. The two numerals that form the number 21 are 2 and 1. Add 2 and 1, and you get 3. Treat the number 24 the same way: 2 + 4 = 6. Then repeat the process for the number 27: 2 + 7 = 9. Again you have the number pattern 3, 6, and 9. The number 2 in the center of the pyramid is a reminder. It reminds you to start each corner number with a 2 and then tack on the numbers that give you the sums 3, 6, or 9.

Now give students an opportunity to build Pharaoh 369's pyramid. On the next page you will find a paper cut-out model of the Pharaoh's pyramid. This hands-on experience will make the concept more memorable. During multiplication practice, put the completed pyramids on students' desks as a reminder of the pattern that threes follow.

Build Pharaoh 369's Pyramid

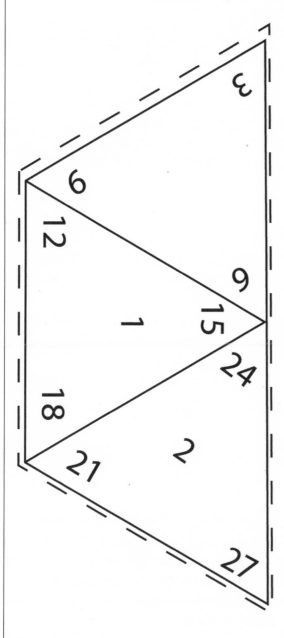

Make a copy of the figure to the left. Then follow the dotted lines and cut out the figure. Make a fold along the line from 12 to 15. Make another fold along the line from 15 to 18. Now bring the edge printed with a 3 and 6 to the edge printed with a 24 and 27 to form a pyramid. Tape these edges together. You now have a model of the 3, 6, 9 pyramid.

PRACTICING WITH THE PYRAMID FACES

Now practice with the pyramid faces. Start with the face that has a 3, 6, and 9 printed on it. Starting at the lower left corner, 3, imagine climbing to the top of the pyramid where you find a 6, then slide down the other side to the 9. Repeat this climb for the other two triangles. (Explain to students that each number they come to is the product of multiplying 3 times that number position. For example, the fourth position that we arrive at in climbing and sliding down the pyramid is the number 12—the product of multiplying 3 x 4. Notice the explanatory equations next to each triangle corner.)

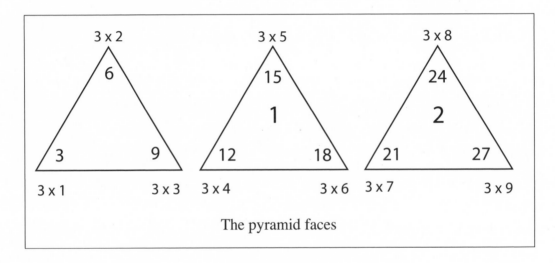

The pyramid faces

THE PYRAMID GAME, MULTIPLYING BY 3

1. You need three to five people to play this game.
2. Get nine Popsicle® sticks or pennies.
3. Use masking tape on the floor to lay out the triangles you see in the preceding illustration (include the numbers you see inside the triangles, but leave out the explanatory multiplication equations on the outside of the triangles). Make each triangle side about three or four feet long.

4.   Copy the spinner below.

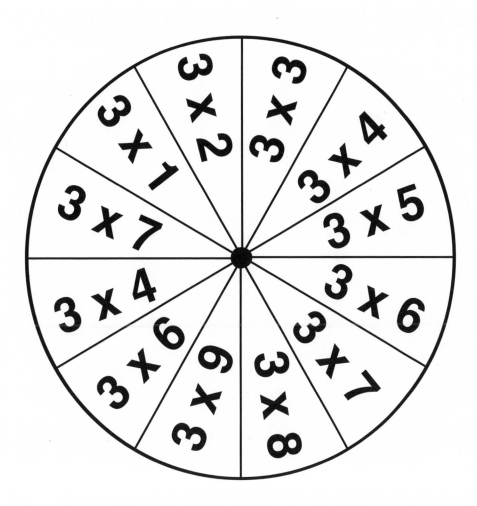

5.   Glue the spinner to a piece of cardboard. Then cut out the
      spinner along the outside edge. Push a tack through the center
      of the spinner and put a piece of tape over the tack to secure it.

6.   Point a pencil at the spinner.

To play the pyramid game:

One person is the referee and spins the spinner, calling out the
multiplication problem that the pencil points to. The other students
have been walking in a circle around the group of triangles.
Students run to the spot on the triangle that represents the product
of the multiplication problem. The first student to put his foot on
the correct answer gets a Popsicle® stick. When the nine Popsicle®
sticks have been handed out, the student with the most sticks
becomes the new referee.

Multiplying by 4

 Rhythm is a powerful memory aid. For example, you probably learned
the alphabet using rhythm. Ask any child or adult to recite their ABCs,
and you will hear it sung to the tune of *Twinkle, Twinkle, Little Star*. The
words in this familiar tune have been replaced with letters. The discoverer of this
mnemonic shortcut has helped countless children learn the alphabet.

You can also use rhythm to help children memorize the products of 4 x 1, 4 x
2, 4 x 3, all the way up to 4 x 9. Instead of *Twinkle, Twinkle, Little Star*, use the
tune *She'll Be Comin' Round the Mountain*. Replace the words in this song with
the products in the correct order:

        Four,   eight,   twelve, six-teen,   t-w-e-n-t-y, twenty-four
        She'll be   comin'   round   the mountain when   she   comes,

        twenty-eight,   t - h i r t - y -two,   t h - i - r - t - y - six
        She'll be comin'   round the   mountain   when she comes ...

If a child needs the product of 4 x 7, she counts through the first seven
numbers in the song, which will take her to 28, the product of 4 x 7.

Multiplying by 5

To learn how to multiply by 5s, have children memorize the following list by saying it out loud. You'll hear a rhyming cadence. This cadence makes it easy to remember.

5 and
1 and 0
1 and 5
2 and 0
2 and 5
3 and 0
3 and 5
4 and 0
4 and 5

In looking at this list, notice the pattern. After saying 5, you start with 1s on the left repeated twice. Then 2s repeated twice. Then 3s repeated twice and 4s repeated twice. The left column follows a pattern of 1, 2, 3, 4. The right column has alternating patterns of 0 and 5. Pointing out this pattern to students may make it easier for them to remember the organization.

The first line is the product of 5 x 1 or 5. The second line is the product of 5 x 2 or 1 and 0, which is 10. The third line is the product of 5 x 3 or 1 and 5, which is 15. This pattern continues to the end.

Multiplying by 6

To teach the times tables for 6s, use a combination of rhyming, chaining, and substitution. The story you are about to read has a rhyming pattern for some products, i.e., *twelve* and *elves*. Or products use substitutions, i.e., *forty-two* has been changed to *for two*. Finally, the story format contains a chain of events that make it easier to remember. Have children memorize the following story:

6 (6) sacks were carried by
12 (12) elves and
18 (18) queens
up 24 (24) floors.
These 30 (30) were thirsty and
36 (36) sodas they sucked.
For two (42) dollars, yes,
For eight (48) quarters,
They climbed 54 (54) more floors.

This story contains the products, in order, of 6 x 1, 6 x 2, 6 x 3, 6 x 4, 6 x 5, 6 x 6, 6 x 7, 6 x 8, and 6 x 9.

THE TIMES 6 STORY EXPLAINED

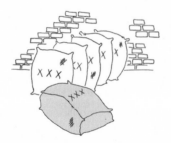

In the first line, *6 sacks were carried by …*, 6 is the product of 6 x 1. The word *sacks* is a substitution for six, making it easier to remember that 6 starts the story.

Then come *12 elves*. Twelve is the product of 6 x 2. The word *elves* rhymes with 12, making it easier to remember 12.

In the line *18 queens,* 18 is the product of 6 x 3. The word *queens* rhymes with 18, again making it easier to remember the 18.

Then we have *24 floors,* where 24 is the product of 6 x 4, and the word *floors* rhymes with 24.

Next comes *These 30 were thirsty.* The number 30 is the product of 6 x 5, and *thirsty* is a sound-alike substitution for 30.

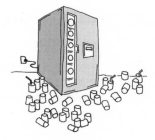

In the line *36 sodas they sucked,* the number 36 is the product of 6 x 6.

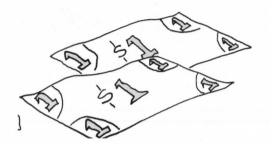

In the line *For two dollars,* the words *For two* are a sound-alike substitution for 42, the product of 6 x 7.

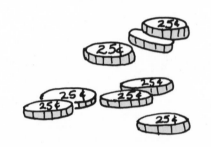

The same technique is used in the next line, *For eight quarters.* The words *For eight* are a substitution for 48, the product of 6 x 8.

Finally comes the line *They climbed 54 more floors.* The number 54 is the product of 6 x 9, and the word *floors* rhymes with 54.

When the story is memorized, if a child needs the product of 6 x 3, he counts through the story until he comes to the third number in the story: *"6* (count 1) sacks were carried by *12* (count 2) elves and *18* (count 3) queens." Eighteen is the third number in the story and the product of 6 x 3.

To help children learn the rhyme, have students tell the story out loud while physically acting it out. This will make it easier for them to visualize the sequence.

Multiplying by 7

To teach the times tables for multiplying by 7s, use two mnemonic techniques: substitution and chaining. First, we will substitute images for numbers. If you read Chapter 11, you are already familiar with those images.

    We usually think of substitution mnemonics as finding a sound-alike that can be turned into an image, but in this case we're going to use a look-alike. Each number will be assigned an image (also known as a pictogram) suggested by the shapes of the numbers. The number 1 has the silhouette of a candle. Number 2 follows the outline of a swan. A 3 on its side is similar to the top of a valentine heart. Four is the sail on a sailboat. Five is a hook. Six is a coiled snake. Seven is represented by a boomerang. Eight has the shape of a snowman. Nine is a balloon with the string dangling. Now check yourself to see if you can remember the images for the numbers 1-9. Write down the pictogram image for each number:

1

2

3

4

5

6

7

8

9

Refer to Chapter 11 for illustrations of the pictogram numbers. Chapter 11 also explains how to teach these pictograms to children.

The next step is chaining. The products of 7 x 1, 7 x 2 … all the way up to 7 x 9, are chained together—or rather, their images are chained together in the context of a story:

A boomerang (7) comes whizzing by, which represents **7.**

It knocks a candle (1) off the back of a sailboat (4), a pictogram for **14.**

The candle (1) lands on the back of a swan (2), which is **21.**

The swan (2) is hit by a snowman (8) falling from the sky, number **28.**

The snowman's heart (3) pops out and is impaled on a hook (5), an image for **35.**

The line on the hook leads back to the sailboat (4) which is about to run over the swan (2), number **42.**

The sailboat (4) sails over the swan, which holds its breath and turns into a balloon (9), which gets stuck on the bow of the boat, a pictogram for **49.**

The balloon is popped by a hook (5) held by a snake (6), number **56.**

The snake (6) is startled by the balloon blast and is left with its heart in its mouth, number **63.**

Here are all the images in the series:

When the story is memorized, if a child needs the product of 7 x 3, she counts through the story until she comes to the third pictogram in the story: "A boomerang (7) knocks a candle off a sailboat (14), and the candle lands on the back of a swan (21)—21 is the product of 7 x 3."

Multiplying by 8

  Here's a substitution and chain method for multiplying 8s. The substitutions start at 8 x 1 and go through to 8 x 9. Have children memorize the following story:

The ogre *ate* (8)
6 teens (16),

and *24* (24) hours later

he was *thirsty too* (32)
for tea (40).

Then this *fatty ate* (48)
50 socks (56)

and was *sick for* (64)
72 (72) days.

After the story is memorized, if a child needs the product of, say, 8 x 3, he counts through the story until he comes to the third number in the story: "The ogre ate (8) 6 teens (16) and 24 (24) hours" … and 24 is the product of 8 x 3.

Some numbers are substitutions, like *sick four* in place of 64, and other numbers are simply woven into the story like the 24 in 24 hours.

As in previous mnemonic techniques that use stories, have students act the story out as they tell it to make the experience more kinesthetic and thereby more memorable.

Multiplying by 9

Multiplying by 9 involves finger manipulation. Often, 9s are one of the harder multiplication series for children to learn. With the following method, children will be able to multiply by 9 in less than two minutes!

Hold both of your hands up, palms facing you. Let's say you want to multiply 9 x 2. Starting on the left hand, count over two fingers and fold that finger down.

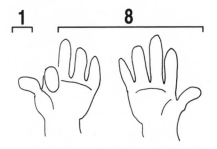

Notice that you have one straight finger on the left of the folded finger and eight straight fingers on the right side of the folded finger (make sure to count your right hand). One finger to the left and eight fingers to the right stands for 18, the product of 9 x 2.

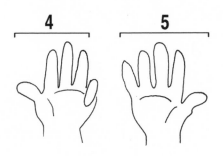

Now try 9 x 5. With palms facing you, count from the left over five fingers and fold that finger down (it should be the pinky finger on your left hand). On the left side of the folded finger, there are four straight fingers, and on the right side, there are five straight fingers, which represents 45.

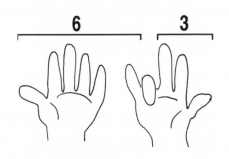

Still not convinced? Try 9 x 7. Count over seven fingers and fold down that finger (ring finger on your right hand). You should see six straight fingers on the left side of your bent finger and three straight fingers on the right side of your bent finger which stands for 63.

This system works when you multiply 9 times 1, 2, 3, 4, 5, 6, 7, 8, and 9.

Multiplication Twister Game

Multiplication twister is similar to the well-known Twister® game. In Twister®, children stretch to reach color spots with their hands or feet in response to a spinner that indicates the color. In multiplication twister, children stretch to reach the products produced by multiplications. Multiplication twister makes times tables a physical experience.

To play multiplication twister you need:

1. A times table (if the referee doesn't yet know the products)
2. Two 10-sided number dice (provided as cutouts)
3. One die with the markings H and F (provided as a cutout)
4. One multiplication twister play area

THE TIMES TABLE

X	0	1	2	3	4	5	6	7	8	9
0	0	0	0	0	0	0	0	0	0	0
1	0	1	2	3	4	5	6	7	8	9
2	0	2	4	6	8	10	12	14	16	18
3	0	3	6	9	12	15	18	21	24	27
4	0	4	8	12	16	20	24	28	32	36
5	0	5	10	15	20	25	30	35	40	45
6	0	6	12	18	24	30	36	42	48	54
7	0	7	14	21	28	35	42	49	56	63
8	0	8	16	24	32	40	48	56	64	72
9	0	9	18	27	36	45	54	63	72	81

To use the times table, find the two numbers being multiplied. Locate one number in the top row, and the other along the left side. Slide a finger from the top row down and another finger from left to right. Your fingers will meet at the product.

Ten-Sided Number Dice

Use a copy machine to make two copies of the number die. Cut along the outer edge of each die. Fold one die along each line. Put a dab of rubber cement on each non-numbered tab. Make the necessary folds to create a decahedron die (ten-sided die). The tabs should be inside, where they will hold the die together. Repeat the process for the second die. You now have two dice.

The H And F Die

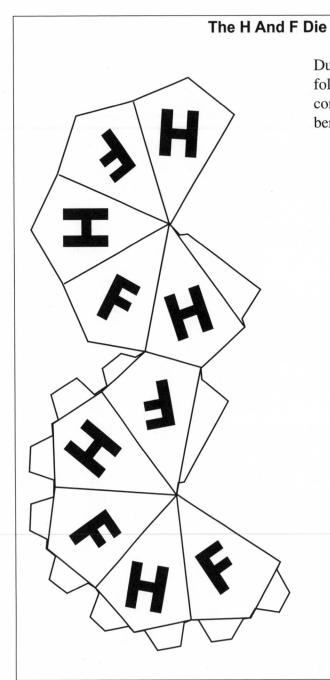

Duplicate the H and F die. Cut, fold, and glue the same way you constructed the ten-sided number die on the previous page.

THE MULTIPLICATION TWISTER PLAY AREA

The following pattern of numbers in circles can be drawn on a playground with chalk, outlined on an old bed sheet with an indelible marker, or fashioned out of paper plates taped securely to the floor. The number pattern is shown below.

Let's say you are using chalk on a playground. Make the circles six inches in diameter. The distance between circles is one foot in the horizontal and vertical directions. This creates a play area six-and-a-half feet wide by eleven feet long. Small children might require a smaller play area. Reduce the size or distance between plates to make it easier for small students to reach the numbers.

0	2	4	6	8
9	7	5	3	1
0	6	2	8	4
5	1	7	3	9
9	3	7	1	5
4	8	2	6	0
0	2	4	6	8
1	3	5	7	9

Rules for Multiplication Twister

1. You need three people to play. One person acts as the referee.
2. Players face each other from opposite ends of the playing area. The referee rolls the three dice and calls out the body part and two numbers. For example the referee might call out: "Hands (H on the die represents hands while F represents feet), four and six." Both players try to follow the referee's directions.
3. Each player tries to place the called-out body parts on a vacant circle. The circles chosen represent the product of the called-out numbers. If the two numbers called out are 4 and 6, the resultant product would be 4 x 6 = 24. Players then try to cover a 2 and a 4. If the referee called out hands, players will place their left hand on the first number in the product, in this case 2, and their right hand on the second number in the product, in this case 4. If the product is a single digit, then the right hand would cover that number, and the left hand would be kept off the playing field.
4. There can never be more than one hand or foot on any one circle. If two players reach for the same circle, the referee must decide who reached it first. The other player must find another vacant circle that represents the correct product.
5. The referee determines if the called-out body parts cover the correct product. To do this, the referee can use a times table to quickly calculate the correct product. If the product was 48 and it was to be covered by hands, the left hand should cover a 4 and the right hand an 8. If the called-out body part was feet, and the product was 48, then the left foot should cover a 4 and the right foot an 8.
6. Any player who falls or touches the mat with an elbow or knee is immediately eliminated. In a two-player game, the game ends and the remaining player is the winner, who then becomes the new referee.

A Final Note on Teaching the Multiplication Tables

If you learned multiplication tables with rote memorization, you are going to have to relearn the tables with new mnemonic methods. Most brains resist relearning something when they already have a method worked out, because of a lack of motivation. Your brain says you already know how to do it. So your motivation has to be that it will make you a more efficient teacher. The children you teach will master their multiplication tables in a fraction of the time that this task normally takes. Moreover, they'll learn practical examples of mnemonic techniques that can be used for other memory tasks.

Getting Silly with the Solar System

In this chapter:

*   Memorize the planets and their order in the solar system.

Helping youngsters memorize the planets and their order is a great way to teach them the mnemonic techniques of mapping and substitution. Warning: Don't tell students that they're going to learn the order of the planets in the solar system. Wait till you're near the end of the exercise to divulge the secret. They'll be surprised when they realize that they learned something while being silly and having fun.

The Body Map System

 First you need a mapping system. We will use a body mapping system. Ten distinctive places have been chosen on the body.

1. Top of the head
2. Eyes
3. Mouth
4. Neck
5. Shoulders
6. Belly button
7. Fanny
8. Thighs
9. Knees
10. Feet

LEARN THE BODY MAP SYSTEM WITH A GAME

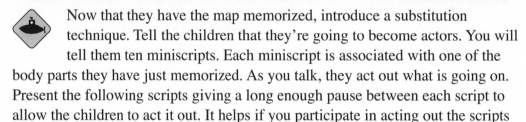

Teach the body mapping system with a game. Have children start by clapping their hands twice on top of their head. Then have them touch their eyes twice, then tap their mouth twice, and so on until they get to their feet. After they have done it several times, see if they can do it from memory. Then speed up the tapping and see if they can keep up. When you get going really fast, you will probably get a lot of laughter.

Miniscripts for the Planets

Now that they have the map memorized, introduce a substitution technique. Tell the children that they're going to become actors. You will tell them ten miniscripts. Each miniscript is associated with one of the body parts they have just memorized. As you talk, they act out what is going on. Present the following scripts giving a long enough pause between each script to allow the children to act it out. It helps if you participate in acting out the scripts along with them.

1. Imagine that the sun's rays are burning down on top of your head, and your hair catches on fire.
2. Stuck in your eye is an old-style mercury thermometer.
3. Vines start growing out of your mouth as in a scene from an alien movie.
4. Rub your neck with your hands. Do you feel little dirt balls forming?
5. On each of your shoulders you have a candy bar, Mars® bars. Try to open the wrappers on these candy bars without using your hands.
6. Your belly button has a jewel in it, and you start belly dancing.
7. You sit down on a Grecian urn. (You may need to explain what an urn is and have children pretend to sit on this invisible urn.)
8. While sitting on the urn, it rains on your thighs. Drum with your fingers on your thighs like raindrops plopping.

9. Suddenly, Neptune, the king of the sea, plunges a pitchfork into your knee, and you leap up.
10. While standing there massaging your Neptune-stabbed knee, the Disney dog Pluto comes and starts sniffing at your feet, and you use your foot to push him away.

BE SURE CHILDREN HAVE THE STORY DOWN PAT

Have everyone pair up. One child acts out the story while the other child makes sure they include all parts of the story in the proper order. Remind them to use their body map to jog their memories about what happens in each part of the story. Then have everyone switch roles.

EXPLAINING TO CHILDREN HOW THEY LEARNED THE ORDER OF THE PLANETS

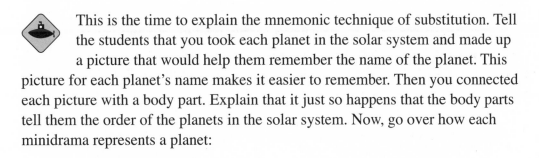 This is the time to explain the mnemonic technique of substitution. Tell the students that you took each planet in the solar system and made up a picture that would help them remember the name of the planet. This picture for each planet's name makes it easier to remember. Then you connected each picture with a body part. Explain that it just so happens that the body parts tell them the order of the planets in the solar system. Now, go over how each minidrama represents a planet:

1. The *sun* igniting your hair represents the Sun as the center of the solar system.
2. The *mercury thermometer* in your eye represents Mercury.
3. *Vines* growing out of your mouth are a sound-alike for Venus.
4. There's *dirt* on your neck, and another word for dirt is Earth.
5. The *Mars® candy bars* on your shoulders represent Mars.
6. The *jewel* in your belly button is a sound-alike substitution for Jupiter.

7. You *sat on an urn* sounds like Saturn.
8. *Rain* on your thighs sounds like Uranus.
9. *Neptune* stabs your knee with his trident, and the next planet is Neptune.
10. *Pluto* the dog sniffing at your feet represents the planet Pluto.

Ask questions, like those that follow, to see if the students understand the mnemonic technique.

*   Go back to each body place—top of head, eyes, mouth, and so on—and describe the action that's occurring there. After describing the action, tell me what planet it represents.
*   What is the fifth planet from the sun? A child simply counts down from the sun at the top of his head to the fifth body place, his belly button. Then he imagines what is attached to his belly button, a jewel. Finally, he translates the substitute picture into the planet it represents—jewel is a sound-alike for Jupiter.
*   What planets are on either side of the Earth? Knowing that earth (dirt) is on the neck, a child simply thinks, "Mouth is the body part on one side of the neck, shoulders are on the other side. Mouth has *vines,* which is Venus, and the shoulders have *Mars® candy bars,* which are Mars."

If the students have trouble understanding the pictures attached to each body place, show them the illustration of Mr. Solar System on the following page. Point out how each of the body locations they memorized has a picture attached to it.

Mr. Solar System

Earth History from Eons to Epochs

In this chapter:

- Memorize terms used to describe the Earth's geological history.
- Remember the order in which these terms are applied.

Memorizing Eons

Scientists divide the Earth's history into two main chapters called eons. The first chapter is the Precambrian eon, which covers everything from the origin of the Earth, 4.6 billion years ago, up to 570 million years ago. The Phanerozoic eon covers from 570 million years ago to the present:

Precambrian	Phanerozoic

Origin of the Earth
4.6 billion years ago

570 million
years ago

Present

  Use substitution and chaining to remember the names and order of the Earth's major history chapters, the eons. Visualize a *praying camera* (Precambrian). This camera is taking a picture of a *fan* on a *zoo* (Phanerozoic). Look at the illustration on the next page if you are having trouble coming up with an image.

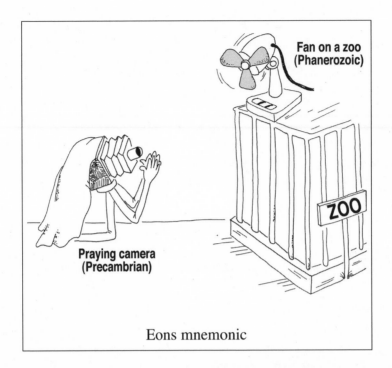

Eons mnemonic

Memorizing Eras

The Phanerozoic eon is divided into three subchapters called eras: the Paleozoic, Mesozoic, and Cenozoic eras.

The Paleozoic was 570 million to 230 million years ago. The Mesozoic went from 230 million to 70 million years ago. The Cenozoic started 70 million years ago and goes to the present.

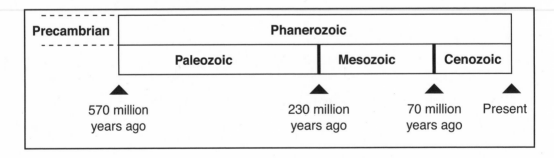

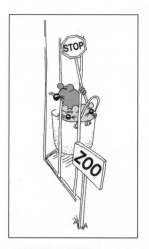

To remember the three eras of the Phanerozoic eon, go back to the substitute image for this eon, a fan on top of a zoo. Now, visualize a pail inside the zoo (*pail + zoo =* Paleozoic). Inside the pail are mice that are also in the zoo (*mice + zoo =* Mesozoic). The mice are holding signs in the zoo (*signs + zoo =* Cenozoic).

Most beginning students of earth history stop here. If you want to go further, here's information that puts more detail into the Earth chapters.

Memorizing Periods and Epochs

The Paleozoic, Mesozoic, and Cenozoic eras are divided once more into sub-subchapters. These sub-subchapters are called periods or epochs. When teaching these sub-subchapters, point out where periods and epochs have similar endings like -ian, -assic, and -ocene.

Most of the substitutions are heavily schmurgled.

Eras	Periods and epochs	Substitutions
Paleozoic	Cambrian period	Camera
	Ordovician period	Hard doves
	Silurian period	Sill (on a window)
	Devonian period	Devil
	Carboniferous period	Carbon
	Permian period	Perm (at a hair salon)

Mesozoic	Triassic period	Tree-asses (donkey)
	Jurassic period	Jury-asses (donkey)
	Cretaceous period	Crutches
Cenozoic	Paleocene epoch	Palace
	Eocene epoch	E (large letter E)
	Oligocene epoch	A leg
	Miocene epoch	Magazine
	Pliocene epoch	Policing
	Pleistocene epoch	Plastic
	Holocene epoch	Halloween

Here's a chaining technique for remembering the order of the six periods in the Paleozoic. You have a *camera* (Cambrian) taking a picture of frozen *hard doves* (Ordovician) on a window *sill* (Silurian). The *devil* (Devonian) pops up and fries the doves into *carbon* (Carboniferous), with little *perms* (Permian).

The Mesozoic's three periods story starts with a *tree* filled with *asses* (Triassic) which is judged by a *jury* of *asses* (Jurassic) who are all on *crutches* (Cretaceous).

The seven epochs of the Cenozoic are chained into a story that starts with a *palace scene* (Paleocene) with a huge *E in the scene* (Eocene). It grows *a leg* (Oligocene) that jumps on a *magazine* (Miocene), police start *policing the scene* (Pliocene), and they string *plastic* around a *scene* (Pleistocene), of *Halloween* (Holocene) characters.

Rock Bingo: Geology

In this chapter:

- Remember the names of eighteen rocks.
- Classify rocks according to the three ways in which they form—igneous, metamorphic, and sedimentary.
- Give three examples of each type of rock.

Most geology texts start by explaining the rock classification system. Then they go on to introduce specific rocks. In this chapter, we learn specific rock names first. The reasoning for this progression is that it's more concrete to hold a rock in your hand and learn its name than it is to learn an abstract classification system.

Meet the Rocks

 To start becoming rock literate, you're going to learn the names of eighteen rocks and how to help your students do the same. This means you'll have to get the rocks (see the list of recommended rocks later in this chapter). When purchasing rocks, avoid kits with tiny samples glued to a card or encased in plastic. Instead, visit a rock or lapidary store and buy specimens the size of a matchbook. Handling larger rocks without packaging gives the rocks greater kinesthetic and visual input. If possible, take your students with you to a rock store and make it a scavenger hunt for the listed rocks.

Now let's start the memory process. You can memorize the names of rocks in much the same way you memorize people's names. You will use the three S's mnemonic technique—Say, See, Stick.

SAY	Say the rock's name out loud while looking at the rock.
SEE	Turn the rock's name into a sound-alike substitute picture.
STICK	Stick the image you've created onto a unique characteristic of the rock.

Here's how you would memorize the name of a rock like granite using the Say, See, Stick technique. Hold a chunk of granite in your hand. **Say** the name out loud while looking at the granite. Next, come up with a sound-alike substitute for the name *granite* which might be *grains* of *night*. This becomes the substitute image, something you can **see**. Now we need to stick this image to a distinctive characteristic of the rock. In the case of granite this works out beautifully. Notice that granite has freckles of black mineral against a white background. Those black speckles are like *grains* of *night*. **Stick** the grains of night image to the freckles of black. The next time you pick up a piece of granite, look at the distinctive freckles and ask, "What was that feature related to? Oh, now I remember. It looks like *grains of night* which is the sound-alike for *granite*."

In the list on the following page, notice that an interesting fact is given for each rock—to increase concentration, which in turn improves memory. The fact that the Empire State Building, a structure many children have heard about, is built of granite turns granite into something more than a mere rock. Even better would be to point out a building constructed of granite in your own town.

The eighteen rocks in this list represent a cross section of the three main types of rocks.

For a smaller set of nine rocks, choose the rocks in italics.

Say Rock Name	See (substitute)	Stick	Fact
Basalt (Igneous)	Sounds like *bath salts*	A dark gray rock. Imagine the opposite, white *bath salts* sprinkled on a dark rock.	When a volcano cools, basalt forms the plug. Crushed rock under road beds is often made of basalt.
Chalk (Sedimentary)	Same as *chalk*	Chalk is white. It used to be made into blackboard chalk.	Formed from the calcareous remains of tiny sea creatures.
Coal (Sedimentary)	Sounds like *cold*	Coal is a black rock. Imagine a *cold* black night.	Comes from plant material that died thousands to millions of years ago. Burned to heat homes and to make electricity.
Flint (Sedimentary)	Sounds like *flute*	Looks like solid mud. Imagine a solid mud *flute*.	The prehistoric poor person's source for arrowheads. Not as sharp or as tough as obsidian.
Granite (Igneous)	Sounds like *grains* of *night*	A white rock with specks of black. The black speckles against the white in granite look like *grains* of *night*.	One of the rocks used in building the Empire State Building.

Say Rock Name	See (substitute)	Stick	Fact
Limestone (Sedimentary)	Sounds like *limes*	Some limestone is pure white and appears to be made of big crystals. Imagine *limes* reflected in the crystal facets of white limestone.	Made from the bodies of prehistoric creatures that lived in oceans and lakes, pulling calcium carbonate from the water to use in their bones and shells. The stalactites and stalagmites of caves are made of limestone.
Marble (Metamorphic)	Sounds like *marbles*	Marble looks like compacted sugar. Imagine *marbles* made of sugar.	The Taj Mahal is made of marble.
Obsidian (Igneous)	Sounds like *oboe,* a musical instrument	Obsidian is a black glassy rock. Oboes are black instruments. Imagine an *oboe* made of obsidian.	Primitive man chipped obsidian into arrowheads. Modern surgeons use obsidian for heart surgery. It cuts cleaner than steel scalpels.
Pumice (Igneous)	Sounds like *puma*	Pumice is a light porous rock. Imagine a *puma* with pumice in place of its fur coat.	Pumice is so light it floats on water. It can be used as a fishing bobber.

Say Rock Name	See (substitute)	Stick	Fact
Quartzite (Metamorphic)	Sounds like *quarts*	Often white to greyish in color, with a reflective surface. Imagine *quarts* of quartzite.	Comes from sandstone that has been heated and squashed tighter together.
Sandstone (Sedimentary)	Sounds like *sand*	Looks like sand that has been cemented together. Imagine a stone made of *sand*.	Egyptian pyramids are made of sandstone. Thick beds of sandstone form from desert sand, ripple marks suggest formation in moving water, horizontal lines suggest sandstone formed in calm water.
Schist (Metamorphic)	Sounds like *sheet*	A flaky rock. Splits easily into *sheets*.	Gemstones are often found in schist.
Scoria (Igneous)	Sounds like *score*	Imagine this porous red rock shaped into a *score*board.	A light rock used in ground cover around homes. The reddish color is due to traces of oxidized iron, rust.
Serpentine (Metamorphic)	Sounds like *serpent*	Fracture this greenish rock and it has a scale-like surface like that of a green *serpent*.	Occasionally used in jewelry.

Say Rock Name	See (substitute)	Stick	Fact
Shale (Sedimentary)	Sounds like a quiet (*shhh*) kind of *hail*	Can be grayish. Imagine a gray day with shale *hailing* down and landing quietly, going *"shhhh."*	Compacted mud with the water squeezed out. With more heating and compaction, shale becomes slate.
Slate (Metamorphic)	Sounds like *slate* used to make blackboards	Imagine a *slate* blackboard.	Slate cleaves into flat planes that were once used in blackboards.
Soapstone (Metamorphic)	Sounds like *soap*	Soapstone feels like *soap*.	The softest rock. It can be ground into talcum powder.
Tuff (Igneous)	Sounds like *tough*	Tuff is a soft rock—not very *tough*.	The solidified ash of a volcano, blown into the air and usually deposited a distance from the volcano.

Classifying Rocks: Igneous, Metamorphic, Sedimentary

After students have learned all eighteen rock names, they are ready to fit them into the classification system.

Geologists classify rocks into three main boxes:

- Igneous
- Sedimentary
- Metamorphic

How a rock is formed determines which category it belongs to.

1. **Igneous** rocks come directly from molten rock (magma). Igneous rock can solidify quickly as it oozes or is blown out of a volcano, or more slowly as magma cools deep under the Earth's crust.
2. **Sedimentary** rocks start with eroded rocks, which deposit in layers. When the layers are subjected to great heat and pressure, they form a new type of rock.
3. **Metamorphic** rock can start with igneous, sedimentary, or another metamorphic rock. When it's subjected to heat and pressure, it becomes a new rock.

Rocks are in a constant state of living, dying, and rebirth. Rebirth often results in a new type of rock. The following diagram shows the rock cycle:

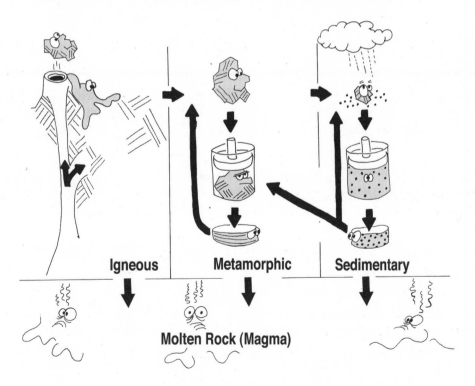

Interacting with the Rock Cycle

MISs Rock

 Don't sit there like a rock. Interact with the rock cycle. Use colored pencils and brighten up the rock cycle diagram on the previous page. Now make a copy of MISs Rock (you'll find her to the right on this page). Then cut out your copy. Using MISs Rock as a marker, have students slide her through the rock cycle as you describe the trip. Ask students the questions below to have them determine which classification system MISs Rock falls into as she makes her journey.

1. Where is she igneous?
2. How does she become metamorphic or sedimentary?
3. Could a metamorphic or sedimentary rock become an igneous rock again?

I. You'll never miss the three major groups of rock if you remember MISs Rock. The MIS stands for metamorphic, igneous, and sedimentary.

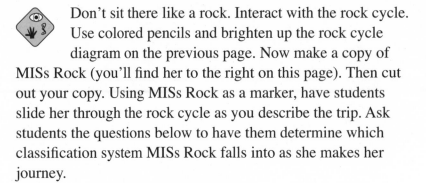

Examples of Igneous, Metamorphic, and Sedimentary Rock

   Our next memory goal is to be able to give three examples of rock found in each classification system and to explain how the rock was formed. By now, students should have memorized the nine representative rocks presented at the beginning of the chapter.

Igneous rocks are represented by obsidian, scoria, and granite. They solidify from a molten or a partially molten state.

Here's the igneous memory device. Igneous sounds like *egg* and *knee*. Imagine a man balancing an egg on his knee. This will be our igneous man. Now add three items to this picture to represent three igneous rocks: obsidian, scoria, and granite. The image for obsidian is a sound-alike substitution, an *oboe*. Igneous man is playing the oboe. An erupting volcano next to him has a scoreboard mounted on its side. The *scoreboard* is a sound-alike substitution for *scoria*. Next to the volcano is a piece of night that is disintegrating into *grains* of *night,* the sound-alike substitution for granite.

The volcano in this image is the clue as to how igneous rock forms. Igneous rocks either cool from molten magma by bubbling out of a volcano or solidify deep under the crust from magma.

Igneous man

Sedimentary rocks include sandstone, limestone, and chalk. These rocks are formed from sediment, or fragments of rocks, or living organisms and are often eroded or transported by water.

The substitution for sedimentary is *sad men in tar*. So imagine two frowning men standing up to their ankles in tar. If you were standing in tar you would probably be sad. Now add three representative sedimentary rocks: sandstone, limestone, and chalk. These two sad men are juggling *sand* (sandstone), a piece of *chalk* (chalk), and a *lime* (limestone).

The sand is a clue as to how sedimentary rock is made from broken-down rock that is cemented back together.

Sedimentary men

Metamorphic rock occurs when heat and pressure modify igneous, sedimentary, or even other metamorphic rocks.

The substitute for metamorphic is *metal morphing*. Imagine a metal robot morphing (changing) into a man. Three representatives of metamorphic rock are quartzite, slate, and marble. Imagine the robot holding a quart pitcher (quartzite). As our robot transforms, he is holding a blackboard slate (slate). When he finally morphs into a man he is holding marbles (marble).

Finally, imagine a piston. This piston is pressuring the robot to change into a man. Pressure is the clue. It's a factor in the formation of metamorphic rock.

Metamorphic man

When students have memorized the igneous man, the sedimentary men, and the metamorphic man, they should be able to give three examples of rock in each geological category and a brief explanation of how they were created. The following game will help cement this knowledge.

Rock Bingo!

 Games are a great way to create more interest in a subject. Rock bingo is a geology game that will help students memorize rocks and their geological classification system.

Items needed:

1. One game board for each player (you will find a game board on the next page that can be reproduced).
2. A deck of cards with the rock names written on them. (Cut up one copy of a game board to get these cards.)
3. A set of rocks for each player.
4. One set of marked rocks (you could glue rocks to a permanent game board). This is used as a reference when students challenge — when one student tells another that the wrong rock has been put on the board. A knowledgeable rock referee could also fulfill this role.

Rock Bingo Game Board

Igneous	Metamorphic	Sedimentary
Obsidian	Serpentine	Chalk
Basalt	Schist	Coal
Scoria	Slate	Flint
Tuff	Soapstone	Limestone
Granite	Marble	Sandstone
Pumice	Quartzite	Shale

How to Play Rock Bingo (Level 1)

1. Three to four students can play. One player is the referee.
2. Set the rocks out on a table.
3. Shuffle the cards and then turn them face down in a pile.
4. Players take turns choosing cards. Say, for example, Player 1 picks up the card for obsidian—he then has five seconds to find the rock and place it on the game board in the appropriate space. Afterward, he puts the card into a used-card pile. The rock referee determines if it's the correct rock. If not, it's returned to the table. Then it's Player 2's turn.
5. If a player turns over a card and already has that rock, that's his turn and he doesn't get to take a rock.
6. The first person to get a complete column of igneous, sedimentary, or metamorphic rocks yells, "Igneous!" or "Sedimentary!" or "Metamorphic!" whichever category is filled.
7. If no one gets a complete row the first time through the deck, the cards are reshuffled and the game continues.

How to Play Rock Bingo (Level 2)

This level encourages students to learn characteristics of the rocks that go beyond just knowing the name. What you need to play:

1. All the items needed for the Level 1 version.
2. Fact cards. You can either cut out the fact cards from the book (refer to the charts in the section Meet the Rocks) or use index cards with one fact written on each card—for example, "What rock was used to build the Egyptian pyramids?" On the opposite side of the card, write the correct answer. In this case, the pyramids were built out of sandstone.

The rules:

1. Lay out the rocks and give players a rock bingo card like the one used in the Level 1 version.
2. Shuffle the fact cards and lay down the deck, fact side up.
3. Player 1 picks up the first card in the deck and reads the fact, then chooses a rock for his rock bingo card. If the other players think Player 1 has chosen an incorrect rock, they can challenge. If challenged, Player 1 turns over the card he has just picked up to check the answer. If he has made a mistake, he removes the rock from his rock bingo card. Then it's Player 2's turn.
4. If no one gets a bingo the first time through the deck, the cards are reshuffled and the game continues.

Stalagmites and Stalactites

Two geological structures found in caves are stalagmites and stalactites. They look like ice cream cones made out of limestone. One comes up from the floor. The other hangs from the ceiling. To remember the difference between a stalagmite and a stalactite, circle the *g* in stalagmite. The *g* stands for ground. Stalagmites come up from the ground. Now circle the *c* in stalactite. The *c* stands for ceiling. Stalactites come down from the ceiling.

The Yucatan Peninsula of Mexico has a giant underground river system that flows through caves. These caves are loaded with stalagmites and stalactites, yet these limestone formations can only form in dry caves. How did they get there? The answer is that 10,000 years ago, during the ice age, the seas were lower and the caves were air filled. A fact for rock bingo level 2.

Memorize Eight Elements
That Make up Most Rocks

Eight elements make up 99% of all rocks: oxygen, silicon, aluminum, iron, calcium, sodium, potassium, and magnesium. Using substitution, association, and chaining, you can remember these eight elements. The associations, or substitutions, are as follows:

- Oxygen: oxygen cylinder
- Silicon: sand
- Aluminum: soft drink can
- Iron: barbells (as in pumping iron)
- Calcium: bones in a skeleton
  (bones are made of calcium)
- Sodium: soda
- Potassium: pot
- Magnesium: magazine

Now chain the items together: A skeleton (calcium) has a pot (potassium) on her skull. She's wearing an oxygen cylinder (oxygen) on her back. In one hand she holds an aluminum can (aluminum) out of which soda (sodium) is pouring. The other hand holds a barbell (iron). A magazine (magnesium) covers her pelvis, and she's standing on sand (silicon).

17

Clouds and the Atmosphere

Weather memory includes being able to:

- Identify nine common clouds.
- Remember the order of the colors in a rainbow.
- List five layers of the atmosphere in proper order.

Three Cloud Shapes

To make it easier to identify clouds, we will start by learning a chunk of three clouds. First, clouds are classified by shape. The three main shapes are:

- Cumulus
- Stratus
- Cirrus

CUMULUS

Cumulus clouds are shaped like cotton balls or cauliflower. These are the puffy clouds children love to find images in. (In Latin, cumulus means heap.)

To remember the name for a cumulus cloud we are going to use the Say, See, Stick system which is a substitution method.

SAY	Have kids say the name of the cloud out loud. Let's use *cumulus* as an example. You could simply have them repeat the word over in their minds—but saying it out loud increases the stimulus, which helps the brain pay attention, which increases retention (refer to the sidebar at the end of this chapter).
SEE	Turn the cloud name into a sound-alike word you are familiar with. Cumulus sounds like cue-mule. Imagine a *cue* stick being held by a *mule* at a pool table.
STICK	Stick the image to the cloud being named. Imagine cumulus clouds on a billiard table. The *cue* stick is being used by a *mule* in an attempt to sink the clouds into the corner pocket:

Now see if your students understand how this memory technique works: Show a picture of a cumulus cloud and ask, "Where is this cloud in your substitution picture?" They should reply, "It's on a billiard table. A mule with a cue stick is trying to sink it into the corner pocket." They should understand that the *cue* and *mule* are substitutions that help them remember it's a cumulus cloud.

This Say, See, Stick method will be used for the rest of the clouds.

STRATUS

Stratus clouds are flat or layered clouds. (In Latin, stratus means layer.) They often cover large areas of the sky like a blanket.

SAY	Stratus
SEE	A sound-alike substitution for stratus that's easy to visualize is *straw*. Imagine a mat of straw.
STICK	Imagine the flat stratus cloud as being a flat layer or mat of *straw*.

CIRRUS

Cirrus are the highest clouds, from about three to eight miles high. They look like curled wispy mare's tails. (In Latin, *cirrus* means curl of hair.)

SAY	Cirrus
SEE	Cirrus sounds like *sea rush*.
STICK	Imagine cirrus clouds, which look like curling waves, as a *sea rush*ing to shore.

A QUICK CLOUD TEST

Draw a:

1. Cumulus cloud
2. Stratus cloud
3. Cirrus cloud

More Cloud Names

Once children know names for the three main cloud types, they're ready for more. Cloudologists, more commonly called meteorologists or weather people, add prefixes to the main cloud types to create labels for different clouds.

Three prefixes are used in cloud identification: nimbo-, cirro-, and alto-. Nimbo refers to a rain cloud. Alto and cirro both have to do with the height of clouds. Alto clouds are mid level in the atmosphere, roughly one to four miles up. Cirro clouds are high-level clouds found from about three to eight miles high.

When one of these three prefixes is attached to one of the three main cloud types, it defines another type of cloud. For example, altostratus are medium-high clouds about one to four miles high in the atmosphere, with the flattened or layered appearance you'd expect of a stratus cloud. Cirrostratus are also flattened clouds, but they're found at a higher elevation—around four to eight miles high.

To remember what the three prefixes mean, use Say, See, Stick:

NIMBO

SAY	Nimbo
SEE	Nimbo sounds like *hymn* and *bow*.
STICK	Imagine a preacher singing a *hymn* while holding a *bow* in the rain. The rain represents the characteristic of this prefix.

ALTO

SAY	Alto
SEE	Alto sounds like *altar*.
STICK	Alto clouds are midrange clouds. Imagine an Aztec pyramid rising into the sky topped by an *altar*. The altar is midway up in the atmosphere.

CIRRO

SAY	Cirro
SEE	Cirro sounds like *zero*.
STICK	Since cirro refers to the highest clouds, visualize lots of *zeros* at the outer edge of the atmosphere.

Attaching prefixes to basic cloud types gives you the following combinations:

- Nimbocumulus
- Nimbostratus
- Altocumulus
- Altostratus
- Cirrostratus
- Cirrocumulus

If you add the three clouds we learned at the beginning of the chapter—cumulus, stratus, cirrus—you now have nine clouds you can recognize by name.

Notice that there are two combinations of clouds and prefixes that aren't included in this list, nimbocirrus and altocirrus. There's no nimbocirrus because the conditions under which cirrus clouds form, high in the atmosphere, means they lack sufficient moisture to produce rain that will reach the ground. There's no altocirrus because cirrus clouds form at altitudes outside the alto range.

Cloud Quiz

After teaching children the Say, See, Stick technique for remembering cloud names, go over the pictures that each cloud name brings to mind. Follow this up with the cloud quiz. Fill in the names of nine common clouds on the following cloud chart:

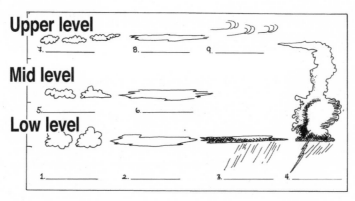

The answers to the cloud quiz are:

1. Cumulus
2. Stratus
3. Nimbostratus
4. Nimbocumulus
5. Altocumulus
6. Altostratus
7. Cirrocumulus
8. Cirrostratus
9. Cirrus

ASK QUESTIONS ABOUT THE CLOUDS

Now is the time to ask questions about the clouds. If a student has trouble, stop and ask, "What substitute picture comes to mind when you hear the cloud name?"

1. Which is higher, a cirrus or altostratus cloud?
2. If you were playing baseball, which cloud would you rather have over you, a nimbocumulus or a cirrocumulus?
3. If you were flying in a jet at high altitude, would you be more likely to be flying through stratus or cirrus clouds?
4. If you were a farmer with parched crops, which would you rather see: stratus, nimbocumulus, or altocumulus?

Remembering the Colors in a Rainbow

 To remember the order of colors in a rainbow, use the initial memory technique that's also known as an acronym. Say the following name out loud:

ROY G. BIV

Each letter in ROY G. BIV indicates the first letter of a color:

Red, Orange, Yellow, Green, Blue, Indigo, Violet

Next time you look at a rainbow, see if you can distinguish the seven colors in order.

Remembering the Layers of the Atmosphere

Scientists love to divide things up and then give names to the pieces. The atmosphere is divided into the following layers:

Layer	Description
Exosphere	The layer farthest from the Earth. It contains a few rarefied gases and continues on into outer space.
Thermosphere	Here's where meteors start to burn up and the aurora borealis forms.
Mesosphere	This layer is marked by a maximum temperature of 50 degrees F, dropping to -130 degrees F near the outer edges.
Stratosphere	This area contains the ozone layer.
Troposphere	The lowest layer—Here is where clouds and weather occur. It also contains about 75% of the gases in the atmosphere.

  To remember the order of these layers, use substitution and chaining. Start with substitution. Since the word for each layer ends in *sphere*, let's find a substitute word for just the beginning part of the word. Refer to the chart on the next page.

Layer	Description
Exosphere	Xs and Os (like the ones you would find in a tick tack toe game)
Thermosphere	Thermos
Mesosphere	Mice
Stratosphere	Straight (like a straight line)
Troposphere	Tropical

Now chain the substitution words into a short story:

In the *tropics* (troposphere) a *straight* (stratosphere) line of *mice* (mesosphere) stand in front of a giant *thermos* (thermosphere) covered with *X*s and *O*s (exosphere).

Vocalization Increases Concentration

Novice tennis players practicing backhand shots showed little improvement when told to simply concentrate. But they showed rapid improvement when told to say the word *ready* out loud when the ball machine was about to fire the next ball, the word *ball* when they saw the ball launched from the machine, the word *bounce* when they saw the ball hit the court, and the word *hit* when they saw the ball smack their racquet during a backhand swing. Saying key words out loud helped the tennis players concentrate.

It's Alive! Six Functions That Determine Life

In biology how do you determine if something is living?

- Memorize the six functions that determine life

Six functions are necessary for something to be considered living. Here's the checklist used to determine if something is living:

√	1.	Takes in nutrients
√	2.	Uses energy to do work
√	3.	Reproduces
√	4.	Gets rid of wastes
√	5.	Grows
√	6.	Reacts to outside changes

The Living Checklist

1. Taking in nutrients includes a child eating a peanut butter and jelly sandwich, a whale filtering plankton from the sea, and a fungus consuming a dead tree.

2. Using energy occurs when a child plays on a swing, a cheetah dashes after an impala, and an amoeba slides through slime.
3. Reproducing occurs when your pooch produces a litter of puppies, when a termite queen pumps out a thousand pupae, and when a pea plant produces peas.
4. Growing is shown in the lawn grass you mow weekly, the giant clam that began as a pinhead-sized clam, and the boa constrictor that started out the size of a worm.
5. Getting rid of waste is evident in all the poop that a barnyard of animals makes, in the carbon dioxide you breathe out, and in the oxygen a plant gives off.
6. A reaction to outside change is flexing your knee when the doctor hits it with a little rubber mallet, a pollywog diving to the bottom of a pond in response to a shadow, and a dandelion bending toward the light.

Memorizing the Six Functions of Life

  To remember the six functions that define life, memorize the following story. This story uses the mnemonic techniques of association and chaining:

A boy eats (takes in nutrients), does push-ups (uses energy to do work), and then splits into two little men (reproduces). These two men grow (grow) until they're big enough to pick up a garbage can and take it outside (get rid of waste). Outside, it starts to rain, so they put up umbrellas (react to change).

Now repeat the story from memory, and explain how each image represents a function of life. Remember, if you simply read this story, it will stay on the porch of temporary memory. It won't make it across the threshold into long-term memory unless you work with it.

WORKING WITH YOUR DEFINITION OF LIFE

Look at the following questions. Use your mental checklist for the six functions of life to answer each question.

1. Is your brother or sister living?
2. Is a redwood tree alive?
3. Is a rock alive?
4. Is a virus alive? (This is a tough one even for biologists to answer.)
5. Is a city alive?
6. Can you design an alien that's missing one of the functions we use to determine life?

19 Biological Classification System Made Easy

In this chapter:

- Memorize the five kingdoms of biology.
- Memorize the classification system used in biology.

Biologists are fond of lumping and splitting.

Here's lumping in action: "Hmmm, let's put garden snails, crocodiles, blue belly lizards, giant clams, blue-ringed octopuses, rhinos, and humans in the animal box." Then, "In the plant box put the dandelions, redwood trees, orchids, and cactus." Lumping takes a bunch of life forms with similar characteristics and puts them in the same group.

And here's splitting: "Let's put some dividers in these big boxes. How about giant clams, garden snails, and octopuses in the mollusk section? Crocodiles, rhinos, humans, and blue belly lizards in the chordate cubby. Wait! Put another divider in that chordate cubby. Now, put rhinos and humans in the mammal niche and that crocodile can go with the blue belly lizard in the reptile file."

At an early stage children learn to classify life. They look for similar outward characteristics: "Furry, four legs, pointy teeth, tail, retractable claws. Got it! It's a kitty." Even if it is a classic Siamese, a calico, or Alice's grinning Cheshire cat, they get lumped under the classification of cats. Like children, early biologists looked for obvious similarities and differences when lumping and splitting. But with time, classification systems were based on more subtle relationships—evolutionary relationships. Children are also familiar with this type of classification system. "Let's see, grandpa is Mom's dad. Then there's uncle

Ralph, Mom's brother. That makes Ralph's kids my cousins." A family tree is a detailed splitting of evolutionary relationships.

Five Kingdoms of Biology

In biological classification, the biggest category, where everything is lumped together is called *life*. But then the splitters go to work. Life is split into groups called kingdoms. Biologists recognize five kingdoms:

- Plantae (plants)
- Animalia (animals)
- Protista (e.g., single-cell algae, like plankton)
- Fungi (e.g., mushrooms)
- Monera (e.g., bacteria)

To remember these kingdoms, use mapping and substitution mnemonics, starting with a mapping technique.

Remember how the Greek poet Simonides remembered speeches, as was explained in Chapter 2? He imagined himself strolling down a familiar street. At distinct locations along this street, he put images that would jog his memory for the next point in his speech. This was an example of a mapping system.

Instead of a street, let's use a castle. A castle seems appropriate because kingdoms are often associated with them. Imagine a castle and five distinct locations:

1. Moat
2. Drawbridge
3. Castle wall
4. Tower on the castle wall
5. Central palace

These five locations give us places on which to put images that represent each kingdom.

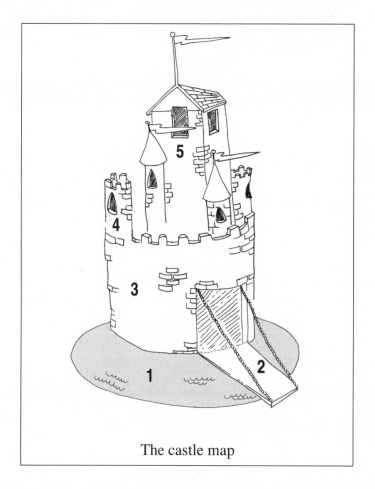

The castle map

Next, use a substitution technique. Make a sound-alike substitution for each kingdom. Plantae is easy. Plantae sounds like *plant,* which is exactly what it represents, plants. In position four, the wall tower, imagine a profusion of plants growing out of the tower. These plants represent Plantae.

Some of the substitutions are not so easy. Monera needs to be schmurgled to create a sound-alike, which might be *money ran.* Imagine a dollar bill running around position one, the moat.

The following chart lists substitution images for the five kingdoms and the location of each image on the castle.

Location	Kingdom	Kingdom Images
Moat	Monera	Monera sounds like *money ran*. Imagine money, a dollar bill with legs, running around the moat.
Drawbridge	Protista	Protista sounds like *protest*. Imagine a bunch of protesters standing on the drawbridge, waving signs in protest.
Wall	Fungi	Fungi sounds like *phone tree*. Imagine a tree with a huge phone in place of the leaves. This tree is growing out of the side of the castle wall.
Tower	Plantae	Plantae sounds like plant. Imagine ivy, cattails, and lilies growing all over the tower on the castle wall.
Central palace	Animalia	Animalia sounds like *animals*. Imagine giraffes, elephants, and crocodiles as the animal representatives. They are hanging all over the central palace.

Kingdoms in biology

KINGDOMS IN BIOLOGY EXERCISES

After looking at the kingdoms in biology illustration, use these exercises to test and improve memory for the five kingdoms:

1.   Explain how each image depicts one of the five kingdoms.
2.   Use colored pencils to brighten up the castle and the images associated with it.
3.   Draw a castle and sketch the image associated with each kingdom at the appropriate location on the castle.

Splitting up Things Even More: Kingdom, Phylum, Class, Order, Family, Genus, Specie

Biologists don't stop with kingdoms. Each kingdom is split into six smaller categories. The labels for these categories, in order of larger to smaller, are: phylum, class, order, family, genus, and specie. The smaller the categories get, the more similarities you find in a group. Here's how human beings shake out in a biologist's version of a family tree:

Kingdom: Animalia (includes humans, chimpanzees, gorillas, lemurs, elephants, possums, kangaroos, rats, pigs, shrews, flamingos, gooney birds, finches, tortoises, sharks, rattlesnakes, crocodiles, spiders, jellyfish, sponges, tapeworms, clams, and lice)

Phylum: Chordata (animals with backbones—includes humans, chimpanzees, gorillas, lemurs, elephants, possums, kangaroos, rats, pigs, shrews, flamingos, gooney birds, finches, tortoises, sharks, rattlesnakes, and crocodiles)

Class: Mammalia (animals that suckle their young—includes humans, chimpanzees, gorillas, lemurs, elephants, possums, kangaroos, rats, pigs, and shrews)

Order: Primates (supposedly, critters with more developed brains—includes humans, chimpanzees, gorillas, and lemurs)

Family: Hominidae (includes humans, chimpanzees, and gorillas)

Genus: Homo (humans are the only ones left; the rest are bones from the past)

Species: sapiens (that's us)

To remember the categories in a biological classification system, use the initial memory technique known as an acrostic, an initial mnemonic technique:

King Philip's Class Ordered Family Genius Specials

The first letter of each word in the above sentence stands for the first letter of the corresponding word in the classification system:

King (Kingdom) *Philip's* (Phylum) *Class* (Class) *Ordered* (Order) *Family* (Family) *Genius* (Genus) *Specials* (Species)

Notice that the words in this acrostic are identical or at least close in sound to the words you're trying to memorize. This gives you two ways to remember the material. You can use the first letter of each word to jog your memory, or you also have a sound-alike word to help your recall. *King* makes it easy to remember kingdom. *Genius* reminds you of genus.

When you can make an acrostic that is close or exact in sound to the target words you want to remember, it makes interpretation of the acrostic easier.

Cell City: Names and Functions of Cellular Organelles

At around the fifth grade, young biologists are introduced to cell structure. In this chapter we're going to:

- Learn the names for nine cellular components.
- Be able to list nine major cellular components from memory.
- Label a diagram of a cell with the correct names from memory.
- Explain the function of each cellular component.

A cell is like a minicity. It has city limits, factories, transport routes, warehousing areas, power plants, waste-disposal systems, and a blueprint department. Some cells also have solar energy panels and encircling walls. In the following descriptions of function, we're going to use the analogy of a city to explain what different cell parts do.

Knowing the names for nine parts of a cell and their functions provides students with a road map through Cell City.

First, familiarize your students with the general layout of an idealized cell.

Cutaway View of an Idealized Cell

As you look at the cutaway view of an idealized cell on the next page, say the name of each cell component out loud. Then have students say the name out loud.

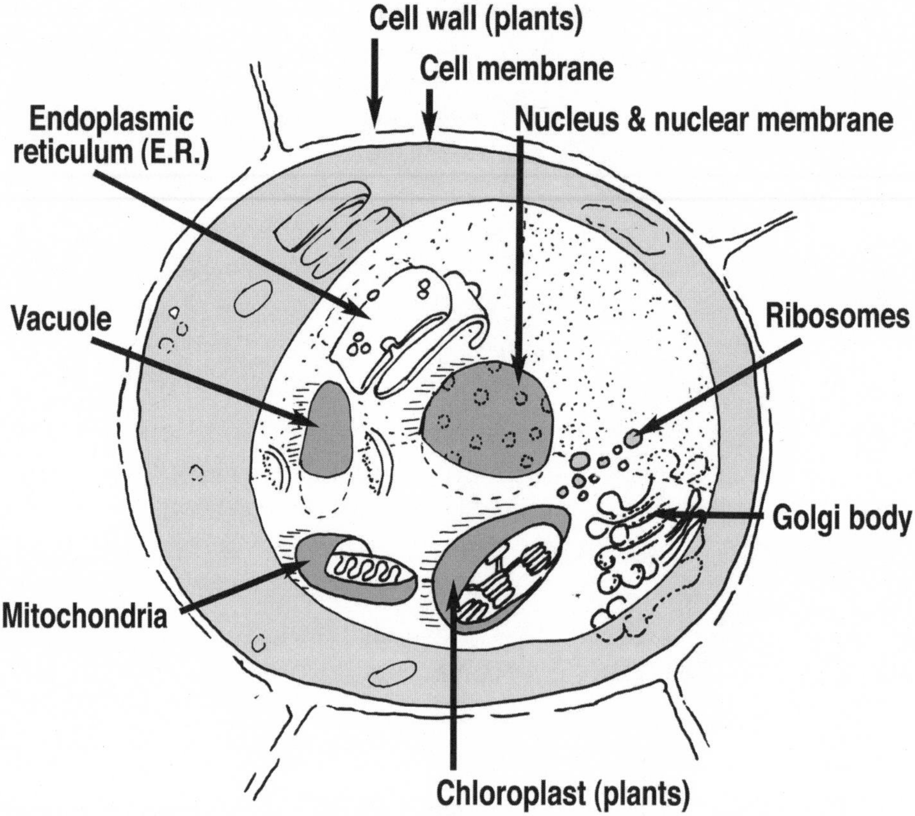

Cell wall (plants)
Cell membrane
Nucleus & nuclear membrane
Endoplasmic reticulum (E.R.)
Ribosomes
Vacuole
Golgi body
Mitochondria
Chloroplast (plants)

The Cell Cards

Now we are going to look at each cellular component individually. Cards are presented for the cell parts. Again we will use a version of the Say, See, Stick technique. The mnemonic method being used here makes two substitutions for each cell part. One substitution is for the cell name, another for the function. Then both substitutions are stuck together. Refer to the explanatory card on the next page to understand how this works.

SAY	The name of the cell part. Pronunciation in parentheses if it is necessary.
SEE	Turn the cell name into a sound-alike word you are familiar with and can visualize.
STICK	This stick section is a little different from previous chapters. It starts with a short description of the cellular part and may also include a simple diagram. But then comes the most important part, what the cellular component is or does. Our goal is to remember the function of cellular parts. At this point an analogy is made for the cellular function, comparing it to a city's infrastructure (e.g., the nucleus is like the blueprint department in a city). Finally there is a mnemonic illustration that sticks the name of the cellular part to its function in the cell.

As you work through the upcoming cards, close your eyes after each card and visualize the mnemonic image. Have students explain what that image represents.

SAY	Cell membrane
SEE	Sounds like *cell mom brain*. Imagine a jail *cell* (cell). Inside is a mom holding an apple pie, with the top of her head opened like the hood of a car, exposing her brain, *mom brain* (membrane).
STICK	A cell membrane is like the surface of a very thin water balloon. It holds in liquids and tiny cell organelles. It is the boundary or city limit of Cell City. Imagine the jailed *cell mom brain* holding a sign that reads Cell City Limits. The jail bars represent the function of the membrane—to hold everything inside.

SAY	Nucleus (NU-klee-us)
SEE	Sounds like *new claws* (nucleus). Imagine a cat with new claws—so new the price tags are still in place.
STICK	The nucleus is like another water balloon inside the bigger cellular water balloon. It has its own membrane. The nucleus is where blueprints for the cell are stored. It is also Cell City's copy center, the location where cellular reproduction starts. Imagine a cat with *new claws* holding a blueprint, which represents a function of the nucleus, which is the storage area of the cell's blueprints.

SAY	Mitochondria (mi-to-KON-dree-a)
SEE	Sounds like *mitt on a con tree*. Imagine a catcher's mitt on a convict who's sitting in a tree.
STICK	Like other cell organelles, this mitochondria has its own membrane, again a balloon within a balloon. Slice off the top of a mitochondria and you will see a membrane folded back and forth like a ribbon inside. Mitochondria are Cell City's power plants. They produce chemicals that power the cell. Cells with a high-energy requirement, like muscle, contain many large mitochondria. Imagine a baseball *mitt on a con* who's sitting in a *tree*. This tree thrusts through the roof of a factory with big smokestacks. The smokestacks represent the power-plant function of this organelle.

SAY	Golgi apparatus (GOL-gee a-pa-RA-tus)
SEE	Sounds like *goalie*. Imagine a hockey goalie.
STICK	This golgi apparatus is composed of membrane sheets stacked on top of each other. A cutaway view shows that these sheets are hollow. Cellular materials are collected in the folds of these sheets, which may then form tiny balloons. The golgi apparatus packages cellular substances and moves them to the surface of the cell, where they are expelled. One of its tasks is to package garbage and get rid of it, making it Cell City's garbage collector. Imagine a hockey *goalie* whacking a garbage can. The can represents one of the functions of this organelle—removing waste from the cell.

SAY	Ribosomes (RYE-bo-soms)
SEE	Sounds like *rib* if you skip the later syllables. Imagine ribs on a skeleton.
STICK	When viewed under a powerful microscope, ribosomes show up as distinct dots or clumps in the intercellular liquid or on the surface of the endoplasmic reticulum. Cell City's mini cellular factories, ribosomes, convert substances into proteins, one of the building blocks of the cell. Imagine a skeleton with distinctive *ribs*, coming out of a factory that produces milk. He's even carrying a carton of milk. Milk contains protein, which is one of the items that ribosomes make.

SAY	Endoplasmic reticulum (en-do-PLAS-mik re-TI-cue-lum)
SEE	Endoplasmic reticulum is usually shortened to E.R., which sounds like the *ER*, or emergency room, in a hospital.
STICK	Endoplasmic reticulum, E.R., is composed of membrane folded back and forth upon itself like a stack of sheets. E.R. is Cell City's road system for transporting materials between cellular sites. Some E.R. is studded with ribosomes, as shown in this illustration. Imagine emergency room (*ER*) personnel rolling a patient on a gurney. The gurney is being pushed down a road. The road represents the transport nature of E.R.

SAY	Vacuoles (VA-cue-ols)
SEE	Sounds like *vacuum oil*. Imagine a vacuum cleaner sucking oil from a gushing oil derrick.
STICK	Vacuoles look like balloons inside the cell. Sometimes they are tiny. Sometimes they take up most of the cell. The function of a vacuole is to contain materials. Imagine a *vacuum* cleaner sucking up *oil* from a gushing oil derrick. Storage containers behind the vacuum cleaner represent the function of vacuoles in Cell City: to act as containers for cellular materials.

SAY	Chloroplast (KLO-ro-plast)
SEE	Sounds like *color blast*. Imagine a rainbow, crayons, and a painter's palette with a bomb underneath ready to explode.
STICK	Chloroplasts look like balloons containing flattened pancakes stacked on top of each other. Chloroplasts are found in plant cells where they convert sunlight into stored energy, something like a solar panel. Imagine a *color blast* going off next to a solar panel. The solar panel represents Cell City's alternative form of producing energy from the sun.

SAY	Cell wall
SEE	Sounds like what it is. Imagine a jail *cell wall*.
STICK	Cell walls surround the exterior membrane in plant cells like a shoe box containing a water balloon. These walls can be boxy, oval, circular—many different shapes. They add support and protection. A tree's structure is made up of lots of cell wall material. This wall surrounds a Plant Cell City. Imagine a jail cell wall surrounding Cell City to protect it.

List Nine Cellular Components from Memory

 To list the cellular components and their functions from memory, learn the following story:

1. You visit a mom in jail. She has her hair pulled back to reveal her brain (*cell mom brain* = cell membrane). She's holding a sign through the bars that reads Cell City Limit (the cell membrane's function is to contain materials). She drops the sign …

2. … on a cat with shiny new claws (*new claws* = nucleus). The cat is holding a blueprint (the function of the nucleus is to contain replication materials for the cell). The cat rolls the blueprint into a ball and throws it …

3. … into a mitt on a convict sitting in a tree (*mitt on con in tree* = mitochondria). The tree pierces the roof of a power plant (the function of mitochondria is to provide energy to the cell). In front of the power plant …

4. … is a goalie (*goalie* = golgi apparatus). The goalie slap shots a garbage can away from the goal (the function of the golgi apparatus is to remove waste products from the cell). The garbage can …

5. … hits a skeleton in the ribs (*ribs* = ribosomes). The ribbed skeleton is holding protein, milk, as he comes out of a factory that processes milk (the function of ribosomes is to make proteins). The skeleton …

6. … falls onto a gurney and is wheeled by ER doctors and nurses (*ER* = endoplasmic reticulum). The gurney goes along a road (the function of the E.R. is to provide transport between cell parts and provide a surface for things like ribosomes to attach to). The road …

7. … is blocked by a vacuum cleaner that is sucking up the oil from a gushing derrick (*vacuum oil* = vacuoles). Behind the

derrick are storage containers (the function of vacuoles is to store cellular products). A storage container …

8. … falls over on a jail cell wall (*cell wall* = cell wall). The walls quiver under the impact but hold up (the function of the cell wall is to protect). Then out of the cell come …

9. … a rainbow, crayons, and paint palette. All these colors are blasted out of the cell (*color blast* = chloroplast). The colors land on a solar panel (the function of chloroplasts is to convert sunlight into energy that can be used by the cell).

Now repeat the story and explain how each image relates to the name of a cellular component and its function.

Additional Exercises

 All of the following exercises rely on sense mnemonics. The more senses employed, the more students will remember the cellular terms and their meanings.

- Color the cell diagram in the beginning of the chapter with colored pencils.
- Take a sheet of paper and cut a hole in it just big enough to expose the cell diagram at the beginning of the chapter, but small enough to hide the words. Point at a cell organelle, and ask for its name and function.
- Have students look at the idealized cell drawing at the beginning of this chapter. Then have them attempt to draw a cell from memory.
- Copy the list on the following page. Have students draw an arrow from the cellular component to the role it plays in Cell City:

Cell City	**Cell Component**
Boundary or city limits	Chloroplast
Rigid walls	Nucleus
Road or transport system	Golgi apparatus
Factories	Cell membrane
Blueprint storage	Cell wall
Warehouses	Ribosomes
Garbage company	Mitochondria
Power plant	E.R. (endoplasmic reticulum)
Solar energy plant	Vacuoles

Answers: Boundary or city limits (cell membrane), Rigid walls (cell wall), Road system (E.R.), Factories (ribosomes), Blueprints (nucleus), Warehouses (vacuoles), Garbage company (golgi apparatus), Power plant (mitochondria), Solar energy plant (chloroplast).

21

On a First-Name Basis with Dinosaurs

In this chapter:

- Learn to recognize ten dinosaurs by name.
- Memorize key facts for each dinosaur.
- Play two dinosaur games.

A Young Dinosaur Expert

At 4½-years old, a young test subject could name twenty-one dinosaurs, including the diet, habitat, locomotion, appearance, defense mechanisms, and other information of each. His parents had read dinosaur books to him for three hours a week, one and a half years before he was tested. He also had dinosaur models and nine dinosaur books in his collection.

 Learn dinosaur names using the same method you'd use for learning people's names: Say, See, Stick:

SAY	Say the dinosaur's name five times to get the pronunciation.

SEE	Turn the name into something you can see. If necessary, smurgle the name or syllables until you get a word that's at least an approximation. The dinosaur name, ankylosaurus, for example, starts with ankyl- which sounds the same as *ankle*. It's easy to see an ankle. This may be all you need. You don't necessarily need a substitution for the dinosaur's entire name, just a place to start.
STICK	This section takes a look at our prehistoric friends as we narrow down to a distinctive feature. Stick the image you've made out of the dinosaur's name onto this outstanding feature. Next time you see the dinosaur, look at its outstanding feature, and recall what substitute image you attached. This helps you recall the name.

In developing mnemonic imagery for a dinosaur's name, notice that the last part of many dinosaur names end in the same letters. One of those endings is -*osaurus* (this ending is derived from the Greek word *sauros,* which means lizard). Since many of the endings are similar, imagery for the last part of the name has only been provided when the name doesn't have an -*osaurus* ending.

Meet the Dinosaurs

The cards found in this section use the Say, See, Stick technique for remembering the names of ten dinosaurs. Each card contains an illustration of what the dinosaur was thought to look like, as well as a mnemonic illustration that will make it easier to remember the dinosaur's name. These cards also contain facts about the dinosaurs.

SAY	**Ankylosaurus** (an-KIE-lo-SOR-us).
SEE	The first part of ankylosaurus sounds the same as *ankle*.
STICK	At almost 20 feet in length, the ankylosaurus looks scary, but he's a vegetarian, a plant eater. For protection he is built like an armadillo. Bony plates cover his body. He has bony plates for eyelids. Even the end of his tail contains heavy bones. To defend himself, he could swing his tail like a baseball bat to break a meat eater's shins. An outstanding feature are the bony plates at the end of his tail. Imagine him swinging his tail at your ankle. The *ankle* image gives you the sound for the first part of his name—*ANKYL-*osaurus.

SAY	**Brachiosaurus** (BRA-key-o-SOR-us)
SEE	The first two syllables of brachiosaurus sound like *bra* and *key*.
STICK	This is one of the heaviest dinosaurs. At 77 tons, she weighs more than ten elephants. Notice that the front legs are much longer than the rear legs. Longer front legs made it easy for this leaf eater to reach high into the trees with her even longer neck. An outstanding feature is the length of this dinosaur's neck. Imagine a bra covered with keys around this dinosaur's very long neck. The *bra* and *keys* jog your memory for BRA-CHI-osaurus.

SAY	**Parasaurolophus** (PAR-a-so-ROL-a-fus)
SEE	The first two syllables of this creature's name sound like the *para* in parachute and *Zorro*, the masked movie hero.
STICK	This dinosaur lived in herds. The crest on his head was hollow and could have been used to make different sounds, like those of a trumpet. An outstanding feature is the crest. Imagine a parachute wrapped around the crest. Zorro is tangled in the lines. The *para* and *Zorro* jog your memory for the first two syllables in PARA-SAURO-lophus. Note that this dinosaur's name ends differently from other dinosaurs we have seen.

	Pachycephalosaurus (PAK-ka-sef-fuh-lo-SOR-us)
SAY	
SEE	The first syllable in this dinosaur's name sounds like *pack*.
STICK	These dinosaurs had thick skulls. The tops of their heads were built like helmets with up to ten inches of bone. They are thought to have used their thick heads in butting contests with others of their kind, much like rams do today.
	The outstanding feature is the bony head. Imagine an ice pack on this animal's head, which he'd probably need after butting heads all day. *Pack* jogs your memory for the first syllable in PACH-ycephalosaurus.

SAY	**Corythosaurus** (ko-RITH-o-SOR-us)
SEE	The first syllable of corythosaurus sounds like *core*.
STICK	The front toes of this creature resemble fingers. But the crest, which may have been brightly colored to help this herd animal stay with its group, is the most prominent feature. The outstanding feature is the crest. Imagine this dinosaur grating an apple to the core with its crest. A ribbon of apple spirals off the core. *Core* prompts COR-ythosaurus.

	Plesiosaurus (PLEE-zee-o-SOR-us)
SAY	
SEE	The first syllable sounds like *police* or *please*.
STICK	This dinosaur is a fifty-foot swimming meat eater. When it was cruising the seas millions of years ago, its long neck probably looked like a periscope sticking above the waves. The outstanding feature is the head on a snakelike neck. Imagine a police officer's hat on the top of the head. Our plesiosaurus police has stopped a speedboat and says, "Please, pull over." You have two triggers to get you thinking about the first part of this dinosaur's name, *police* and *please*, which starts PLES-iosaurus.

SAY	**Spinosaurus** (SPINE-o-SOR-us)
SEE	The first syllable sounds like *spine*.
STICK	This guy's a meat eater. The sail on his back was eight feet high. The sail may have been used like a radiator to cool this dinosaur on hot days after he had been chasing lunch. An outstanding feature is the sail. Imagine having X-ray vision and looking through this animal's back, where the sail is connected to the spine. Saying *spine* will remind you of SPINE-osaurus

SAY	**Stegosaurus** (STEG-o-SOR-us)
SEE	The first syllable sounds a little like *steak*.
STICK	Here's a vegetarian with a tail that packs a wallop. Big bony plates on the stegosaurus's back lead down to a spiked tail. The stegosaurus could swing its tail to hold off a meat eater. The outstanding feature is the spiked tail. Imagine a big juicy steak impaled on the stegosaurus's spiked tail. To reinforce this image, have the stegosaurus trying to use a stake to remove the steak. *Steak* or *stake* starts STEG-osaurus.

SAY	**Triceratops** (try-SER-a-tops)
SEE	Syllables in this dinosaur's name sound like *tricycle* and *tops*.
STICK	The frill around this vegetarian's neck was used to gain leverage in biting off thick branches. For protection, the triceratops has a bulldozer-sized body and three wicked horns. Two outstanding features are the horns and the tank-like body. Imagine the bulky triceratops on a tricycle with a top spinning on its center horn. The *tricycle* and *top* will help remind you of the TRI-cera-TOPS name.

SAY	**Tyrannosaurus** (tie-RAN-o-SOR-us)
SEE	The first two syllables sound like *tire* and *rhino*.
STICK	The most famous of the dinosaur meat eaters. In Latin, tyrannosaurus means terrible lizard. The teeth were the size of butcher knives. The outstanding feature of the tyrannosaurus is her big jaws and teeth. Imagine a tire hanging from this creature's jaws like a swing. A rhino is swinging in the tire. *Tire* and *rhino* sounds like the beginning of TYRANNO-saurus.

The Dinosaur Memory Game

Now that you know the dinosaurs, it's time to play with them. To play this game you need:

1. A dinosaur spinner
2. Dinosaur cards
3. Ten pennies

DINOSAUR SPINNER

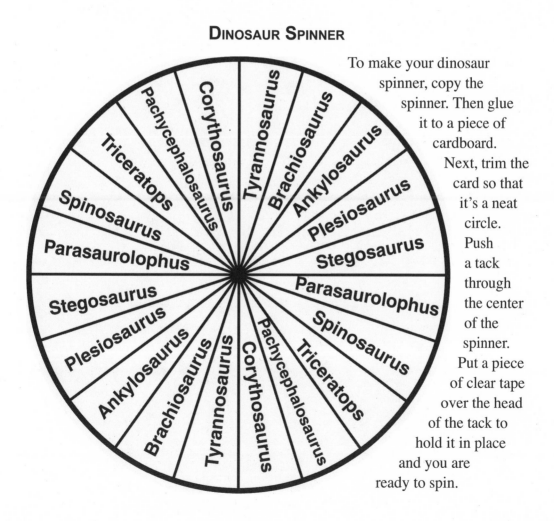

To make your dinosaur spinner, copy the spinner. Then glue it to a piece of cardboard. Next, trim the card so that it's a neat circle. Push a tack through the center of the spinner. Put a piece of clear tape over the head of the tack to hold it in place and you are ready to spin.

CARDS FOR THE DINOSAUR MEMORY GAME

Use a copy machine to duplicate the dinosaur cards that follow. Glue the copies onto a piece of cardboard. Cut out each card. On the back of the card, print the correct dinosaur name. An alternative to printing the dinosaur's name is to make copies of the mnemonic substitution images found earlier in the chapter and glue these to the back of the cards. For example, on one side of a card you have the illustration of a triceratops, and on the other side, the image of the triceratops riding a tricycle and spinning a top on its horn.

RULES FOR THE DINOSAUR MEMORY GAME

1. This game is played with two or three players. If desired, the third player can act as a referee.
2. Lay the dinosaur cards on the floor with the illustration of the dinosaur face up.
3. Put the spinner on a smooth surface, like a book. Place a pen on the book pointing at the spinner. One player spins the spinner. When the circle stops moving, the players look at which dinosaur name the pen is pointing at. Then all the players try to be the first to put their hand on the correct dinosaur card.
4. When a player touches a card she has to keep her finger on that card—even if it is the wrong choice.
5. To be sure that a player has chosen the correct card, turn it over and check the name or the mnemonic image, depending on what is included on the card. The first player to touch the correct card receives a token, one penny.
6. A game is over after the ten pennies have been handed out. The person with the most pennies is the dinosaur master for that game. If you are playing with a referee, the dinosaur master takes the place of referee for the next round of play.

To expand the dinosaur game, check out books from the library on dinosaurs. Look for interesting dinosaurs that aren't in the original ten featured in this book. Use a copy machine to reduce or enlarge pictures of new dinosaurs, to make additional cards for your dinosaur game. Use the Say, See, Stick technique to teach these new dinosaurs. You'll also need to make a new spinner that includes the names of these new dinosaurs. Notice that the spinner in this book has space for twenty dinosaur names, the names are repeated on the spinner. You could also make a larger spinner the size of a pie plate and put more names on the spinner.

The Dinosaur Facts Game

Expand students' dinosaur knowledge with this game. What you will need:

1. Dinosaur cards (same cards used in previous game)
2. Dinosaur fact cards
3. Five pennies

DINOSAUR FACT CARDS

Duplicate the dinosaur fact cards. Glue these copies to cardboard, and cut out.

1. Vegetarian 2. Almost 20 feet long 3. Covered by bony plates 4. Defense was swinging club-like tail **Ankylosaurus** (an-KIE-lo-SOR-us)	1. Leaf eater 2. Front legs much longer than rear 3. Long neck 4. Weighed as much as ten elephants **Brachiosaurus** (BRA-key-o-SOR-us)
1. Fifty feet long 2. Meat eater 3. Lived in the ocean 4. Flippers **Plesiosaurus** (PLEE-zee-o-SOR-us)	1. Vegetarian 2. Bony ridge plates to protect back 3. Spiked tail used for defense **Stegosaurus** (STEG-o-SOR-us)

1. Lived in herds
2. Hollow crest
3. Crest may have been used like a trumpet to communicate

Parasaurolophus
(PAR-a-so-ROL-a-fus)

1. Meat eater
2. Cooling system on back
3. Sail on back 8 feet high

Spinosaurus
(spine-o-SOR-us)

1. Vegetarian
2. Frill around neck used for protection
3. Frill on neck used to gain leverage to bite off branches
4. Three-horned defense

Triceratops
(try-SER-o-tops)

1. Lived in herds
2. Ten-inch thick skull
3. Butted heads like rams

Pachycephalosaurus
(PAK-ka-sef-fuh-lo-SOR-us)

1. Crest on head
2. Front toes resembled fingers
3. Plant eater

Corythosaurus
(ko-RITH-o-SOR-us)

1. Meat eater
2. Teeth the size of steak knives
3. Eyes facing forward make it better at judging distance to prey

Tyrannosaurus
(tie-RAN-o-SOR-us)

RULES FOR THE DINOSAUR FACT GAME

Three players are needed. Players read the fact cards beforehand. Now, lay the dinosaur cards on the floor with the illustration of the dinosaur facing up. Shuffle the fact cards and put them in a stack. One person acts as the fact reader. Drawing a fact card from the stack, the reader chooses one clue to give to the other players, e.g., weighed as much as ten elephants. The facts on the card can be presented in whatever order the reader chooses. Using the clues, the other two players try to be first to touch the correct dinosaur card. If the first fact isn't enough information, the reader gives another clue. Speed to the card determines who gets the token, but players must stay with the first card they touch. If one player chooses the wrong dinosaur, the remaining player is given one more clue to help in making a decision. Play for five pennies, with the winner becoming the new dinosaur fact reader.

Students can make their own fact cards as they learn more about dinosaurs. These cards would then be shared with new players before starting play. This turns the game into part research and part show and tell for the students. Kids could even have dinosaur-card trading sessions.

Expanding Dinosaur Memory

 Spiders know that a single strand is not an effective fly-catcher. That's why they make webs. Memory works in a similar manner. By involving more senses in learning a subject you increase the memory strands that lead back to the information. To increase the number of memory strands for dinosaurs you might try the following:

- Color the dinosaurs on the cards. No one is sure what colors dinosaurs were, so be creative. What color do you think a predator like tyrannosaurus would have been? What about a herd-living animal like parasaurolophus?
- Substitute dinosaur figurines for the cards in the dinosaur game. This adds dimensionality. Figurines are sold in nature stores and on the Web.

- Read books on dinosaurs. Two choices would be *The Big Book of Dinosaurs, a First Book for Young Children,* by Angela Wilkes, or *The Visual Dictionary of Dinosaurs,* publisher Dorling Kindersley.
- Construct a dinosaur model skeleton.
- Construct a dinosaur diorama.
- Visit a dinosaur museum exhibit.
- As mentioned, students can create their own fact cards for dinosaurs. The Web contains many sources for collecting information on dinosaurs.

The Mr. Bonz Game: The Human Skeleton

In this chapter:

- Memorize the names and locations of twenty bones found in the human skeleton.
- Play the Mr. Bonz Game.

There are 206 bones in an adult human skeleton. A beginner who knows just 20 of these bones has a good start on the whole skeleton. For these 20 bones, the Say, See, Stick mnemonic technique works well.

Mr. Bonz

Give your students a copy of the Mr. Bonz illustration on the following page. You may want to blow it up larger on a copy machine. Ask them to color Mr. Bonz according to the color key next to the illustration. As they color each bone, have them *say* the name of that bone out loud.

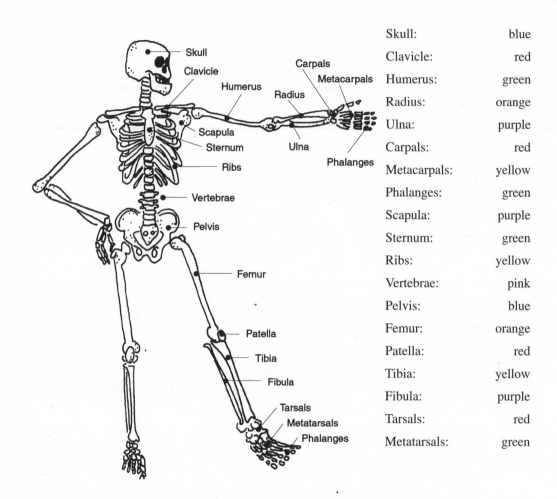

Skull:	blue
Clavicle:	red
Humerus:	green
Radius:	orange
Ulna:	purple
Carpals:	red
Metacarpals:	yellow
Phalanges:	green
Scapula:	purple
Sternum:	green
Ribs:	yellow
Vertebrae:	pink
Pelvis:	blue
Femur:	orange
Patella:	red
Tibia:	yellow
Fibula:	purple
Tarsals:	red
Metatarsals:	green

USING SAY, SEE, STICK ON MR. BONZ

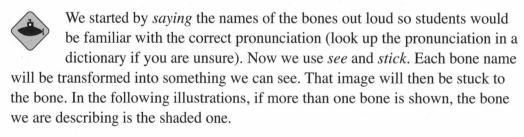

We started by *saying* the names of the bones out loud so students would be familiar with the correct pronunciation (look up the pronunciation in a dictionary if you are unsure). Now we use *see* and *stick*. Each bone name will be transformed into something we can see. That image will then be stuck to the bone. In the following illustrations, if more than one bone is shown, the bone we are describing is the shaded one.

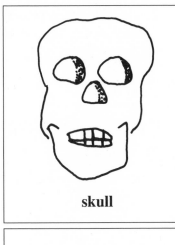

skull

Skull sounds like *scull*, what youngsters do when they're learning to swim. Imagine a skull, sculling water.

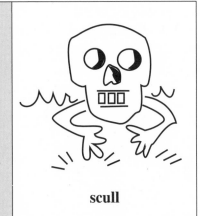

scull

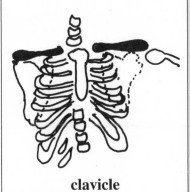

clavicle

Clavicle sounds like *clay vehicle*. Imagine two clay vehicles, one on each of your clavicles.

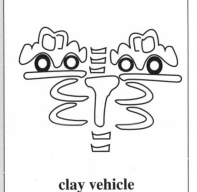

clay vehicle

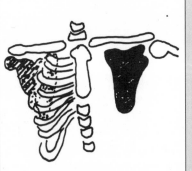

scapula

Scapula sounds like *scalpel*. Imagine a scalpel, sticking in one of your scapulas—ouch!

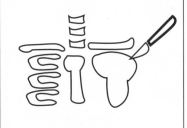

scalpel

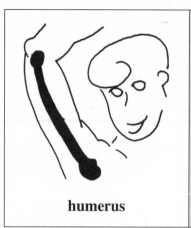

Humerus sounds like *humorous*. Imagine that the arm bone connected to your scapula is laughing, humorous.

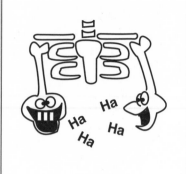

humerus

humorous

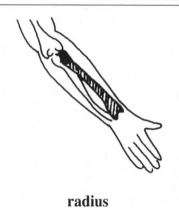

Radius sounds a little like *radio bus*. Imagine a bus shaped like a radio balanced on your forearm.

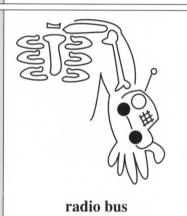

radius

radio bus

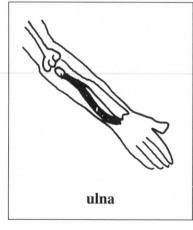

The sound-alike for **ulna** is *hula*. Imagine a hula girl suspended from your arm by her arms.

ulna

hula

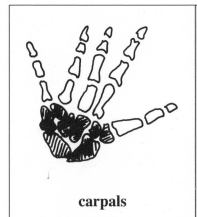

carpals

Carpals sounds like *car pills*. Imagine a car with two giant pills sitting in the front seat. This car sits on the base of your hand.

car pills

metacarpals

Metacarpals sounds like *metal car pools*. Imagine a metal car in the shape of a pool. This car-pool sits on the middle of your palm.

metal car pools

phalanges

Phalanges sounds a bit like *flamingos*. Imagine flamingos sitting on each of your digits.

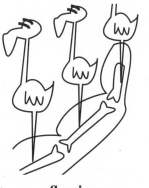

flamingos

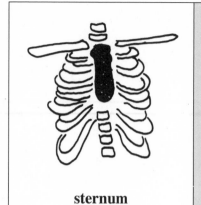

Sternum sounds a little like *steer nun*. Imagine a steer in a nun's habit sitting right in the middle of your chest.

sternum

steer nun

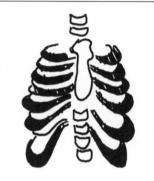

Ribs are *ribs*. Imagine a spare rib dinner. Most kids won't need a memory device for this one.

ribs

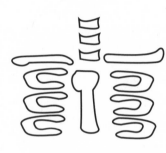

ribs

Vertebrae sounds like *fur tub bray*. Imagine fur lining a bath tub and a donkey sitting in it braying. Mount this image on the spinal column.

vertebrae

fur tub bray

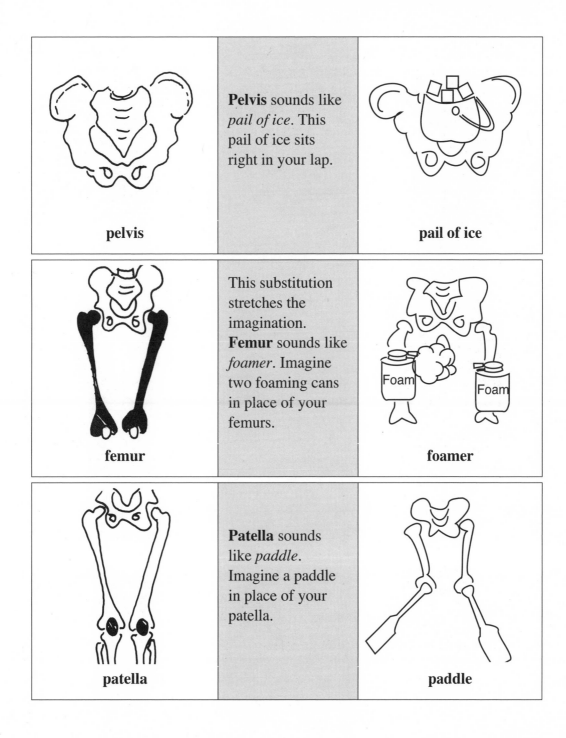

pelvis

Pelvis sounds like *pail of ice*. This pail of ice sits right in your lap.

pail of ice

femur

This substitution stretches the imagination. **Femur** sounds like *foamer*. Imagine two foaming cans in place of your femurs.

foamer

patella

Patella sounds like *paddle*. Imagine a paddle in place of your patella.

paddle

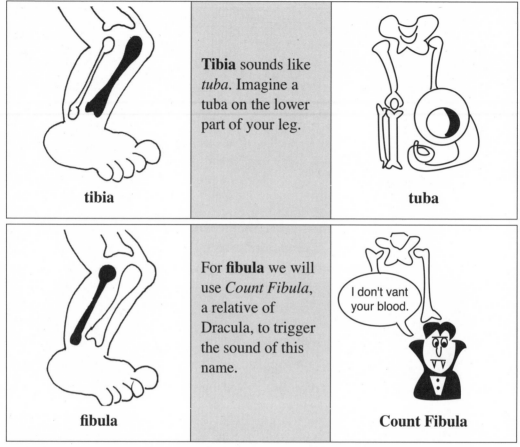

tibia	**Tibia** sounds like *tuba*. Imagine a tuba on the lower part of your leg.	tuba
fibula	For **fibula** we will use *Count Fibula*, a relative of Dracula, to trigger the sound of this name.	I don't vant your blood. **Count Fibula**

The use of *Count Fibula* is a rhyming mnemonic technique rather than a substitution. Fibula is a hard word to use substitution on. To help reinforce this image, have the count say, "I don't vant your blooood." Obviously this is a fib (fibula). Kids often get the fibula and the tibia mixed up. To help them keep their bones straight, imagine *Count Fibula* (fibula) playing the *tuba* (tibia). Obviously Count Fibula would be behind the tuba, as the fibula is behind the tibia.

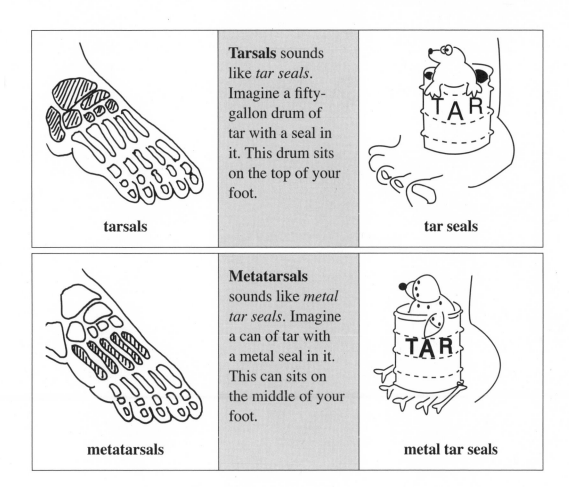

LABEL MR. BONZ

On the next page you will find a full illustration of the skeleton, Mr. Bonz. Work your way down the skeleton, drawing arrows to the different bones you learned in this chapter. Next to the arrow make a quick thumbnail sketch of the substitute image used to remember the name of the bone. Finally put down the correct name for the bone your arrow points to.

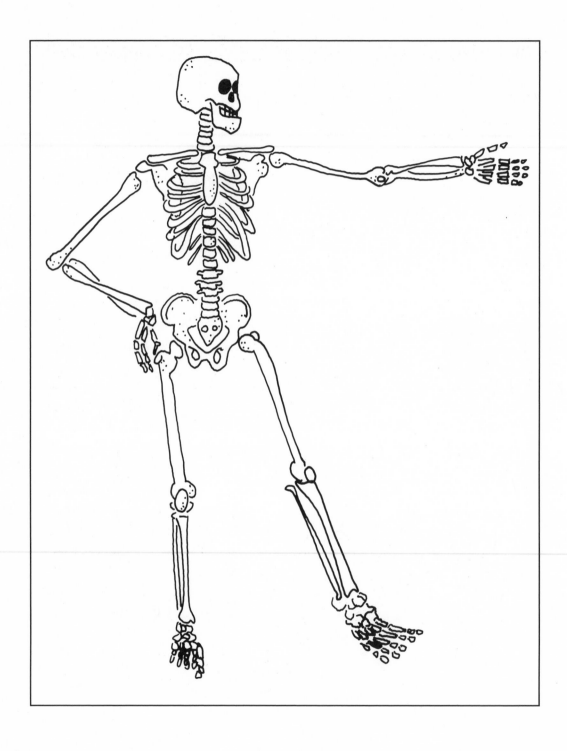

The Mr. Bonz Game

 This game will add excitement to the task of learning human anatomy. To play this game you need:

1. A Mr. Bonz game spinner
2. Three sets of Mr. Bonz skeleton cards
3. A pencil

MR. BONZ GAME SPINNER

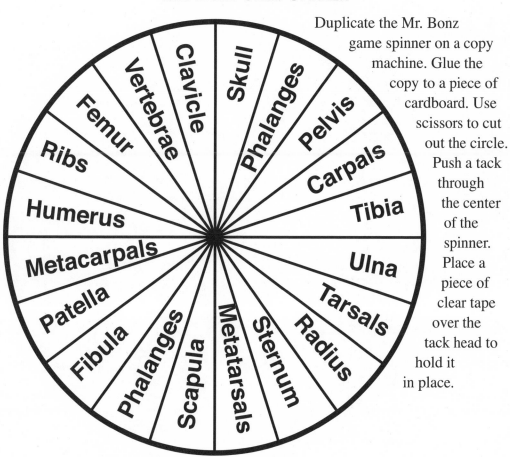

Duplicate the Mr. Bonz game spinner on a copy machine. Glue the copy to a piece of cardboard. Use scissors to cut out the circle. Push a tack through the center of the spinner. Place a piece of clear tape over the tack head to hold it in place.

Mr. Bonz Game Cards

Use a copy machine to make three copies of the twenty Mr. Bonz Game cards, for a total of sixty cards. Cut out the cards. Fold the shaded tab to the back side of the card and tack it down with a dab of glue. This shaded section contains the name of the bone and in parentheses the sound-alike substitution image. An alternative way to make cards is to snip off the shaded portion, and in place of it paste copies of the mnemonic images representing the bones. These images can be found earlier in the chapter.

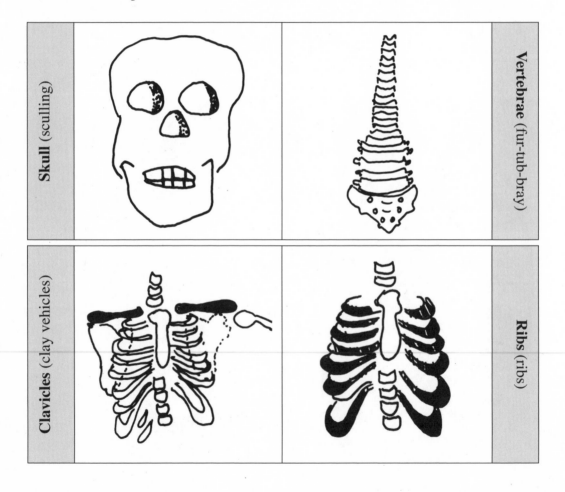

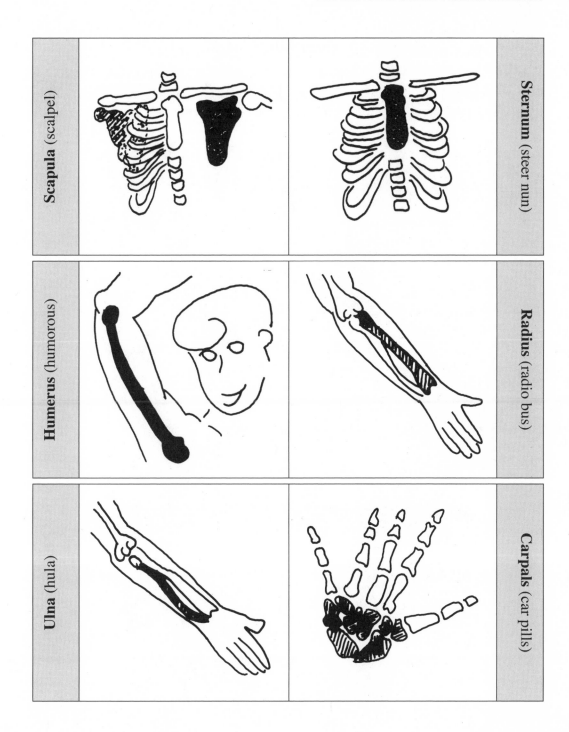

Scapula (scalpel)

Sternum (steer nun)

Humerus (humorous)

Radius (radio bus)

Ulna (hula)

Carpals (car pills)

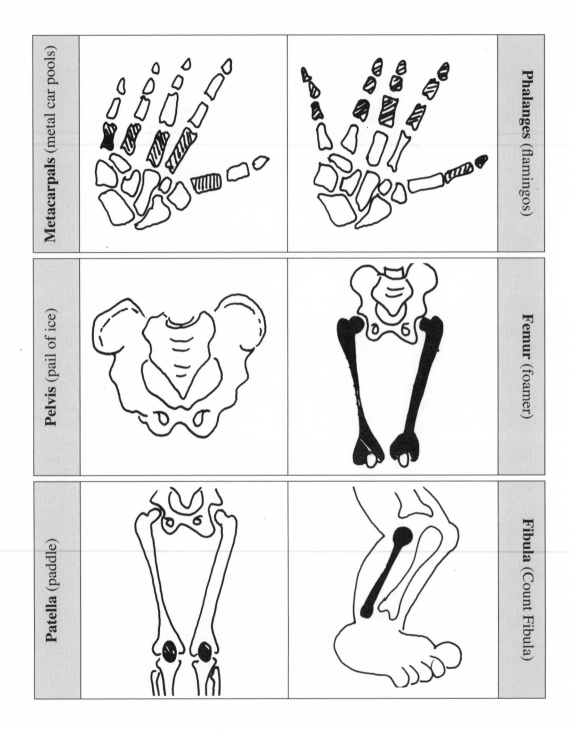

Metacarpals (metal car pools)

Phalanges (flamingos)

Pelvis (pail of ice)

Femur (foamer)

Patella (paddle)

Fibula (Count Fibula)

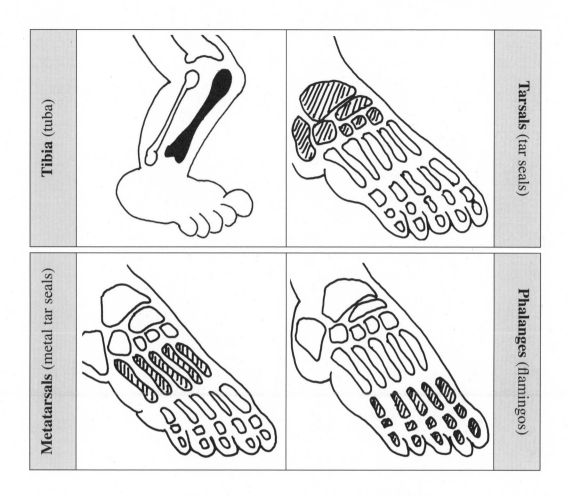

RULES FOR THE SKELETON GAME

The object of the game is to assemble a complete skeleton (twenty bones) from the skeleton cards. You can play with two or three players. With three, the third acts as the referee.

1. Lay out the sixty cards with the bones facing up. For example, with the pelvis card facing up, on the other side of the card would be the correct name, or the mnemonic image for pelvis.

2. Place the spinner on a smooth surface. Lay a pencil next to the spinner with the point facing the circle. One player twirls the spinner. When the spinner comes to rest, the pencil will be pointing at a bone name. Let's say it's *femur*. Both players try to be the first to get their finger on a femur card. Since there are several femur cards, it is the first person on the card who gets to take that card. This is where a referee is helpful. Now the other person spins.

3. When a player puts her finger on a card that is her choice, no changing until the next spin. This prevents players from hopping from card to card. You can also play a version where a player who chooses the wrong card has to forfeit a card.

4. There are many bone cards on the table. As the game progresses, a player may pick up three of the same card. Let's say you have three femurs. When you have this number, and it is your turn to spin, you can exchange any two similar cards for another card on the table that you need to complete your skeleton. The discarded cards go back into play on the table.

5. There will be times when a player will spin and the bone that's selected on the spinner is no longer on the table because they have all been picked up. In that case, spin again.

6. The first person to assemble a complete skeleton yells "Mr. Bonz" and wins.

Make the Skeleton Game More Physical

 While the previous version of the game is active, this section gets the whole body involved. To play this game you need:

1. The Mr. Bonz game spinner
2. A pencil
3. Twenty pennies

RULES FOR THE FULL-BODY SKELETON GAME

1. This game is for three players. One player acts as referee, who does the spinning and also determines who is the first person to get the correct answer.
2. The referee spins the spinner and calls out the selected bone.
3. Players then use their own bodies, placing their finger on the spot where the correct bone is located. The first person to put their finger on the correct bone gets a point. The referee determines who is first to get that point and gives that player a penny.
4. The person with the most pennies at the end of the game becomes the referee for the next game.

23 Forty-Three Presidents in One Day

In this chapter:

- Memorize the presidents' names in order of their presidency.
- Play any of several presidential memory games.

  In elementary school it can take weeks for children to learn the names of the presidents. Using the following mnemonic technique, they can learn the presidents' names—in order of their presidencies—in under an hour. The mnemonic technique uses substitution and chaining. Each president's name is first substituted with a sound-alike word that's easy to picture. Thus, Kennedy becomes *can of tea*. Eisenhower becomes *eyes in a tower*. Clinton becomes *clean tin*. When each president's name is something that can be visualized, a story is made, starting with the first president. In going through the story, each president is linked to the next in a chain.

Tell to a child the following short story, which is broken into four segments. Tell the child that after each segment she is going to repeat the story back to you. If you're working with a group of children, have them pair up. One child tells the story to her partner and then the partner has his turn. If a child is stumped, the other child gives a clue. (It works better if children learn the story before you explain its purpose. They delight in the discovery that it's a list of all the presidents' names. If they learn the purpose first, they spend more time trying to figure out the riddle of which president each part of the story refers to rather than memorizing the story.)

The Presidents' Story

You come to a big white house (the white house represents where the presidents live) and crammed in the doorway of the white house, you see a **washing** (#1 Washington) machine. A man has his **Adam's** (#2 Adams) apple caught under the lid of the washing machine. A **chef and his son** (#3 Jefferson) are trying to pull the man out of the washing machine. The chef gets **mad at his son** (#4 Madison); he gets into a boat and away the **man rows** (#5 Monroe). He comes to **a dam** (#6 Adams). On the other side of the dam are giant **jacks** (#7 Jackson). A **van** pulls up to the jacks, and a **bureau** falls out (#8 Van Buren). Out of a bureau drawer pops a **hairy sun** (#9 Harrison). The sun is wearing a huge **tie** (#10 Tyler).

Stop and repeat back this first section of the story from memory.

The tie has **polka** (#11 Polk) dots. The dots are measured by a **tailor** (#12 Taylor). The tailor turns and starts to **fill more** (#13 Fillmore) gas into a tank. **Pears** (#14 Pierce) start falling out of the nozzle. The pears fall into a big **blue cannon** (#15 Buchanan). The cannon fires, and out come **Lincoln** (#16 Lincoln) pennies. The pennies rip holes in long **johns** worn by the **sun** (#17 Johnson). Out of the holes fall chunks of **granite** (#18 Grant). The granite lands on a pile of **hay** (#19 Hayes). From under the hay runs the cartoon cat **Garfield** (#20 Garfield). Garfield scratches an **author** (#21 Arthur). The author picks up a meat **cleaver** (#22 Cleveland) and chases his **hairy son** (#23 Harrison).

Stop and repeat the first section and the second section from memory.

His hairy son grabs the meat **cleaver** (#24 Cleveland) and hits a big **mac in a can** (#25 McKinley). Out of the can pops a **rose** made of **velvet** (#26 Roosevelt). The rose of velvet falls onto some sticky **taffy** (#27 Taft). The taffy melts under a **wild sun** (#28 Wilson). The wild sun gets **hard** (#29 Harding) and out pops a **college** (#30 Coolidge). The college grows **hooves** (#31 Hoover) and gallops over **rows of velvet** (#32 Roosevelt). The rows of velvet are shaded by a **tree** in the shape of a **man** (#33 Truman).

Stop and repeat the first, second, and third sections from memory.

The tree-man looks up at **eyes in a tower** (#34 Eisenhower). Out of the tower falls a **can of tea** (#35 Kennedy). The can of tea lands on long **johns** worn by a **sun** (#36 Johnson). The long johns are being **knit** by the **sun** (#37 Nixon). The knitter is run over by a model T **Ford** (#38 Ford). The Ford's door opens, and out comes a **cart** (#39 Carter). The cart holds a wildly firing **ray gun** (#40 Reagan). The ray gun ignites a **bush** (#41 Bush). The bush is used to **clean** a **tin** (#42 Clinton). The clean tin is put over another **bush** (#43 Bush).

Stop and repeat all sections from memory.

When students can repeat the entire story, explain the substitution memory technique. Then show where each president appears in the story.

MAKE THE PRESIDENTS' STORY MORE INTERACTIVE

- While telling the presidents' story, have children physically act it out.
- When teaching the presidents' story in a classroom setting, have students pair up and take turns telling the story. One child says, "There is a big white house, and at the entrance there's a washing machine (Washington)." Then the next child picks up the story, "And there was a man with his Adam's apple caught under the lid (Adams)." And so on.

- If you have four children per group, you can play competitive presidents. Each child tells a piece of the story as in the previous example. The difference is that if someone forgets or tells the story out of sequence he sits down. Who can go the farthest in the story?
- Give students a pack of forty-three cards, each with a president's name on it. The goal of the presidents' card game is that four students, working as a team, lay the cards out on the floor in correct order. They are competing against another team with the same goal. A noncompetitive version of the game is to have teams try to beat their personal best times. This game also offers an opportunity to teach teamwork skills.
- Photocopy pictures of the presidents' faces. Blow these pictures up large enough to make masks. On the inside of the mask, write several interesting facts about the president (e.g., President Lincoln was born into poverty. His mother and father were barely literate, yet he taught himself law in his spare time and became a leading lawyer in the state of Illinois.). Now, as the presidents' story is being told, have children step into line when they hear the name of the president whose mask they are wearing. Then each child tells a fact about his president.

The Bill of Rights Game

In this chapter:

- Learn the first ten amendments to the Constitution of the United States and be able to list them in proper order.
- Play the Bill of Rights game.

Your parents, teachers, and friends have greatly influenced what kind of person you are now. But many other influences in your life are unseen. How about the amendments to the Constitution of the United States, for example? Think about it. Your parents have created you and guided you through many years, but the laws of the land shape their behavior—and thus yours too, in ways you might not have thought about. As a part of understanding how you have become who you are, it helps to understand these laws. Let's start with the first ten amendments to the Constitution of the United States, also known as the Bill of Rights.

The paragraph you've just read demonstrates a major factor in motivating students to remember what you're teaching—making the subject itself personally relevant. We are interested in, pay attention to, and remember information that we perceive as having relevance to our lives. For most students, the amendments are abstract and far removed from their own experience. We can change that with personally relevant examples and with the immediacy of turning the amendments into a game.

In this chapter we'll use a combination of mnemonic techniques. First, we need a pegging system. Then we'll use substitution to turn the abstract amendments into images that can be stored in the pegging system.

Rhyming Pegs

  The first step in memorizing the amendments is to create a filing system. We will create one that serves two purposes. It will keep the amendments in order, plus it will act as a retrieval cue. Since each amendment is already numbered we have our order, but we are going to replace each number with an image. For the numbers one through ten, we'll use images whose names rhyme with the numbers. Do you know the nursery rhyme:

One, two, buckle my shoe
Three, four, open the door
Five, six, pick up sticks
Seven, eight, close the gate
Nine, ten, a big fat hen

If you know the rhyme, you already know half the rhyming words that we are going to use in our pegging system. Have your students memorize the list of rhyming pegs that follows:

1. Bun

2. Shoe

3. Tree

4. Door

5. Hive

6. Sticks

7. Heaven

8. Gate

9. Sign

10. Hen

Check to see how many number images your students can recall:

1

2

3

4

5

6

7

8

9

10

If they can recall them in order, have them try jumping around. What is the rhyming word for 8? The rhyming word for 3? How about 9? When students can quickly call out the correct rhyming word for each number, you're ready to move on to the amendments.

Numbers As Patterns

As a child, Picasso saw numbers as patterns. The number 2 was a folded dove wing. Zero was an eye.

The Amendments

  Each amendment starts with a simply worded version of the law that a grade schooler can understand. This is followed by an explanation of the reasoning behind the law and what things could be like without the protections of the amendment. Now we come to the memory part. Each amendment is turned into a substitute image. Then this image is pegged to the correct amendment number.

FIRST AMENDMENT

> Citizens are guaranteed freedom of
> speech, assembly, press, and religion.

In some countries you can end up in prison if you speak your mind, get a group together for a demonstration, write anything against the ruling party, or practice a religion other than that decided on by the country. The First Amendment protects you. How different would your upbringing have been if you'd had to worry about these four things? There would be no late night talk show hosts like Jay Leno. You'd have to be careful about what you said in front of others because they might pass your comments on to the secret police. You'd never read about mistakes made by the ruling party. If you disagreed with what was going on, you wouldn't be able to get a group of people together to discuss it. All churches would be the same, or maybe the ruling government wouldn't allow any religion.

To remember the first amendment, turn it into a substitute image. Imagine a person talking (freedom of speech) to a group of people (freedom of assembly), typing on a computer keyboard (freedom of the press), while sitting on a cross (freedom of religion).

Next step, peg the amendment. What rhyming word goes with the number 1? Remember, it's a bun. Put the bun into the substitute image for the first amendment. How about having the speaker eating a bun and spewing pieces all over his keyboard and the assembled people while seated on a cross?

Here's the retrieval process when someone asks, what's the first amendment?

1.   Say, "One is a bun."
2.   Ask yourself, "Where's the bun?"
3.   Answer, "It's being eaten by a man who's trying to speak (freedom of speech) to a group (freedom of assembly) while typing on a computer keyboard (freedom of press) and sitting on a cross (freedom of religion)."

SECOND AMENDMENT

> As part of a state militia (mini-army), people have the right to bear arms (weapons).

The founding fathers had a problem—the king of England. If a king could restrict who had arms (weapons), he could guarantee that weapons were held only by his soldiers. This gave him a lot of power. If, on the other hand, the people of a state had the right to have weapons, as put forth in the second amendment, it would make the ruling party more cautious. A ruler could expect resistance if he decided to kill the first born in every family, or take away the property of people with the letter *I* in their name, or make you leave the country because of your religion.

The substitute image for the second amendment is a bear holding a gun (right to bear arms):

What rhyming word goes with the number 2? Two is a shoe. So we need to collage a shoe into the substitute image for the second amendment. Imagine your gun-toting bear wearing shoes.

THIRD AMENDMENT

> Soldiers will not be quartered in homes
> in peacetime.

In the good old days, the king could give you roommates. He might do this because he was concerned about your loyalty. All of a sudden you would find soldiers living in your house. This would put a damper on any thoughts you might have about speaking or taking any action against the government.

The substitute image for the third amendment is a huge soldier trying to get into a small dollhouse with a peace symbol on the door. He's too big to get in (no soldiers quartered in homes in peacetime).

What rhyming word goes with the number 3? Three is a tree. Put the dollhouse in a tree with the soldier standing next to it.

FOURTH AMENDMENT

> You are protected against unreasonable search and seizure.

In some countries, government soldiers or the police can simply stop you and start searching through your stuff, without having any reason. Say they find something interesting, like your Rolex watch. They decide to seize the watch, to take it from you. Say goodbye to the watch. The fourth amendment makes this an illegal action in the United States.

A substitute image for the fourth amendment is a man held by an octopus (unreasonable seizure). The octopus is using a searchlight to search through the man's pockets (an unreasonable search).

What rhyming word goes with the number 4? Four is a door. Imagine your octopus-wrapped man trying to escape through a door.

FIFTH AMENDMENT

Serious crimes get a jury trial. No one will be tried for the same crime twice (put in double jeopardy). No one will be forced to testify against themselves, and private property will not be taken for public use without just (fair) compensation.

The fifth amendment covers a lot. First, you are guaranteed a jury trial if the crime is serious, like murder, kidnapping, counterfeiting—anything for which you could go to jail for a looooong time. It's believed that the more people involved in determining guilt or innocence (there are twelve on a jury), the less likely it is that someone will do something sneaky, like letting the guilty party go or convicting an innocent person.

Next, we have protection against double jeopardy, being tried in court twice for the same crime. Let's say you're accused of a crime and go to trial. You're found innocent. The problem is that the local lawyers and judges don't like you. They decide to try you again, and again, and again. Even if you weren't in jail, this would pretty much ruin your life. This is why lawyers and police want to be especially careful if they decide to bring someone to trial. If they don't have enough evidence the first time around, they blow their chances of bringing that person to court again on the same charges. Even if they find new evidence, like a videotape of that person in the act, they cannot charge a person for the same crime if they got off the first time.

We've probably all heard the famous lines on police shows, "… and you understand anything you say can be used against you in a court of law …." These lines protect your fifth amendment rights. You don't have to say anything to the police or in court. This is called, "taking the fifth amendment." When you are accused of a crime in the United States, the idea is that you are innocent until proven guilty. It is up to the legal system to prove your guilt. You cannot be forced to help in that process.

Finally, let's say that you live in a place where they have decided to build a dam to provide electricity for 100,000 homes. Government officials cannot say, "Leave. We need your land." But they can say, "Leave. We will pay a reasonable amount for your land." When a project is determined to be important for the public good, government officials can take your personal property, but they have to give you a reasonable payment.

A substitute image for the fifth amendment is as follows. Imagine a man squashing another man with a big mirror while a jury looks on (a jury trial is guaranteed for serious crimes). The man who dropped the mirror is wearing a teeshirt with the universal symbol for *no,* and he's looking at his own image saying, "He did it" (you can't be forced to testify against yourself). A large Jeopardy game board is next to the jury (you cannot be tried for the same crime twice—double jeopardy). Near the jury is a workman paying a man for his house which sits in the scoop of a bulldozer (property cannot be taken for public use without a reasonable payment).

What rhyming word goes with the number 5? Five is a hive. Imagine the man in front of the mirror with a beehive on his head.

Sixth Amendment

> You are guaranteed the right to a speedy trial by a jury of your peers. You have the right to be defended by counsel (attorney) and confront your accusers.

Evil dictators don't like the sixth amendment. First, it prevents them from making you wait for months or even years before your case goes to trial. If you were held in prison during that time, you might as well be guilty. You would probably lose your job, and without money to pay your rent or mortgage, you'd lose your house. Your family—even your dog—might leave. Even if you eventually went to trial and were declared innocent, you would have suffered terribly. The sixth amendment protects you by guaranteeing a speedy trial. Second, the wicked dictator might stack the jury in his favor or not even have a jury. Again the sixth amendment comes to your rescue, by guaranteeing that you'll get a jury of your peers. Peers are ordinary citizens, not people hand-picked by the dictator. This amendment is one reason why lawyers on both sides of a case are involved in the jury-selection process from a random pool of citizens. Third, the corrupt dictator might give you a trial, to make it look like he's fair, but you don't have anyone to represent you who understands the laws of the country. What would it be like to be in a courtroom charged with a crime, when you know nothing of the laws?

The sixth amendment makes sure you have a representative who understands the laws, which is the right to legal counsel. Finally, this foul dictator tells you there are witnesses to your crime, but he wants to protect their identities so you're not going to know who they are. How could you defend yourself? There's no way to prove these people are mistaken or lying, because you don't even know who they are. The sixth amendment says you get to face your accusers and challenge their testimony.

The substitute image for the sixth amendment is a courtroom with a clock behind the judge (right to a speedy trial). Next to the judge is a jury box filled with pears (right to a jury trial of your peers). In front of the jury is a lawyer with boxing gloves (right to defense from legal counsel). Finally, you are sitting in the witness box and facing the person who has accused you of a crime (right to confront your accuser).

What rhyming word goes with the number 6? Six is sticks. Imagine the judge holding a stick in his hand and pointing it at the clock.

SEVENTH AMENDMENT

> You have the right to a jury trial for sums over $20.

The important part about this amendment is not the twenty bucks, it's that you can get a jury trial to settle problems that involve money. Imagine a country where there's no way to set things right when a mechanic takes your money and doesn't fix your car, or when you buy something on the Internet that isn't what was advertised, or you work for someone and she decides not to pay you. Just like the fifth amendment, the inclusion of a jury is to give the court an impartial third party who decides what should be done to make things right. By the way, $20 in 1801, several years after the amendments were accepted, would be equivalent to about $200 today.

The substitute image for the seventh amendment is a jury box filled with jurors (right to a jury trial) with $20 bills raining down on them (for sums over $20).

What rhyming image word goes with number 7? Seven is heaven. Imagine a cloud with an angel on it to represent heaven. The angel is raining down $20 bills on your jury.

EIGHTH AMENDMENT

> You are protected from excessive bail or fines.
> You are also protected from
> cruel and unusual punishment.

To make sure you show up on the date of your trial, the court can give you a choice. You can go to jail or pay bail. Bail is money held to guarantee that you will return to the court. If you show up, the bail is refunded. If you are a no-show, the money is forfeited, and you are in big trouble. The eighth amendment prevents a judge from setting a bail that is way out of line with the supposed crime. Maybe you are accused of cutting down your neighbor's roses. The judge, a rose lover, says go to jail until your trial, or pay a million dollars in bail. The bail is excessive considering the crime (you are protected from excessive bail).

You are also protected from excessive fines. Let's say you *are* convicted of ravaging the roses. The judge can't fine you outside of what would be reasonable (protection from excessive fines).

Writers of the eighth amendment were also concerned about punishment. There were some pretty unusual and cruel punishments around the world: torture, public dissection, burning at the stake, cutting off hands and ears. The founding fathers wanted to avoid sadistic or inappropriate treatment of the convicted (no cruel or unusual punishment).

The substitute image for the eighth amendment is a man locked in stocks (protected from cruel and unusual punishment by today's standards). He's being fed from a bale of hay (protection from excessive bail or fines).

What rhyming word goes with the number 8? Eight is a gate. Imagine a fence around your cruel and unusual punishment scene. There is a gate in the fence with a bale of hay impaled on it.

NINTH AMENDMENT

> Just because a right isn't listed in the Constitution doesn't mean that the people have given it to the government.

The ninth and tenth amendments were written by worried people. They had seen how many kings ruled. Most kings had a way of adding more and more power to their position. This amendment made it clear that even if the Constitution didn't list a right, the people still retained that right. Smart move. Some rights weren't even imagined back then. For instance, what would happen if the government decided to limit your playing basketball, television watching, or computer use? These are not rights listed in the Constitution. But the ninth amendment says that any rights not signed over to the government are still retained by the people. So, thank the ninth amendment for protecting your right to play basketball, watch television, and cruise the Internet. The ninth amendment is sometimes called "The People's Rights Amendment."

A substitute image for the ninth amendment is two people holding a sign that reads "Power to the People" (people's rights).

What rhyming word goes with the number 9? Nine is a sign. Imagine your two people holding onto right turn street signs (people's rights).

TENTH AMENDMENT

> Powers not given to the United States by the Constitution are left for the states or the people.

The designers of the Constitution were nervous guys. Following through on their intentions behind the ninth amendment—not wanting the federal government to go grabbing rights that had not been assigned to it—in the tenth amendment they protected the states. It guarantees that states can set their own taxes, decide how voting is carried out, and enforce laws particular to that state. This is why cars are cheaper in Oregon than in California—no state tax. It's also why some states have the death penalty and others don't. The vagueness of this amendment has made it one that has often been in contention, such as during the Civil War, when some states tried to secede from the Union. This amendment is sometimes called the "States' Rights Amendment."

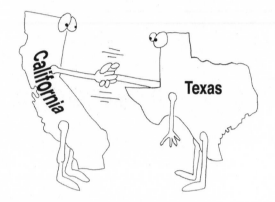

The substitute image for the tenth amendment is two recognizable states shapes shaking right hands (states' rights).

What rhyming word goes with the number 10? Ten is a hen. Imagine a hen held between your two-state image.

AMENDMENTS CHECK

Check your memory for the Bill of Rights. Here's the mental process for remembering which number goes with which amendment, using the second amendment as an example:

1. Someone asks, "What's the second amendment?"
2. You think, "The rhyming peg for 2 is a shoe."
3. Then you ask yourself, "Where is that shoe?"
4. The answer, "It's on a bear's foot. The bear is carrying a rifle. This image represents the right to bear arms."

When students have the pegged amendments memorized, they are ready to play the Bill of Rights game.

Beginner's Bill of Rights Game

 This beginner game on the Bill of Rights tests students on both their pegging and substitution system in a hands-on, fun way. To play the game you need:

1. Three players
2. A set of Bill of Rights cards
3. A Bill of Rights referee sheet

BILL OF RIGHTS CARDS

You will find the Bill of Rights cards on the adjacent page. Copy this sheet and enlarge it by 200% (make it twice as large). Then cut out the cards so that each card has an amendment on it. These are your Bill of Rights cards.

First Amendment	Second Amendment	Third Amendment
Fourth Amendment	Fifth Amendment	Sixth Amendment
Seventh Amendment	Eighth Amendment	Ninth Amendment
Tenth Amendment		

REFEREE SHEET FOR BILL OF RIGHTS GAME

Make a copy of the sheet on the next page.

One's a bun, 1st amend.	Two's a shoe, 2nd amend.	Three's a tree, 3rd amend.
Four's a door, 4th amend.	Five's a hive, 5th amend.	Six is sticks, 6th amend.
Seven's heaven, 7th amend.	Eight's a gate, 8th amend.	Nine's a sign, 9th amend.

Ten's a hen, 10th amend.

1. Freedom of speech, assembly, press, religion
2. Right to bear arms
3. No quartering of soldiers in homes in peacetime
4. No unreasonable search and seizure
5. Jury trial for big crimes, no self-incrimination or double jeopardy, payment for property taken for public use
6. Right to speedy trial, confront accuser, jury of peers
7. Jury trial for sums over $20
8. No cruel or unusual punishment, or excessive bail or fines
9. People's rights
10. States' rights

Rules for Beginner's Bill of Rights Game

1. Shuffle the amendment cards and spread them face down on a table.
2. Players take turns choosing cards. Let's say player #1 turns over the card for the eighth amendment. Player #2 then describes the mnemonic image that goes with the amendment of that number. For the eighth amendment, the player would say, "The substitute image for the eighth amendment is a guy clamped in stocks being fed from a bale of hay." Then that player translates what the substitute image means, "This image means that we are protected from cruel and unusual punishment, as represented by the stocks, and we are protected from excessive bail and fines, as represented by the bale of hay."
3. The referee uses the referee sheet to verify that the player is correct.
4. If correct, the player keeps the card, otherwise it's placed at the bottom of the stack and it's the other player's turn.
5. Play continues until all the cards are gone.
6. The winner becomes the new referee.

Advanced Bill of Rights Game

This game is similar to the beginner's version of the game described on the previous pages, except there is an additional set of cards for this level. These cards are called wild cards. Wild cards pose situations. From the situation, players determine which amendment applies. For example:

> There's a story in the newspaper that a fire at the local army base burned down the soldiers' barracks. Anyone with a spare room will have to let soldiers stay with them until the barracks are rebuilt. Will you have new roommates? Which amendment applies?

The answer is the third amendment, no quartering of soldiers in homes in peacetime.

To play the game you need:

1. Three players
2. A set of Bill of Rights cards (the same cards used in the beginner version of the game)
3. A Bill of Rights referee sheet (also found in the beginner's version of the game)
4. Wild cards

WILD CARDS

Make a copy of the wild card sheets you find on the following pages. Copy on heavy stock paper so you cannot see through the cards. Cut out each card along the lines. On the blank side of each card write WILD CARD.

GOOD NEWS ONLY!	UNI-RELIGION
A police officer calls up the local newspaper and says, "Don't write anything bad about the mayor or I will come down and put you in jail." Which amendment protects you?	In some countries you are only allowed to worship one religion. If you worship another religion, you could be put in jail. What protects us from that happening in the United States?
First amendment	First amendment

GUNS ALLOWED

In some countries, only the government's military and the police are allowed to have guns. This isn't the case in the United States because of which amendment?

Second amendment

ROOMMATES WITH HELMETS

There's a story in the local paper that anyone with a spare room will have to let soldiers stay with them because a fire burned down the barracks on the army base. Do you have to give up your spare room?

Third amendment

PEANUT BUTTER SANDWICH

You are walking to school. Two police officers suddenly grab you. They go through your book pack and find several sandwiches. They say they will keep the sandwiches as evidence. Which amendment protects you?

Fourth amendment

SURPRISE! HOUSE FOR SALE

The federal government is building a freeway that goes right through your backyard. They want to pay for it but you don't want to sell. Who is going to win, and which amendment applies to this situation?

Fifth amendment

WHAT HARDWARE STORE?

It's late at night. A police officer stops you on your way home from the movies. He asks you to tell him if you broke into the hardware store. You decide not to say anything. You are protected by which amendment?

Fifth amendment

SECOND TIME AROUND

You are accused of robbing a bank, and the jury finds you not guilty. As you walk out of the court room, the police put you in handcuffs. They say they are charging you for the same crime again. Can they do this? Why or why not?

Fifth amendment

JUDGING THE JUDGE

Your brother is accused of a crime for which he could go to prison for the rest of his life. The judge decides not to use a jury. He thinks it will be too hard for citizens to decide guilt or innocence. The judge will decide. Which amendment prevents this?

Fifth amendment

BAD BETTY?

The police aren't sure whether you are Bad Betty, the bank robber. So they put you in jail for a month while they look for evidence. Is there an amendment that can help you?

Sixth amendment

FOAMING FOUNTAINS

You are accused of dumping soap into the local fountain. The only witness against you says he is going on vacation to Hawaii. The judge says, "We know what the witness said, so we will just use it as evidence against you." Can the court do this? Which amendment?

Sixth amendment

COMPANY SECRETS

At a company where your mom worked, the director says she stole company secrets when she left to start her own business. Your mom says baloney! The case goes to trial, and she finds a jury made up of members on the board of the company she left. Which amendment protects her?

Sixth amendment

LOUSY SKATE PARK

Your dad paid $9,000 to have a skate park built in your backyard. The builders didn't follow the contract, and you got a lousy skate park. The builders say, "Tough luck." Your dad says he's going to have a jury decide what's fair. Can he take it to court?

Seventh amendment

SWEET TOOTH

Your friend is accused of stealing a case of candy bars. The judge in the case says, "You are to be put in jail or pay a bail of $10,000." What amendment says this judge is out of line?

Eighth amendment

SENTENCED TO A STOMACHACHE

Your friend is convicted of stealing ten boxes of candy. The punishment the judge decides on is, "You will eat ten boxes of candy in one hour." Why is this judge out of line?

Eighth amendment

BAN TELEVISION

The U.S. Congress decides that a lot of TV watching isn't good for U.S. citizens. They decide to control all television watching in the country. Can they do this? Which amendment protects against this?

Ninth amendment

CHEAPER IN OREGON

If you buy a car in California, you're charged a sales tax. In Oregon there is no such tax. What amendment allows for this difference?

Tenth amendment

WE'LL COUNT OUR WAY

In the presidential election in 2000, the state of Florida had ballot counts that were called into question. The state representatives said they would handle how the recount was done and that the federal government had to stay out of it. Which amendment supports them?

Tenth amendment

Rules for the Advanced Bill of Rights Game

1. Mix the wild cards. Then set them on the table in a stack, with the words *WILD CARD* face up.
2. Spread the amendment cards out on the table. The word *amendment* should face up.
3. Now the referee calls out an amendment number.
4. The other two players try to be first to put a finger on the correct card. The referee decides who was first. That player then has a choice. She can explain what the amendment is and have the referee determine if she's correct, or she can choose a wild card.
5. If she chooses a wild card, the referee removes the first card from the wild card stack and reads the situation to the player. The player then has to explain what amendment applies to the situation and why. The referee judges whether the player is correct. If correct, the player gets the card.
6. The player with the most cards at the end of the game is the new referee.

Additional Rhyming Pegs

If you wish to learn more constitutional amendments, here are some more rhyming pegs:

11.	television	21.	here's my son
12.	elf	22.	lots of goo
13.	thirsting	23.	out at sea
14.	fording	24.	near the shore
15.	lifting	25.	a splashy dive
16.	sewing	26.	lots of kicks
17.	deafening	27.	dough is leavening
18.	aiding	28.	dig some bait
19.	knighting	29.	time to dine
20.	penny	30.	dirty

A peg's effectiveness depends on a child's ability to create a strong visual image. For example, for 18, aiding, you might suggest visualizing a Red Cross person providing first aid to someone. You would then use your first aider as the visual element to put into any substitute picture.

The Easy Way to Remember U.S. States and Capitals

In this chapter:

- Memorize the fifty U.S. states and their capitals.
- Play the states and capitals card game.

Some time between fourth and sixth grades, children take on an awesome memory task—memorizing all fifty U.S. states and their capitals. It's also a challenging time for parents. You might be caught off guard when asked, "Mom, what's the capital of Kansas?" Even if you know the answer, you may well be at a loss as to how to make this task easier for your children. Connecting capitals to states is hard. That's because there's no logical reason for Frankfort to be the capital of Kentucky or for Salem to be the capital of Oregon. To learn these facts, most children use rote repetition, dully repeating the state and capital until the information sticks. A more interesting and faster way to accomplish this task is to use the mnemonic techniques of substitution, chaining, and association.

Memorizing States and Capitals

SUBSTITUTION ON STATES AND CAPITALS

Let's start with substitution. Say you want to remember that the capital of Washington is Olympia. First, sound out Washington: *Wash-ing-ton*. Do the individual syllables stand for anything other than the state? When we break a word down into syllables, we're listening for something we can turn into a picture. That picture will represent or substitute for the state. For Washington, use the first two syllables, *wash-ing*, to jog the memory. A concrete image like *washing machine* makes a good substitute image for Washington.

We could have also added an image for the word *ton* at the end of Washington, but often all that's necessary for retrieving a piece of information is a place to start. For that reason we won't bother making an image for the word *ton*.

Next, create a picture for the capital, Olympia. Olympia sounds like Olympic, so use an image of the *Olympic* symbol to represent Olympia.

CHAIN STATES AND CAPITALS TOGETHER

Now chain the two images together. The more action you use in this chain, the better. Imagine a washing machine shaking all over the floor, with an Olympic symbol sticking out the lid and swirling around.

Washington (substitution: *washing* machine)
Olympia (substitution: *Olympic* symbol)

Now when someone asks, "What's the capital of Washington?" imagine your washing machine. What is sticking out of it? The Olympic symbol for Olympia.

Some states and capitals aren't as easy as Washington and Olympia. Difficult states and capitals have names that don't immediately bring an image to mind. For example, the state of New York and the capital of Albany require an additional technique, called *schmurgling*. Schmurgling means being sloppy when you say the word. Pretend you're chewing gum as you say the name of the state out loud. Does the schmurgled word sound remotely familiar to another word? Try it on New York. Doesn't it sound a little like *new yolk?* Next, schmurgle Albany, and you might hear *all bunny*. Now for the chain: Imagine a new yolk at the center of a broken egg, and bunnies throwing eggs at each other.

New York (substitution: *new yolk*)
Albany (substitution: *all bunny*)

When All Else Fails, Use Association

Sometimes it is hard to find a substitute image for a word, even with schmurgling. In these cases, use another mnemonic technique, association, in which one thing makes you think of another. Try it on New Mexico. The association for New Mexico is a *new sombrero,* a hat often associated with Mexico. Then use substitution on the capital, Santa Fe, which gives us *Santa* in his *sleigh*.

Chain the two pictures together, and you have a new sombrero landing on Santa in a sleigh.

New Mexico (association: *new sombrero*)
Santa Fe (substitution: *Santa's sleigh*)

WALK STUDENTS THROUGH THE STATE-CAPITAL CHAIN IMAGES

The state and capital system needs to be presented in a specific order for the best retention. The steps of presentation are critical. In the beginning, walk students through each step. Let's do it for Kentucky:

1. Say the name of the state out loud, "Kentucky."
2. Give students the substitution for Kentucky, *canned turkey.*
3. Have them repeat, "Kentucky sounds like canned turkey."
4. Now ask them to say the name of the capital, "Frankfort."
5. Tell them that the substitution for Frankfort is *franks* (hot dogs) made into a *fort.*
6. Have them repeat, "Frankfort sounds just like a frank fort."
7. Now present the image (there's a complete set of images in this chapter). The picture for Kentucky is *canned turkeys* (Kentucky) surrounded by a wall of *franks* forming a *fort* (Frankfort).

8. Have students take a mental snapshot of the picture, then tell them, "Close your eyes for ten seconds and keep the image of canned turkeys in a frank fort in your mind."

Teach the states and capitals in blocks of ten.

RETRIEVING STATE-CAPITAL CHAINS FROM MEMORY

After presenting ten state-capital chains, quiz students to make sure they retain the images. "What's the capital of Illinois?" "What's the capital of Maine?"

How they retrieve mnemonically stored information is important. Talk them through the process several times:

1. "When you hear Kentucky, ask yourself, What does Kentucky sound like? Say *canned turkey.*"
2. "Close your eyes and imagine canned turkeys."
3. Ask, "What is going on with these canned turkeys? What action or picture do you see attached to them?"
4. Tell them, "In your mind, you see the canned turkeys surrounded by a fort of hot dogs, *frank fort.*"
5. Have students say, "The canned turkeys are surrounded by a frank fort. Frankfort is the capital."

ENSURE THAT STUDENTS *SEE* THE IMAGES

If the state and capital memory system is to work, students need to be able to see the images with their eyes closed. To be sure they're visualizing the state-capital chain, ask them to make sketches of some of the state-capital chain images from memory. Drawing helps lock the relationships in their minds.

Puzzling Through the States

After presentation of the first ten states, students will understand the substitution-chain concept. You can simply continue the process until you have taught all fifty states. But here's an exercise that adds variety:

1. List the next ten state-capital pairs on a sheet of paper or blackboard.
2. Show one image that represents one of the listed state-capital pairs, but don't tell students what it is (students haven't seen these images yet). Explain that it's a puzzle.
3. Have them try to figure out which state and capital is represented.
4. If ten states is too hard or presents too many choices, reduce the number to three or five.

Presenting some of the state-capital chain images as puzzles encourages attentiveness. You still need to go through the memory sequence taught at the beginning of this chapter to fix the images in students' minds, but solving puzzles is fun. And as all teachers know, when learning is fun, you remember more.

In the previous exercise, you can divide students into teams and give each team the task of solving the puzzles. This social interaction increases the number of senses involved.

For some state-capital pairs, have children develop their own substitution images and chain them together. Stick with the easy states, ones where the names don't require much manipulation to create images (for example, Arkansas and Little Rock, Oregon and Salem, Washington and Olympia, Maine and Augusta, Idaho and Boise). Using the easiest states increases chances of success in early attempts to use substitution to create an image. Success builds confidence, and confidence encourages students to try the mnemonic techniques on other subjects. Have students share their creations with the class. Students often come up with brilliant substitutions.

IMAGES FOR STATES AND CAPITALS

In a moment you will see the substitution-chain images for all fifty states and their capitals. The following diagram explains how the state-capital cards are set up:

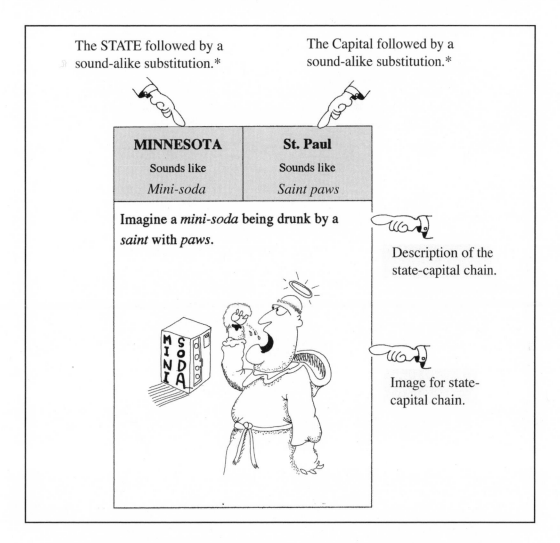

The STATE followed by a sound-alike substitution.*

The Capital followed by a sound-alike substitution.*

MINNESOTA	St. Paul
Sounds like	Sounds like
Mini-soda	*Saint paws*

Imagine a *mini-soda* being drunk by a *saint* with *paws*.

Description of the state-capital chain.

Image for state-capital chain.

The state-capital cards are in alphabetical order by state. For presentations to a class, photocopy the images and transfer them to plastic film for overhead-projection.

* Some states and capitals use the mnemonic technique of association. Others use substitution for the state and association for the capital or vice-versa. Explanations of these variations appear in the shaded boxes.

ALABAMA sounds like *Alley* and *bam*	**Montgomery** sounds like *Mountain* and *gum*	**ALASKA** sounds like *A lost key*	**Juneau** sounds like *Shoe* and *snow*

Imagine firecrackers in an *alley* going *bam*. The alley is filled with a *mountain* of *gum*.

Imagine Eskimos looking for *a lost key*. Nearby are *shoes* worn by a *snow* man.

ARIZONA sounds like *Arrow zone*	**Phoenix** sounds like *Feet* and *nicks*	**ARKANSAS** sounds like *Ark* and *saw*	**Little Rock** sounds like *Little rock*

Imagine arrows in an *arrow zone* marked by signs. *Feet* with *nicks* are in the zone.

Imagine Noah's *Ark* being *sawed* by a *little rock*.

CALIFORNIA sounds like *Cauliflower*	**Sacramento** sounds like *Sack of cement*	**COLORADO** sounds like *Cold radio*	**Denver** sounds like *Den* and *fur*

Imagine a *cauliflower* about to be smashed by a *sack of cement*.

Imagine a *cold radio* covered with icicles. Nearby is a *den* filled with *fur*.

CONNECTICUT sounds like *Cut a net*	**Hartford** sounds like *Heart* and *Ford*	**DELAWARE** sounds like *Deli* and *wire*	**Dover** sounds like *Dove* and *fur*

Imagine scissors *cutting a net* being held by a model T *Ford* covered with *hearts*.

Imagine a *deli*catessen with barbed *wire* going out the window. A *dove* in *fur* sits on the wire.

FLORIDA sounds like *Flower*	**Tallahassee** sounds like *Tall Lassie*	**GEORGIA** sounds like *George*	**Atlanta** sounds like *Ant land*

Imagine a man offering a *flower* to a *tall Lassie*.

Imagine *George* Washington on a dollar. An ant from *Ant Land* is holding the bill.

HAWAII sounds like *Highway*	**Honolulu** sounds like *Honey* and *loo loo*	**IDAHO** sounds like *Eye* and *hoe*	**Boise** sounds like *Boys*

Imagine a *highway* where *honey* drips on two *loos* (loo is the name for toilet in England).

Imagine an *eye* with a *hoe* in it. Two *boys* are trying to pull the hoe out.

ILLINOIS sounds like *Hilly* and *noses*	**Springfield** sounds like *Spring field*	**INDIANA** sounds like *Indian*	**Indianapolis** sounds like *Indian, apple,* and *ice*

Imagine *hilly* terrain covered with *noses* and *springs* in a *field*.

Imagine an *Indian* seated on an *apple* on a cube of *ice*.

IOWA sounds like *Eye water*	**Des Moines** sounds like *Day* and *mowing*	**KANSAS** sounds like *Cans*	**Topeka** sounds like *Toes* and *peek*

Imagine an *eye* dripping *water* on grass with a new *day's* sun pushing a *mower* over the grass.

Imagine *cans* with *toes peeking* out.

KENTUCKY sounds like *Can* and *turkey*	Frankfort sounds like *Frank* and *fort*	LOUISIANA sounds like *Little weasel*	Baton Rouge sounds like *Bat on rouge*

Imagine a *can* with *turkey* heads sticking out. This can is encircled by a hot dog *(frank) fort*.

Imagine a *little weasel* swinging a bat at a *bat on rouge*.

MAINE sounds like *Mane*	Augusta sounds like *A gust*	MARYLAND sounds like *Marry* and *land*	Annapolis sounds like *Apple* and *ice*

Imagine a horse's *mane* blown about by *a gust* of wind.

Imagine a couple *marrying* on an *apple* made of *ice*.

MASSACHUSETTS sounds like *Mass of chewed steps*	Boston sounds like *Boss* and *ton*	MICHIGAN sounds like *Mushy gun*	Lansing sounds like *Lance singing*

Imagine a *mass of chewed steps* being eaten by a *boss* who weighs a *ton*.

Imagine a bowl of *mush* with a *gun* shooting mush at a *singing lance*.

MINNESOTA sounds like *Mini-soda*	St. Paul sounds like *Saint Paws*	MISSISSIPPI sounds like *Miss sipping tea*	Jackson sounds like *Jacks* and *sun*

Imagine a *mini-soda* being drunk by a *saint* with *paws*.

Imagine a *miss sipping tea*. Out of the tea leap toy *jacks* and the *sun*.

MISSOURI sounds like *Misery* or *miss sewing*	**Jefferson City** sounds like *Chef and son*	**MONTANA** sounds like *Mountain*	**Helena** sounds like *hell*

Imagine a *miserable miss sewing* a *chef and his son* together.

Imagine a *mountain* with a devil on top. The devil, an association, represents *hell*.

NEBRASKA sounds like *New brass key*	**Lincoln** association a *Lincoln* penny	**NEVADA** sounds like *No water*	**Carson City** sounds like *Car, sun,* and *city*

Imagine a *new brass* key being inserted into a *penny* with *Lincoln's* face on it.

Imagine a *no water* sign hit by a *car* driven by the *sun* with a *city* in the background.

NEW HAMPSHIRE sounds like *New ham shirt*	Concord sounds like *Concorde* jet	NEW JERSEY sounds like *New Jersey* cow	Trenton sounds like *Tent on*

Imagine a pig (ham) wearing *new ham shirt*. He's getting off a *Concorde* jet.

Imagine a shiny *new jersey* cow wearing a *tent on* her back.

NEW MEXICO association *Sombrero*	Santa Fe sounds like *Santa's sleigh*	NEW YORK sounds like *New yolk*	Albany sounds like *All* and *bunny*

Imagine a *new sombrero,* to represent Mexico, landing on *Santa* as he sits in his *sleigh*.

Imagine the *yolk* of an egg surrounded by *all* these *bunnies* throwing eggs at each other.

N. CAROLINA association: *N. Pole* sounds like *Caroling*	**Raleigh** sounds like *Raw* and *lei*	**N. DAKOTA** association: *N. Pole* sounds like *Da' coat*	**Bismarck** sounds like *Bee's mark*

Imagine *North poles*, to represent North, *caroling*. They are wearing *raw* meat *leis*.

Imagine a *North pole*, to represent North, wearing *da' coat*, while a *bee marks* da' coat.

OHIO sounds like *Oh, hi, oh*	**Columbus** sounds like *Column* and *bus*	**OKLAHOMA** sounds like *Oak* and *home*	**Oklahoma City** sounds like *Oak, home,* and *city*

Imagine an *O* saying *Hi* to another *O*. They are standing on a *column* on a *bus*.

Imagine an *oak* tree filled with *homes*—a whole *city* of homes.

OREGON sounds like *Organ*	**Salem** sounds like *Sail*	**PENNSYLVANIA** sounds like *Pencils* and *vane*	**Harrisburg** sounds like *Hair* and *berg*

Imagine an *organ* with a *sail* mounted on top.

Imagine a *pencil* weather *vane*. A *hairy* man on an ice*berg* is underneath the weather vane.

RHODE ISLAND sounds like *Road island*	**Providence** sounds like *Pray for dents*	**S. CAROLINA** association: *Penguins* Sounds like *Caroling*	**Columbia** sounds like *Column* and *bees*

Imagine a *road* covered *island*. A man kneels on the road *praying for dents* in his car.

Imagine *penguins* to represent South. They are *caroling* on a *column* surrounded by *bees*.

S. DAKOTA association: *Penguins* sounds like *Da'coat*	**Pierre** sounds like *Pier*	**TENNESSEE** sounds like *Tennis* and *sea*	**Nashville** sounds like *Gnash* and *bill*
Imagine *penguins* to represent South. They are trying on *da'coats* on a *pier*.		Imagine a *tennis* game in the *sea*. Nearby ducks are *gnashing bills* in their bills.	
TEXAS sounds like *Tacks*	**Austin** sounds like *Ash* and *tin*	**UTAH** Sounds like *You tall*	**Salt Lake City** sounds like *Salt lake city*
Imagine *tacks* flying into an *ash*-filled *tin* can.		Imagine people saying to a tall person, "*You tall*." She's pouring *salt* into a *lake* near a city.	

VERMONT sounds like *Fur* and *mount*	**Montpelier** sounds like *Mount pail of hay*	**VIRGINIA** sounds like *Virgin*	**Richmond** sounds like *Rich man*

Imagine a *fur* covered *mount*. A nearby *mountain* has a *pail of hay* at the peak

Imagine the *Virgin* Mary talking to a *rich man*.

WASHINGTON sounds like *Washing*	**Olympia** sounds like *Olympic*	**W. VIRGINIA** association: *Cowboy* sounds like *Virgin*	**Charleston** sounds like *Charleston* dance

Imagine a *washing* machine with an *Olympic* symbol rattling around inside.

Imagine a *cowboy* outfit, for West, worn by *Virgin* Mary, who's near a *Charleston* dancer.

WISCONSIN sounds like *Whisk on sun*	**Madison** sounds like *Mad at his son*	**WYOMING** sounds like *Y humming*	**Cheyenne** sounds like *Shy ant*

Imagine a man holding a *whisk* broom on the *sun*. He's *mad at his son*.	Imagine a *Y humming* to a *shy ant*.

Games for Learning U.S. States and Capitals

The State-Capital Card Game

To play this game, you'll need to:

1. Photocopy all of the images for states and capitals (pages 314-326) onto heavy stock.
2. Cut out the state-capital images to make cards. You should have fifty cards.
3. Flip each card over onto the blank side, and write the name of the appropriate state.

Now you're ready to play. Lay out the cards, image side down. Players take turns choosing states. Let's say Player #1 chooses the state of Maine. Player #1 then announces the capital. Then she turns over the card to make sure she is correct. If correct, she keeps the card. If she made a mistake, she puts the card, image side down, back on the table.

If there isn't a lot of room to spread out the cards, stack them and have students take turns drawing a card from the pile. If they give the correct answer, they keep the card. If the answer is incorrect, slip the card back at the bottom of the deck of cards.

STATE PUZZLE GAMES

To teach the geographical location of a state, have children play with geographical puzzles. *Back to Basic Toys* sells a jumbo wooden puzzle of the United States for $21.95 (1-800-356-5360). On each puzzle piece is the name of the state, which you will want to cover with a piece of masking tape. On the under side of the puzzle piece, on another piece of tape, write the name of the state. Have the children try to assemble the puzzle, naming the states as they go along and checking the back of each puzzle piece to see if they are correct.

PLAYGROUND OF THE UNITED STATES

Some schools have painted maps of the United States on their playground. These oversized maps, which are about the size of a school bus, show the division lines between each state. To teach geography on the playground, first divide the class into two teams. Have one team line up on the Canadian side of the border and the other team on the Mexican side. Assign a number to each child. Then say, for example, "Numbers 2 and 8, Arkansas." Children 2 and 8 dash toward Arkansas. The first child there gets a point for her team. A variation on the game is for the teacher to shout out a capital, like "Little Rock," and for the children then to try to be the first one to the state where that capital is found.

26

Know Your Way Around the Seven Continents

In this chapter:

- Learn how to memorize a list of the seven continents from largest to smallest.

The seven largest pieces of land on our planet are called continents. In order of size, they are Asia, Africa, North America, South America, Antarctica, Europe, and Australia.

You can remember the continents in order of size by using the mnemonic techniques of association and chaining.

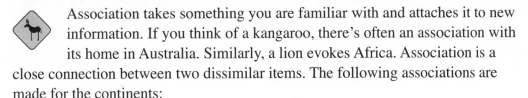

Association Technique for Memorizing the Continents

Association takes something you are familiar with and attaches it to new information. If you think of a kangaroo, there's often an association with its home in Australia. Similarly, a lion evokes Africa. Association is a close connection between two dissimilar items. The following associations are made for the continents:

Asia	Dragon
Africa	Lion
North America	Buffalo

South America	Rain Forest
Antarctica	Penguin
Europe	Eiffel Tower
Australia	Kangaroo

Chaining Continents Together

 To remember all seven continents in order from largest to smallest, chain the associations made up in the previous section into a story:

A dragon (Asia) blows its fiery breath at a lion (Africa). The flaming lion leaps onto a buffalo (North America) and they run into a rain forest (South America) to cool off. This strange sight frightens penguins (Antarctica) who waddle over to the Eiffel Tower (Europe) where kangaroos (Australia) are jumping off the top.

Four Habits That Affect Your Memory

In this chapter:

- Learn how mood affects memory.
- Discover three ways to develop a mood that helps memory.
- Learn how exercise helps memory.
- Find out what foods fuel a good memory.
- Find out how much sleep children need for an optimal memory.
- Learn a mnemonic technique for remembering the four habits that affect memory.

Mood, exercise, meals, and rest all affect memory. These effects are so entwined that it's sometimes hard to separate them.

Mood

Mood affects memory. Three things that affect your mood are:

- Self-esteem
- Beliefs
- Stress

If you have low self-esteem, your memory suffers. Consider this experiment: People were tested for their ability to remember nonsense syllables, then divided into two groups of equal ability. While one group was told that it was good at this memory task, the other was told it was inferior. When the groups were retested, even though they had initially performed equally well, the people in the group who thought they were superior performed better than the group who thought they were inferior. The results of this and similar experiments show that if you think you have a good memory, you'll usually remember better than if you think you have a bad memory.

Clearly, it makes sense to acknowledge when children demonstrate good memory. You might say, "Monica, we haven't seen the Solomons for a week, but you remembered both of their new kitties' names. Good memory!" By praising specific examples of good memory, you reinforce what a child might overlook. This reinforcement bolsters self-esteem and promotes future good performance. Beliefs strongly influence memory performance. Lots of people believe that you're either born with a good memory or not. Remember hearing people say, "I have a lousy memory for names"? Once this idea becomes a belief, no effort is made to remember names. Imagine what could happen if you could get these people to change their thinking to, "I have a lousy process for remembering names. If I could master a better process, I'd remember more names." Mastering a better process is exactly what's done in memory classes all the time. People who would even forget the name of their brother-in-law or next door neighbor are taught a process for remembering names. Using this process, they discover they can recall the names of ten, twenty, or more people they have just met. The skills taught here can change beliefs about memory. The child who learns forty-three U.S. presidents with chaining, or who memorizes the main points in a book, or who pegs the ten amendments to the Constitution has learned that memory can be improved by learning the right process.

Excessive stress also affects mood, which in turn affects memory. When you're exposed to long-term stress, chemicals are released that make it harder to recall information. Researcher Robert Sapolsky reports that glucocorticoids, which are released during periods of high stress, decrease a person's ability to retain long-term memories. These chemicals actually cause parts of the brain to shrivel. While damage caused by short-term exposure to glucocorticoids is reversible, long-term exposure may cause some of the nerve cells responsible for memory to die. Stresses in a child's life that might impede memory include:

- Parents divorced and hostile and disrespectful toward each other
- A hostile environment (e.g., parents often arguing)
- Socialization problems (e.g., having no friends and worrying about it)
- Concerns about school (e.g., emotional or physical safety)

Over time, stress can lead to depression. Depressed children also have a harder time learning. One of the diagnostic clues that a child is depressed is a diminished ability to concentrate. This may be due to rumination. Depressed children often return to thoughts that upset them, making it hard to focus on memory tasks. Restructuring the way people think is one way to help children who are facing a major life stress. *The Optimistic Child* and *Learned Optimism,* by Martin Seligman, offer methods for emotionally immunizing children against depression. The Penn Optimism Program is a school-based program designed to provide positive coping skills for stressful situations (e-mail jgillham@psych.upenn.edu for more information). You can help children develop better memories by helping them develop better moods.

A positive mood makes it easier to remember

Physical Exercise

Experiments comparing sedentary with active people suggest that exercising improves speed of recall and retention. Physical exercise does this in three ways:

- Lowers stress, which interferes with learning
- Releases nerve growth factors that stimulate brain cells
- Increases capillaries in the brain, resulting in more blood and oxygen reaching the brain

One reason that exercise may benefit memory is related to the mood change it promotes. In a National Institute of Mental Health study of over 1,900 people, those who did not exercise were twice as likely to have depressive symptoms as people who regularly did aerobic exercise.

Memory benefits can occur with a brisk walk of thirty minutes, five days a week. As with many other beneficial undertakings, doing too much can have an adverse effect and actually hamper memory.

A brisk walk, thirty minutes a day, five days a week, can help your memory

Missing Out on Exercise

According to the President's Council on Physical Fitness and Sports, only 36% of children in grades 1 through 12 get a daily thirty-minute aerobic workout.

Meals

Good nutrition is a volatile topic. Even nutritionists find it difficult to stay abreast of the research. One day the venerable four-tiered food pyramid is abruptly renovated to six levels with recommendations to eat enough fruit and vegetables to choke a fruit bat. Then we are told that fat is evil—the Darth Vader of the food empire. A little more research, and we find there's good fat and bad fat. Fish swims its way to the top of the protein list, but it turns out that only certain kinds of fish contain the good stuff. Then there's the mega-vitamin controversy. Article after article, even by Nobel laureates, promote taking mega-vitamins while government agencies report that vitamin supplements are a waste of money if you eat a balanced diet.

Considering nutrition's roller-coaster findings, it should come as no surprise that conclusions about the effects of nutrition on memory are also in a state of flux. Adding to the confusion are attempts to extrapolate research findings from rats to people, differences in metabolic and genetic factors among humans, metabolic changes that come with aging, and dubious research by manufacturers who sell "memory pills." Even researchers in the field admit that they take supplements, not because of irrefutable evidence, but because it's cheap insurance. In other words, what we think we know today may change tomorrow. Even so, here are some current ideas on the state of nutrition and memory.

Start with breakfast. In one study, students who regularly ate breakfast improved math scores by 40%. This makes sense. Brains need energy to work. If you skip breakfast, you are going from dinner all the way to lunch, about 16 hours without eating—a minifast. As blood sugar levels drop, your brain begins to run low on fuel needed for memory-intensive tasks. Fuel up with breakfast.

Missing Out on Breakfast

Between 1965 and 1991, the number of youths age 15 to 18 who ate breakfast had dropped from 90% to 75% among boys and from 84% to 65% among girls.

And not just any breakfast will do. As a general rule, before studying, eat low-fat proteins and a small serving of carbohydrates.

An exemplary memory-enhancing breakfast of low-fat protein and carbohydrates is: yogurt, soy milk, soy protein powder, a single egg, and old-fashioned oatmeal. An important benefit of this breakfast is that it's high in the amino acid tyrosine.

Tyrosine improves alertness. It's recommended by the National Academy of Sciences to help bomber pilots to stay awake and to maintain alertness for long assignments. Being wide awake and alert are good for your memory. But tyrosine's benefits are hampered by some foods.

A substance that knocks the wind out of tyrosine's sail is the amino acid tryptophan. Tryptophan competes with tyrosine for entrance to the brain. While tyrosine keeps you alert and awake, tryptophan does the opposite. It makes you feel relaxed and sleepy. Turkey is high in tryptophan. Maybe that's why Thanksgiving dinner makes you feel like having a nap afterward. Tryptophan is also found in carbohydrates like french fries, puffed wheat, and corn chips. Too many carbohydrates dull mental alertness. This doesn't mean that you should give up carbohydrates. But rather, study first, then eat carbohydrate-rich foods before going to sleep or before exercising.

Carbohydrates that raise blood glucose levels slowly are thought to be best for memory tasks. These are known as slow carbs (low glycemic index foods) as compared with fast carbs (high glycemic index foods). The glycemic index is an actual measure of the speed at which glucose levels rise in the blood stream. The glycemic index offers some surprising information. It turns out that white potatoes raise blood glucose faster than plain sugar and white bread raises it more rapidly than ice cream. The sugar spikes that occur in the blood from eating fast carbs may actually interfere with memory on a long-term basis and shove your spirits down into the pits. Examples of slow- and fast-carb foods follow:

SLOW CARBS	FAST CARBS
Apple	Corn flakes
Dried apricots	Instant rice
Banana	Vanilla cookies
Sourdough bread	Mashed potatoes
Oatmeal	Bagel
Brown rice	Dried dates
Spaghetti	Pretzels
Soybeans	French baguette
Nonfat fruit-flavored yogurt	Raisin bran
Orange juice	Crackers

For more information on slow- and fast-carb foods, read *The Glucose Revolution,* by Jennie Brand-Miller, Thomas Wolever, Stephen Colagiuri, and Kaye Foster-Powell.

Next we look at fat. Studies of animals eating saturated animal fat diets show related memory problems. Bad fats include bacon, sausage, hash browns, whole milk, butter, cheese, mayonnaise, fried food, and vegetable oils like corn oil.

But there are also good fats. Anecdotally, fish is known as brain food. It turns out that it is more complicated than that. The beneficial fats in fish are the omega-3 fatty acids. This substance may have long-term benefits to memory. But it isn't found in every fish. Fish high in omega-3 fatty acids include Chinook salmon,

Atlantic mackerel, Pacific herring, blue fin tuna, lake trout, and anchovies. Fish like cod, catfish, flounder, and swordfish are low in omega-3s. Pick your fish wisely.

What about vitamins and minerals? Studies show that giving children multivitamin and mineral supplements raises IQ. Multivitamin and mineral supplements raised intelligence scores of 6-year old children more than eight points compared with giving a placebo. Similar results have been found by giving older children vitamins. These results could be because many children miss important elements in their diet and are running on suboptimal levels of vitamins. The recommendation: multivitamins—as the doctors say, they're cheap insurance.

Finally, think about how much water you drink. Mild dehydration interferes with brain processing. *Health* magazine (June 2000) reported that more than half the nation is walking around in a chronic mildly dehydrated state. Soda, milk, and juices are no substitute for plain water. Drink eight to ten eight-ounce glasses of water every day.

This section has provided a peek into the nutritionist's pantry of food for the brain. There are often interactions between different kinds of food, which you need to understand in order to achieve nutritional balance. For a more in-depth overview of a wide range of food supplements, read *Your Miracle Brain,* by Jean Carper.

A memory-enhancing breakfast: soy milk,
nonfat yogurt, oatmeal, and an egg

Rest

Studies suggest that memory consolidation occurs during sleep. When test subjects were awakened as they fell into REM (rapid eye movement) sleep, recall of previously learned material dropped drastically. The Gesell Institute of Human Development recommends that 10-year olds get at least ten hours of sleep a night.

Students who went to bed after an evening of study remember more than students who cram all night. The best time to study may be before sleeping. One group of students who had studied before noon and were tested eight hours later remembered 9% of what they had learned. Another group of students studied prior to bedtime and after eight hours of sleep recalled 56% of what they had learned.

Studying While Asleep

While sleep may be necessary to fix information learned during wakeful study, there is no proof that you can learn during deep sleep. The U.S. Army spent lots of money to test this possibility. They found no evidence that educational tapes played during sleep resulted in learning.

Most children need at least ten hours
of sleep. Not getting enough sleep can hamper
memory processes.

Remembering the Four Habits That Affect Memory

I. To remember the four habits that affect memory let's use a version of the initial mnemonic technique. We want to remember that mood, exercise, meals, and rest all impact our memory. The first letter of each of these words could be put together to form an acronym, MEMR. But this phrase isn't particularly memorable. How about adding two filler words to create the phrase:

Mood, Exercise, Meals, or Rest—Yes!

The first letter for each word in this phrase spells the acronym:

M.E.M.O.R.Y.

To remember what affects your memory, go through each letter in the word *memory* to remind you of the phrase: Mood, Exercise, Meals, or Rest—Yes!

Become a Memory Black Belt

In this chapter:

• Start working on memory goals.

Anyone can read about karate. Skills that were once guarded secrets are now available in books. But knowing how a spinning 360-degree hook kick is done does not mean that you can do it. To master a martial art, students must follow a regime of diligent practice. The same goes for memory. Knowing how to use your memory does not mean that you can do it. It takes practice. This chapter contains a list of specific memory goals. Charting a child's progress through these levels will focus him on becoming a memory black belt.

The following list covers skills taught in this book. Page numbers on the list show where to go to find out more about a memory task. When students successfully master a skill—for example, demonstrating the use of the Say, See, Stick technique in memorizing the names of ten people—they earn 1 point. If it's a challenging skill, they earn more points (each skill is worth 1 point unless noted otherwise). Children track their progress on a chart at the end of the chapter.

Skills List

ITEM #	CATEGORY	PAGE
	Names	
1	❑ Meet 5 new people, and use each person's name 5 times during conversation.	42

2	☐ Put a phone book under your bed. Every morning, pick 10 names at random. Use the substitution technique on these names to turn them into something you can see (e.g., Jim = gym). Do this for one month. (5 points)	47–50
3	☐ Learn the names of 10 new people you meet this week—using the Say, See, Stick technique. If necessary, go out of your way to meet 10 new people.	53–56
4	☐ Find substitutions for the 60 most common American names.	57–58
Language Arts		
5	☐ Use the hide-and-seek technique on 25 spelling words.	70–71
6	☐ Use the helpful phrase or sentence technique on 25 spelling words.	71–72
7	☐ Use the vocabulary cartoon method to learn 25 vocabulary words.	73–76
8	☐ List 9 parts of grammar (nouns, pronouns, verbs, etc.) from memory and explain what they mean.	81–90
9	☐ Demonstrate the 5 movements that represent a period, comma, quotation marks, question mark, and exclamation point.	91–94
10	☐ Memorize the main points and examples in a book chapter that is 25 pages long. (Each set of 25 pages = 1 point; 50 pages = 2 points; 75 pages = 3 points.)	95–99
11	☐ Memorize the African Animal Facts chain.	101–108

12	❑ Learn 10 words in a foreign language using substitution. (An additional point is earned for each additional 10 words learned with this technique. When choosing words, consider using the list of The First 100 Words to Learn in a Foreign Language, in Chapter 10.)	111–114
Numbers		
13	❑ List the letters that are used to represent the numbers 0 to 9 in the simple consonant code (e.g., 1 = t).	143
14	❑ Using the consonant code, translate the following numbers into words: 71, 69, 995, 1492.	141–145
15	❑ Use the consonant code to turn 2 phone numbers into words.	141–145
16	❑ Learn the mnemonic method for memorizing the multiplication tables, starting with 2s and going to 9s. (3 points)	147–165
17	❑ Memorize the 100-peg mnemonic system. (3 points)	360–361
Science		
18	❑ Use the body peg system to list the planets in the solar system in order.	173–176
19	❑ Name the 2 eons of the Earth's history, followed by the eras, in order of earliest to most recent.	179–181
20	❑ Name the periods and epochs of the Earth's history in order of earliest to most recent.	181–182

21	❑ Using the Say, See, Stick technique, learn to recognize and name 18 rocks.	183–188
22	❑ Name 3 categories that are used to classify rocks, and list 3 rocks from each category.	188–193
23	❑ Identify 9 types of clouds from a chart.	205
24	❑ Give the acronym for the color order in a rainbow.	206–207
25	❑ Name the 5 layers of the Earth's atmosphere, in order.	207–208
26	❑ List the 6 functions that are necessary for something to be considered living.	209–210
27	❑ List the 5 kingdoms of biology.	214–216
28	❑ List the 7 classification categories used in biology, in order.	218–219
29	❑ List 9 cellular components and their functions.	222–234
30	❑ Name 10 dinosaurs from their pictures.	239–248
31	❑ Name 20 bones found in the human body.	259–265
History		
32	❑ List 43 presidents of the United States, in order.	276–277
33	❑ Explain the first 10 amendments of the U.S. Constitution.	281–294
Geography		
34	❑ Provided with a list of the 50 U.S. states, write down the corresponding capitals.	314–326

35	❑ List the 7 continents in order from smallest to largest.	329–330
Habits		
36	❑ List 4 habits that affect your memory.	340
Extra Credit (some suggestions)		
37	❑ List the 9 mnemonic techniques covered in this book and give an example of each.	36–37
38	❑ Use memory techniques to memorize a list of the major lakes of the world: Great Salt Lake, Lake Superior, Lake Michigan, Lake Huron, Lake Erie, Lake Ontario, Lake Titicaca, Caspian Sea, Aral Sea, Lake Chad, Lake Victoria, Lake Tanganyika.	
39	❑ Name the capitals of 30 countries.	
40	❑ List 7 areas of the brain (frontal lobe, parietal lobe, occipital lobe, cerebellum, medulla, pons, and temporal lobe) and their functions.	
41	❑ Learn to recognize 20 great paintings and the artists.	
42	❑ Memorize 3 mathematical constants, like pi or the speed of light.	
43	❑ Memorize 100 pages in a *National Geographic* magazine, so that you can recall what pictures are on which pages. Use the peg mnemonic system. (First you need to memorize the 100 peg mnemonic system in Appendix 3.) (3 points)	
44	❑ Choose your own subject to memorize.	

Achievement-Level Chart

In the martial arts, students practice skills going from simple to complex. As skills are mastered, students are tested. A successful test results in a new ranking denoted by colored belts. A black belt recognizes a high performance level. The following chart, similar to the martial arts method of tracking progress, will help students make a goal to become a Memory Black Belt.

MEMORY SKILLS RANK	POINTS
White	1–3
Grey	4–7
Yellow	8–11
Orange	12–15
Green	16–19
Purple	20–23
Blue	24–27
Brown	28–31
Red	32–35
Red-Black stripe	36–39
Black	40+

Appendix

French Foreign Language Game

In chapter 10, Spanish is used to illustrate mnemonic principles as applied to learning a foreign language. Here's the same information using French. This section contains a referee sheet and cards to play the French foreign language game. Refer to Chapter 10 for information on playing the game.

FRENCH LANGUAGE REFEREE SHEET AND GAME CARDS

Each section of the French language referee sheet begins with an illustration. This drawing represents the substitution image stuck to the item it represents.

Word in French
(phonetic pronunciation)
item represented

Substitution explanation

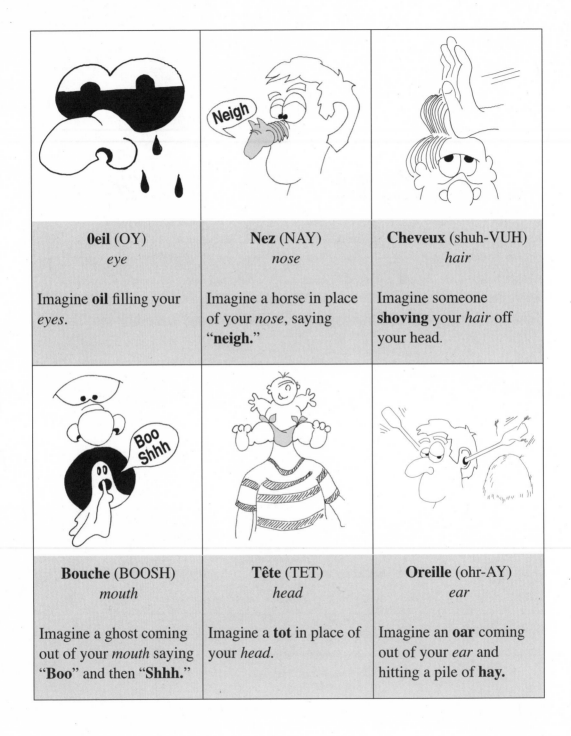

Oeil (OY)
eye

Imagine **oil** filling your *eyes*.

Nez (NAY)
nose

Imagine a horse in place of your *nose*, saying "**neigh.**"

Cheveux (shuh-VUH)
hair

Imagine someone **shoving** your *hair* off your head.

Bouche (BOOSH)
mouth

Imagine a ghost coming out of your *mouth* saying "**Boo**" and then "**Shhh.**"

Tête (TET)
head

Imagine a **tot** in place of your *head*.

Oreille (ohr-AY)
ear

Imagine an **oar** coming out of your *ear* and hitting a pile of **hay.**

Main (MEN)
hand

Imagine five **men** on your *hand*.

Bras (BRA)
arm

Imagine a **bra** draped over your *arm*.

Poitrine (pwa-TREEN)
chest

Imagine **paws** on a **train** on your *chest*.

Estomac (es-toe-MA)
stomach

Imagine an **S** on your *stomach*.

Genou (jhuh-NU)
knee

Imagine **jeans** that are **new** on your *knee*.

Jambe (JHAMB)
leg

Imagine a jar of **jam** in place of each *leg*.

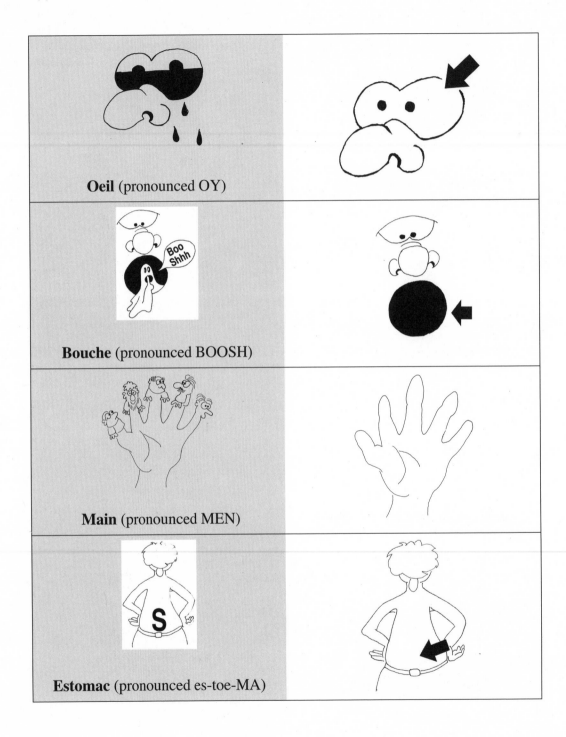

Oeil (pronounced OY)

Bouche (pronounced BOOSH)

Main (pronounced MEN)

Estomac (pronounced es-toe-MA)

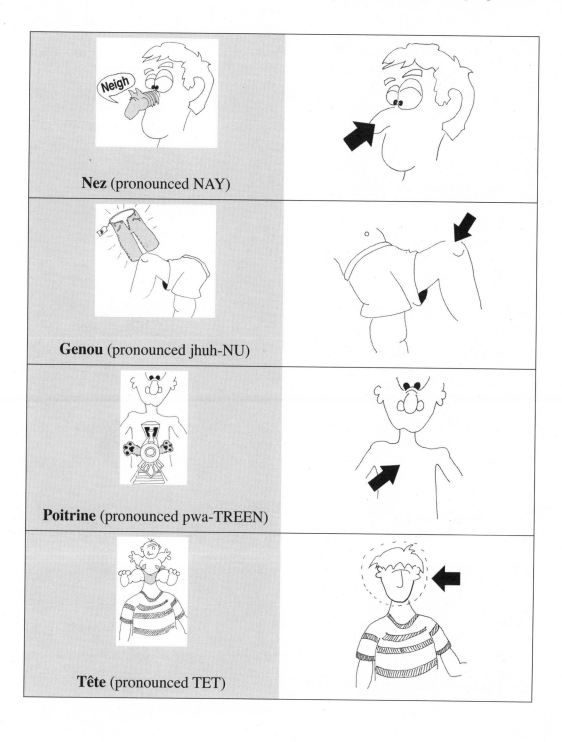

Nez (pronounced NAY)

Genou (pronounced jhuh-NU)

Poitrine (pronounced pwa-TREEN)

Tête (pronounced TET)

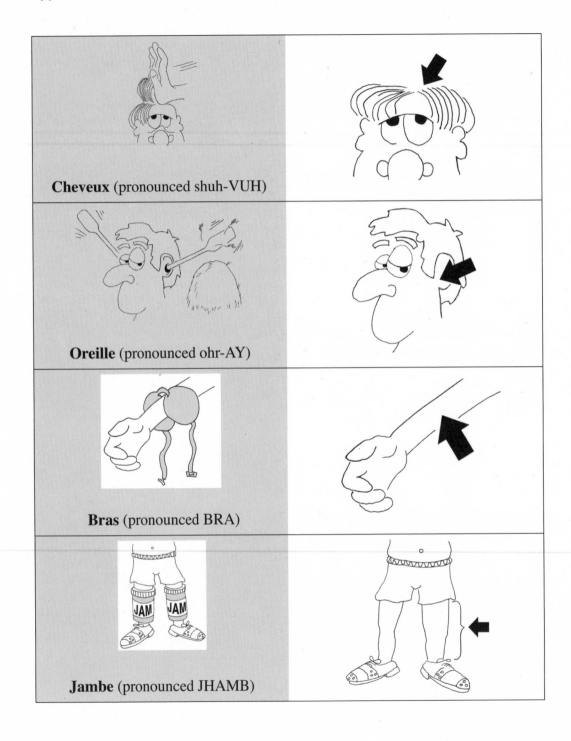

Cheveux (pronounced shuh-VUH)

Oreille (pronounced ohr-AY)

Bras (pronounced BRA)

Jambe (pronounced JHAMB)

Appendix

Auditory Chart for Learning Numbers

Auditory-leaning students prefer to learn through their ears. They may find these charts easier to memorize than the visual-oriented charts presented in Chapter 11. The following chart focuses on rhyming a number with a concrete object: Zero is a Cheerio®, 1 is a bun, 2 is a shoe, 3 is a tree, and so on. In this case, rhyming makes it easy to relate numbers to more familiar items.

As with the visual set of pictograms, there are suggested physical movements to benefit kinesthetic memory. Refer to Chapter 11 for an explanation of how to use the kinesthetic portion of the chart.

0	**1**	**2**	**3**	**4**
Cheerio®	Bun	Shoe	Tree	Door
Roll a Cheerio® with your fingers	Eat a bun	Put on a shoe	Climb a tree	Open a door

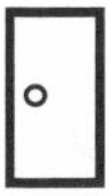

5	6	7	8	9
Hive	Sticks	Heaven	Gate	Sign
Lick honey off your fingers	Rub two sticks together	Look up to heaven	Latch a gate	Wave a sign

Appendix

C

The Original Consonant Code

To understand this appendix, you need to have read Chapter 12. The consonant code presented in Chapter 12 is a simplified version of the original. The original code requires more effort to learn, but it offers advantages. It provides more letter choices when translating numbers into words. This makes it easier to come up with words that evoke images. As mentioned throughout the book, words that readily bring images to mind are easier to remember. The simple code was presented first so that you could make the transition to the original code with the least difficulty. But some of the rules are different.

In the simple version of the code, each digit is assigned a single letter. The original code is based on a different principle.

Rule 1 of the original consonant code:

Specific consonant sounds are assigned to numbers.

Assigning consonant sounds means assigning more than one letter to some numbers. A consonant sound is a basic speech sound produced by the partial or complete obstruction of the air stream by the vocal apparatus. Say the letter *T* out loud. Notice how your tongue taps just behind your top front teeth. Now make the *D* sound. You feel your tongue tap just behind your top teeth. This results in a sound similar to the one you produced for a *T*. In the original code, letter sounds that are similar are grouped with one digit.

Thus the number 1 is represented by both a *T* and a *D*.

$$1 = T \text{ or } D$$

Number 2 is represented by a single letter.

$$2 = N$$

The rationale for a single letter in this case is because none of the other consonants are similar to the *N* sound.

Numbers 3 through 5 are also represented by single letter sounds.

$$3 = M$$
$$4 = R$$
$$5 = L$$

The number 6 is represented by many letters because the letters or letter combinations have similar consonant sounds. Remember, it's a specific sound that's assigned to a digit. Letters are merely symbols for that sound. If more than one letter represents a sound, those letters are grouped with the number, as in the case of the number 6.

$$6 = J \text{ or Sh or Ch or soft G, as in gem}$$

Make a *j, sh, ch,* and soft *g* sound. Notice how your mouth makes the same movement for each sound. This is why number 6 gets more than one letter.

The number 7 is represented by four letters with similar sounds.

$$7 = K \text{ or hard C, as in cold, or hard G, as in golf, or Q}$$

Try saying the letter *k*. Notice how you make the sound. Your throat constricts and then allows an explosive rush of air. This same movement is made for the hard C, hard G, and Q sounds. That's why they're all grouped with the number 7.

The number 8 is represented by two letters.

$$8 = F \text{ or V}$$

The number 9 is represented by two letters.

$$9 = P \text{ or } B$$

The digit 0 is represented by three letters.

$$0 = S \text{ or } Z \text{ or soft } C \text{ as in celery}$$

PEGGING THE CONSONANT CODE

Now that you understand how the code works, here's a method for committing the code to memory using mnemonic techniques almost identical to those found in Chapter 12.

Digit	Consonant Sound	Mnemonic Aid
1	T or D	T and D have *one* down stroke
2	N	N has *two* down strokes—or, it looks like a 2 turned on its side
3	M	M has *three* down strokes—or, it looks like a 3 turned on its side
4	R	R looks like a backwards 4—or, a golfer saying *Fore!* Remember the R in four
5	L	The roman numeral for 50 is L—or, hold up your left hand and stick out your thumb so that your index finger and thumb make the outline of an L (five fingers on hand)

6	J or Sh or Ch or soft G	A cursive J is a mirror image of 6
7	K or hard G	Look closely at a capital K and notice that it's made of two 7s
8	F or V	A cursive F has two loops, like an 8
9	P or B	P is a mirror image of 9
0	S or Z	Both Z in zero and an S looks like a backwards Z

In the simple code, words are built with the vowels *a, e, i, o,* and *u,* as well as the letters *y* and *w.* The original code works the same way but with the addition of the letter *h.*

> **Rule 2 of the original code:**
>
> Some letters have no value. This includes the vowels a, e, i, o, u, and the letters w, h, and y.

Even though some letters have no value, they serve the important role of helping to build words. For example, the number 3 is represented by the letter *m.* By adding valueless letters, the *m* can be turned into words like *ham, me,* or *ma.* To translate this coded word back into a number, look at the first letter that has value in the word; for *ma* that would be the *m,* which equals 3. The *a* in *ma* has no value, so you know that *ma* represents the number 3.

WORKING WITH THE ORIGINAL CONSONANT CODE

Let's turn some numbers into words. Say you want to remember a street number, 3451. First, using the consonant code, translate the numbers into letters.

$$3 = M, 4 = R, 5 = L, \text{ and } 1 = T \text{ or } D$$

The translation of 3451 into letters leaves us with MRLT or MRLD. Let's go with MRLD. At this point the valueless letters come in handy. Insert one or more of the letters *(a, e, i, o, u, w, h,* and *y)* into MRLD to make a word. One possibility is eMeRaLD. To remember the street number, you could visualize an emerald at your destination. When you need the street number, translate the letters in the word *emerald* back into numbers.

e = no value, M = 3, e = no value, R = 4, a = no value, L = 5, D = 1

Now use the code on a number where digits have more than one possible letter to represent them. This time let's try the technique on a friend's telephone number: 918-1014. Again, you start by translating the numbers into letters:

9 = P or B, 1 = T or D, 8 = F or V, 1 = T or D, 0 = S or Z, 1 = T or D, 4 = R

Notice that some numbers, like 9, give you two letter choices. When you have a choice, it's easiest to just choose the first letter. If 9 is the number, and you have a choice of P or B, go with the P. If you have trouble constructing a word, then use your next letter choice. The telephone number 918-1014 translates into the letters PTFDSTR. Now insert valueless letters to create a word or words. One possibility is PeT FooD StoRe. Make an image of your friend working at the counter of a *pet food store.* As with other mnemonic techniques, words that readily bring an image to mind are more memorable. When you need the telephone number, translate the letters in the words *pet food store* back into numbers:

P = 9, e = no value, T = 1, F = 8, o = no value, o = no value,
D = 1, S = 0, T = 1, o = no value, R = 4, e = no value

There's one more rule:

Rule 3 of the original code:

When using the code to turn a number into letters, if the resulting word has silent letters, those letters don't count as numbers.

This means that if you're using the code to translate the number 539 into a word, *lamb* is not an acceptable word. The *b* is silent in *lamb,* so it doesn't represent the 9. This is a sound-based system, so if you don't hear it, it doesn't count. The word *LaMb* equals 53 in the original code. An appropriate word for the number 539 would be *LaMP*. That's because you hear all the consonants in the word *lamp*. This is also the reason that double letters in a word are often worth only one digit. The number 955 is not represented by the word *PiLl*, because the second *l* is silent. *PiLl,* in the original code, is equal to 95. An appropriate translation of the number 955 would be *PiLLow,* in which you hear both *L*s.

Again, the advantage of the original consonant code over the simplified version is that it offers more letter choices to build words. In the simple consonant system, if you were trying to remember the date for the end of the Civil War, 1865, you might come up with these words: eaT FiJi Luau. The original system gives lots more choices, such as DoVe JaiL. Imagine union and confederate soldiers releasing a dove from jail to mark the end of the war.

The following chart shows number translations from 1 to 103. Letters in each word that represent a digit are bold capitals. Remember that silent letters in a word have no value (e.g., the silent *k* in the word *knife* does not represent a digit).

CONVERTING NUMBERS INTO WORDS WITH THE ORIGINAL CONSONANT CODE

1.	Tie	10.	ToeS	19.	TuB
2.	Noah	11.	ToT	20.	NoSe
3.	Moo	12.	TiN	21.	NeT
4.	Rye	13.	ToMb	22.	NuN
5.	Law	14.	TiRe	23.	NaMe
6.	Jay	15.	ToweL	24.	NeRo
7.	Key	16.	DeeJay	25.	NaiL
8.	iVy	17.	DoG	26.	gNaSH
9.	Pie	18.	DoVe	27.	NecK

28.	kNiFe	53.	LooM	78.	CaVe		
29.	kNoB	54.	LyRe	79.	CoB		
30.	MouSe	55.	LiLy	80.	VaSe		
31.	MuD	56.	LodGe	81.	FooT		
32.	MooN	57.	LaKe	82.	FiN		
33.	MiMe	58.	LoaF	83.	FoaM		
34.	MoweR	59.	LiP	84.	FiRe		
35.	MaiL	60.	CHeeSe	85.	FLy		
36.	MuSH	61.	JeT	86.	FiSH		
37.	MiKe	62.	GeNie	87.	FoG		
38.	MoVie	63.	GeM	88.	FiFe		
39.	MaP	64.	JaR	89.	ViP		
40.	RoSe	65.	JaiL	90.	BuS		
41.	RoD	66.	CHooCHoo	91.	BaT		
42.	RaiN	67.	JocK	92.	BoNe		
43.	RaM	68.	CHeF	93.	BuM		
44.	RR (train)	69.	SHiP	94.	BeaR		
45.	ReeL	70.	KiSs	95.	BeLl		
46.	RoaCH	71.	CoT	96.	BeaCH		
47.	RocK	72.	CoiN	97.	BooK		
48.	RooF	73.	CoMb	98.	PuFf		
49.	RoPe	74.	CaR	99.	PiPe		
50.	LaCe	75.	CoaL	100.	DaiSieS		
51.	LooT	76.	CaGe	101.	TeST		
52.	LooN	77.	CoKe	102.	DoZeN		

A CONSONANT PEGGING SYSTEM

  Look at the preceding chart. Notice that it's a pegging system. Specific images are assigned to numbers. There are several uses for this pegging system. But first the consonant pegging system must be memorized. To do this, use the mnemonic technique of chaining. Imagine a *tie* (1) worn by *Noah* (2) who greets a *moo* (3) cow with a loaf of *rye* (4) in its mouth and so on.

Memorization of this pegging system gives students a rapid-fire imagery system for numbers. Let's say you're given the telephone number (394) 257-9286. You could use the mnemonic method described earlier to remember this number. You would translate each number into letters, then assemble those letters into words. Here's an alternative method, a short cut. Divide the telephone number into digit pairs: 39-42-57-92-86. Now apply the images from the consonant pegging system to these digit pairs. The number 39 is MaP. The number 42 is RaiN. By assigning words to all the digit pairs, you get MaP-RaiN-LodGe-BoNe-FiSH. These images are committed to memory with a quick mnemonic chain: a *map* in the *rain* is near a *lodge* occupied by a *bone fish*. You now have the telephone number memorized.

This pegging system can also be used like a mental filing cabinet. Say you're taking chemistry. You decide to memorize the Periodic Table of Elements, in which all the elements are arranged in numeric order and atomic number, starting at 1. The process for memorizing this table, using the element helium as an example, follows:

1. Turn elements into images. The element helium could be represented by a helium-filled balloon.
2. Find the atomic number for the element. Helium's atomic number is 2.
3. Translate the atomic number into an image. The number 2 is represented by Noah.
4. Combine images. Imagine Noah handing out helium balloons to the animals as they enter the ark.

When you want to remember the second element in the periodic table, you think, "Two is represented by Noah. What's he doing? Oh yes, he's handing out helium balloons. The element is helium."

Some elements lend themselves to an immediate image: carbon, gold, aluminum, and neon. Other elements are harder to visualize: lithium, nitrogen, boron, and sodium. Use the mnemonic technique of substitution for difficult elements. Lithium sounds like light-thumb. Imagine a lit-up thumb. Nitrogen sounds like night-Trojan. Imagine a dark night occupied by a Trojan horse. The consonant pegging system enables students to do what many would view as an impossible memory task.

Bibliography

Adler, Bill. *The Student's Memory Book*. New York: Doubleday, 1988.

> A practical memory resource for students in high school and college. Covers the use of memory techniques for such topics as chemistry, economics, biology, physics, and history.

Arnot, Robert. *The Biology of Success*. Little, Brown and Company, 2000.

> Covers such topics as diet, exercise, mood, and circadian rhythm for optimum performance.

Atherton, Herbert M., and Barlow, Jackson J., eds. *The Bill of Rights and Beyond 1791–1991*. The commission on the bicentennial of the United States Constitution.

Bolla, K. I.; Lindgren, Karen N.; Bonaccorsy, Cathy; and Bleecker, Margit L. "Memory Complaints in Older Adults: Fact or Fiction?" *Archives of Neurology* 48 (1991): 61–64.

Brand-Miller, Jennie; Wolever, Thomas M. S.; Colagiuri, Stephen; and Foster-Powell, Kaye. *The Glucose Revolution: The Authoritative Guide to the Glycemic Index, The Ground Breaking Medical Discovery*. New York: Marlowe & Company, 1996.

Burchers, Sam; Burchers, Max; and Burchers, Bryan. *Vocabutoons: Vocabulary Cartoons*. Florida: New Monic Books, 1997.

————. *Vocabulary Cartoons*. Florida: New Monic Books, 1998.

Buzan, Tony. *Use Your Perfect Memory*. 3d rev. ed. Plume, 1991.

Carper, Jean. *Your Miracle Brain*. HarperCollins, 2000.

> Information on how nutritional supplements affect the brain.

Corinda. *Thirteen Steps to Mentalism*. Brooklyn, New York: D. Robbins and Co. Inc., 1996.

> Mnemonic techniques employed by magicians.

Crook, Thomas, and Allison, Christine. *How to Remember Names*. HarperCollins Publishers, 1991.

> A practical approach to remembering people's names, loaded with examples and practice techniques.

DePorter, Bobbi, and Hernacki, Mike. *Quantum Learning: Unleashing the Genius in You*. Dell, 1992.

Dilts, Robert. *Spelling for NLP Practitioners*. Dynamic Learning Publications, 1990.

> A sixteen-page booklet on neurolinguistic programming spelling strategy and the reasoning for its effectiveness.

Ehri, L.; Deffner, N.; and Wisce, I. "Pictorial Mnemonics for Phonics." *Journal of Educational Psychology* 76 (5) (1984): 880–893.

Ericsson, K. A.; Chase, W. G.; and Faloon, S. "Acquisition of a Memory Skill." *Science* vol 208 (1980): 1181–1182.

Faber, Barry. *How to Learn Any Language*. Citadel Press, 1991.

> Memory techniques used by a man who is fluent in 25 languages.

Fry, Edward. *1000 Instant Words*. Laguna Beach Educational Books, 1994.

Goddin, Nell. *Grammar Smart: A Guide To Perfect Usage (The Princeton Review)*. Palma, Erik, ed. New York: Random House, 1993.

Gordon, Barry. *Memory: Remembering and Forgetting in Everyday Life*. A Mastermedia Book, 1995.

> Worried about your memory? Read this book. Explains the malleability of memory. Memory is not a solid file cabinet of information. Contains tests to determine if you have average memory problems.

Gordon, P., Valentine, E., and Wilding, J. "One Man's Memory: A study of a mnemonist." *British Journal of Psychology* 75 (1984):1–14.

Grinder, Michael. *Righting the Educational Conveyor Belt*. Portland, Oregon: Metamorphous Press, 1991.

> This book focuses on the process of teaching and the importance of using visual, auditory, and kinesthetic techniques to get ideas across.

Gruneberg, Michael M. *Link Word Spanish by Association*. Lincolnwood, Illinois: Passport Books, 1994.

> Turns memory theory into practical techniques for learning a foreign language. You can pick up hundreds of words and basic grammar in about twelve hours. Other books in the series cover French, German, and Italian.

Halacy, D. S. *Man and Memory*. Harper & Row Publishers, 1970.

Hermine, Hilton. *The Executive Memory Guide*. New York: Simon & Schuster Audio Division, 1989.

> One audio tape

Hersey, William D. *Blueprints for Memory: Your Guide to Remembering Business Facts, Figures, and Faces*. American Management Association, 1990.

Higbee, K. L., and Kenneth, L. *Your Memory: How It Works and How to Improve It*. Prentice Hall Press, 1988.

> Research on memory and techniques for improvement. Discusses specifically why mnemonics works and yet is not a standard part of school curriculums.

Higbee, K. L. "Novices, apprentices, and mnemonists: Acquiring expertise with the phonetic Mnemonic." *Applied Cognitive Psychology* 11 (2) (1997): 147–161.

Hirsch, E. D., Jr., ed. *What Your First Grader Needs to Know*. New York: Doubleday, 1991.

———. *What Your Second Grader Needs to Know: Fundamentals of a good second-grade education*. New York: Doubleday, 1991.

———. *What Your Third Grader Needs to Know: Fundamentals of a good third-grade education*. New York: Doubleday, 1992.

———. *What Your Fourth Grader Needs to Know: Fundamentals of a good fourth-grade education*. New York: Doubleday, 1992.

———. *What Your Fifth Grader Needs to Know: Fundamentals of a good fifth-grade education*. New York: Doubleday, 1993.

———. *What Your Sixth Grader Needs to Know: Fundamentals of a good sixth-grade education*. New York: Doubleday, 1993.

Howard, Pierce J. *The Owner's Manual for the Brain: Everyday Applications from Mind-Brain Research*. 2nd ed. Austin, Texas: Bard Press, 2000.

Johnson, George. *In The Palaces of Memory*. New York: Vintage Books, 1991.

Lorayne, Harry, and Lucas, Jerry. *The Memory Book*. New York: Stein and Day, 1974.

> A classic on memory. During the Johnny Carson Late Night Show era, Lorayne made appearances during which he demonstrated skills such as remembering everyone's name in the audience. Lucas was a National Basketball Association All-Star. Back-and-forth dialog between these two experts makes for a readable introduction to memory skills.

Lorayne, Harry. *Page a Minute Memory Book*. New York: Ballantine Books, 1985.

———. *Super Memory, Super Student*. Little, Brown and Company, 1990.

Luria, A. R. *The Mind of a Mnemonist*. Translated by Lynn Solotaroff. Cambridge, Massachusetts: Harvard University Press, 1968.

> Part psychology and part history of a man with a phenomenal memory.

Martin, Gary, and Pear, Joseph. *Behavior Modification*. 4th ed. New Jersey: Prentice-Hall, Inc., 1978.

Meish, Goldish. *Making Multiplication Easy*. New York: Scholastic Professional Books, 1991.

Michalko, Michael. *Cracking Creativity: The Secrets of Creative Genius*. Berkeley, California: Ten Speed Press, 1998.

Minninger, Joan. *Total Recall, How to Boost Your Memory Power*. Emmanus, Pennsylvania: Rodale Press, 1984.

> A good mix of theory and practical uses of mnemonics.

Reid, Struan. *Improve Your Memory Skills*. Edited by Stockley, C. London: Usborne Publishing, 1988.

Rupp, Rebecca. *Committed to Memory: How we remember and why we forget.* New York: Crown Publishers, 1998.

> Beautifully written prose and stories make the topic of memory come to life.

Samuels, Mike, and Samuels, Nancy. *Seeing with the Mind's Eye.* Random House, 1975.

Sapolsky, Robert. *Biology and Human Behavior: The Neurological Origins of Individuality.* Springfield, Virginia: The Teaching Company, The Great Courses on Tape, 1998.

> Four audio-cassette tapes. Technical explanation of how memory works at a cellular and biochemical level. Leaves the listener with an appreciation for how little we know.

Searleman, Alan, and Herrmann, Douglas. *Memory from a Broader Perspective.* McGraw Hill, 1994.

Seligman, Martin. *Learned Optimism.* New York: Pocket Books, 1990.

————. *The Optimistic Child.* Boston: Houghton Mifflin Company, 1995.

Spence, Jonathan D. *The Memory Palace of Matteo Ricci.* New York: Elisabeth Sifton Books, Viking, 1985.

Tennesen, Michael. "Water Works." *Health* (June 2000): 89–94.

Thompson, Charles P.; Cowan, Thaddeus; Frieman, Jerome; Mahadevan, Rajan S.; Vogl, Rodney J.; and Frieman, Jeanne. "Rajan: A study of a memorist." *Journal of Memory and Language* 30 (1991): 702–724.

Trudeau, Kevin. *Mega Memory.* Niles, Illinois: Nightingale Conant Corporation, 1992.

> Nine audio-cassette tapes.

Wendon, Lyn. *Letterland Programme One Teacher's Guide*. Cambridge, England: Letterland International, 1997.

> A memory-literate approach to teaching children how to read. Possibly the best phonics material on the market.

Yates, Frances. *The Art of Memory*. Chicago: The University of Chicago Press, 1996.

> A scholarly work on the origin of classical memory systems and how they impacted people from 500 BC up through the renaissance and Elizabethan England. Tells of Peter of Ravenna who used loci systems to remember such things as, "…two hundred speeches or sayings of Cicero, three hundred sayings of the philosophers, twenty thousand legal points."

Memory Skills, Program One, Associations. A BBC-TV production in association with Ambrose Video Publishing Inc., New York:1994.

Memory Skills, Program Three, Sequences. A BBC-TV production in association with Ambrose Video Publishing Inc., New York:1994.

> The videos in this series are an interesting but superficial introduction to memory skills.

Index

A

acronyms 28, 206
acrostics 28, 219
addresses 131
amendments 2; *see also* Bill of Rights
amnesia, infantile 10
aroma 32
association 9, 12, 36, 38
 continents 329–330
 defined 25–26
 functions of life 210
 logical 20
 states and capitals 307, 309–310, 313,
  320–325
 symbol 35
atmosphere layers
 exosphere 207–208
 mesosphere 207–208
 stratosphere 207–208
 thermosphere 207–208
 troposphere 207–208
auditory
 pegs 354
 processors 30

B

Bill of Rights 279, 294–296, 299, 304
 amendments 279–280, 290, 297, 295
  1st 282–283, 297, 299
  2nd 283–284, 294, 297, 300
  3rd 284, 297, 299, 300
  4th 285, 297, 300
  5th 286–287, 290, 297, 300–301
  6th 288–289, 297, 301–302
  7th 290, 297, 302
  8th 291, 297-298, 302–303
  9th 292–293, 297, 303
  10th 292–294, 297, 303

Bill of Rights game, advanced 298,
 304
Bill of Rights game, beginner 295–296
bomber pilots 336
Botswana 1
brain capacity 96
Brand-Miller, Jennie 337
buffalo, cape 102
Burchers, Sam 73

C

Camillo's memory theater 19
capitals
 Albany 309, 321
 Annapolis 318
 Atlanta 316
 Augusta 312, 318
 Austin 324
 Baton Rouge 318
 Bismarck 322
 Boise 312, 316
 Boston 319
 Carson City 320
 Charleston 325
 Cheyenne 326
 Columbia 323
 Columbus 322
 Concord 321
 Denver 315
 Des Moines 317
 Dover 315
 Frankfort 307, 310–311, 318
 Harrisburg 323
 Hartford 315
 Helena 320
 Honolulu 316

Acknowledgments

With special appreciation to: Ellen McNeil, my wife and partner, who patiently read, listened to, and advised me during the decade of development and revisions that went into this book; the LITs (leaders in training) at Deer Crossing Camp, who tested my first memory tools; all the parents who took my adult education super memory classes so they could help their children improve study skills; Sandy Randles, who encouraged me to present my first child-parent seminars and then made the program a reality for years by doing all the organization and promotion to come up with forty participant families; Dr. Robert Pruitt, principal extraordinaire, who supported my fledgling workshops by both booking and participating in the activities with his students and their parents; all the principals, vice principals, teachers, and parent coordinators who supported the workshops that are the foundation for the book, especially: Tony Byrd, Maria Clemo, Jackie DeVille, Bob Enz, Linda Kakes, Jeri Kazmierczak, Cindy McCarthy, Debra Negrete, Susan Olsen, and Lisa Pruitt; the readers of my first rough draft, many of whom have already been mentioned, whose comments helped the revision process: Diane Birkeness, Taran Gagné, Diane Keith, Lois Lazar, and Mary Phoenix; all the students in my super memory classes at Williams Elementary, Farnham Elementary, Hacienda Elementary, Rancho Elementary, Laurelwood Elementary, Graystone Elementary, Encinal Elementary, Oak Knoll Elementary, Randol Elementary, Norwood Creek Elementary, Rachel Carson Elementary, Willow Glen Elementary, Silver Oak Elementary, and Cedar Grove Elementary; and Diana Morley, my enthusiastic editor and proofreader who was talking to friends about the book before it was even printed.

About the Author

Jim Wiltens lives with his wife and son in Redwood City, California, for part of the year and the California High Sierra for the other part. During the school year, he coaches students in Gifted and Talented Education (G.A.T.E.) programs, provides teacher in-services, talks to school assemblies, and works with corporate groups. His topics include super memory practice, leadership skills, goal setting, creativity, and specialized classroom enrichment programs in the sciences and writing. During the other part of the year, Jim can be found at Deer Crossing Camp, Inc. (www.deercrossingcamp.com), as the owner-director of a wilderness summer camp for children. He has worked as a university coach of championship water polo teams, a research marine biologist and commercial diver, an industrial chemist, an adventure guide, and an award-winning columnist on the subject of how to bring out the best qualities in children.

To find out more about Jim's school assemblies, teacher in-services, and workshops for children and adults:

www.jimwiltens.com

jim@jimwiltens.com

phone: 650-369-3902

fax: 650-369-4382

Books by Jim Wiltens

If you want to be a 100% positive parent, put this book at the top of your list. Learn how to get inside kids' heads so that you can be heard. Make changes in a child's behavior without making waves. Create self-propelled kids by tapping into six driving forces behind children's behavior. (190 pages)

Parents and teachers learn how to coach grade schoolers in nine memory skills that make a huge difference in academic success. If you think reading literacy is important, discover the amazing things you can do when you are memory literate. (384 pages)

Five secrets of goal-setting success. Inspire and motivate school-aged children to set and achieve goals. (84 pages)

"Goal Express! could be the most important book you ever give your child."

Mary Brence Martin,
Former Managing Editor, Bay Area Parent Magazine

No More Nagging .... @ $9.95/book =	
Memory Smart .... @ $29.95/book =	
Goal Express! .... @ $9.95/book =	
CA resident add sales tax, 8.25% to book total =	
Shipping first book, $2.50 .... = $2.50	
Shipping additional books, $1.50 each .... =	
Total......... =	

Name: _____

Address: _____

City: _____ State: _____ Zip: _____

Phone (please include area code): (____) _____

Send this form with a check or money order payable to Deer Crossing Press to:

Deer Crossing Press
690 Emerald Hill Rd.
Redwood City, CA 94061